PATRIOTS

AND

HEROES

by

Gerald Reminick

THE GLENCANNON PRESS

MARITIME BOOKS

PALO ALTO
2000

Published by The Glencannon Press
P.O. Box 341, Palo Alto, CA 94302
Tel. 800-711-8985
www.glencannon.com

Library of Congress Cataloging-in-Publication Data

First Edition, first printing.

Patriots and heroes / [compiled] by Gerald Reminick.
    p. cm.
  Includes bibliographical references and index.
  ISBN 1-889901-14-8 (alk. paper)
    1. World War, 1939-1945--Transportation. 2. Merchant marine -- United
States--History--20th century. I. Reminick, Gerald, 1943-

D810.T8 P368 2000
940.54'5973--dc21

                                                    00-026432

ACKNOWLEDGEMENTS

There are many people who helped me in my quest to compile this anthology of *Patriots and Heroes,* initiated in 1996.

Very special thank yous are in order to Professor Joyce Gabriele, my colleague and editor, and Matthew Loughran, Historian of the North Atlantic Chapter of the American Merchant Marine Veterans, for their assistance and support.

I would especially like to thank Leroy C. Heinse, a survivor of the bombing of Bari, Italy; Frank Braynard, Curator of the American Merchant Marine Museum, who asked me to speak at a Merchant Marine reunion and dedication at the United States Merchant Marine Academy; Captain Arthur R. Moore; and George Searle, President of the American Merchant Marine Veterans, for their support as well as my other friends from all over the United States.

I also thank Dolores Perillo, Circulation and Interlibrary Loan Clerk in the Western Campus Library of Suffolk County Community College; the Libraries of Suffolk County Community College; and the United States Merchant Marine Academy Library.

I extend my gratitude to all the Merchant Marine Veterans and their families who contributed stories to this anthology. Without them, there wouldn't have been an anthology. Without them, we wouldn't have won the war!

Finally, I'd like to remember my mother, who recently passed away. She always told me, "Don't worry, you'll win in the end!"

...The work your son gave his life for is the most important work in the war. None of us want to die, but we don't want any American soldier to die either because he didn't have that bullet to fire, or that plane to fly, or that oil or gasoline. So we all go back, knowing it has to be done, and then we carry food and goods to build instead of destroy — safely

Goodbye and our deepest sympathy
Merton S. Barrus
(Letter to the parents of Leslie Vail from a shipmate, courtesy the Oysterponds Historical Society, Orient, New York.)

Contents

INTRODUCTION

At the end of the war, Emory S. Land, Administrator of the War Shipping Administration (WSA) wrote a report on World War II and the involvement of the United States Merchant Marine. Published on January 15, 1946 it was titled: The United States Merchant Marine At War. The first three paragraphs precisely summarize the important role of America's mariners:

> The United States was a member of a fighting team of United Nations that won the greatest war in history. There were three major players who represented the United States on that team: Our fighting forces overseas, the production army here at home, and the link between them — the United States Merchant Marine.
>
> Each of the three was dependent upon the other, and together with their counterparts in other United Nations, a winning combination was evolved which smashed the Axis powers beyond all recovery.
>
> Never before has the maritime power of America been so effectively utilized. Its naval and merchant fleets became the difference between victory and defeat.[1]

The winning combination and the ultimate victory did not come easily. At the turn of the twentieth century, the United States was the world's foremost industrial nation. However, her leadership qualities lagged when it came to maritime development. At the outbreak of World War I, the United States found itself with a shortage of merchant ships. It had become precariously dependent upon foreign nations to move its exports, troops, and war materials.

> Much warning went unheeded until 1914 caught this country
> dozing in isolation with 90% of its overseas commerce in foreign
> bottoms. Quickly most of that 90% was withdrawn by its owners for
> war. The United States paid a billion-dollar freight bill for what space
> could be had in three years to 1917. Mountains of goods piled up.[2]

Congress, realizing the need for U.S.-flag ships, passed the Shipping Act of 1916. This authorized the newly formed U.S. Shipping Board which, in turn, directed the Emergency Fleet Corporation to build ships. More than 2,300 ships were built under its auspices. Ironically, most were completed and delivered after the war was over.

Very little ship construction took place in the U.S. from 1920 to 1936. Tonnage built for the First World War became out-of-date and in poor condition. Once again, America's merchant marine fell behind the other maritime nations of the world. According to the Maritime Administration, "In 1936, our merchant marine was fourth among the six leading maritime nations in tonnage, sixth in vessels ten years of age or less, fifth in vessels with speeds of twelve knots or over."[3]

Reacting to this deterioration in maritime strength, Congress once again moved to rectify the situation and passed the Merchant Marine Act of 1936. This became the cornerstone of a new American merchant marine — one that would be capable of carrying its own trade, compete globally, and provide transport for troops and war materials. It called for five hundred ships to be built over a ten year period. To facilitate this enormous task, Congress created the United States Maritime Commission. Manning for the new ships would come from the officers and seamen of America's merchant marine.

Looked at with disdain, if not outright contempt, the typical seaman was considered a "rough character." In the public eye he was uneducated, alcoholic, and usually settled matters with his fists. Fueling this perception were the union strikes of 1934 and 1936, warring political factions within the unions, struggles between ship operators and seamen, and the bad publicity created by these events.

Concern about the quality of seamen was such that Senator Royal Copeland of New York held closed-door hearings with a view to amending the Merchant Marine Act of 1936. During one such meeting a ship captain pointed out that "Our ships are infested with thugs, thieves, gangsters, dope-runners, drunkards, racketeers of all descriptions."[4]

To understand what a person who chose seafaring as a profession was up against, one must understand the conditions aboard ship. Felix Riesenberg wrote about shipboard life:

> If you don't mind sleeping in a narrow bunk on a dirty mattress crawling with bedbugs and have no objection to crowding into a dark hole deep in the after peak of a ship, over the screw, where the fumes from showers and toilets permeate the air; and if lack of ventilation or light has no terror for you and you like to take your meals in a smelly messroom just off a hot galley, sitting at a narrow bench covered with soiled oilcloth and facing a blank wall not too clean, with a slovenly mess boy shoving a plate of greasy stew over your shoulder — if these things please you and you are thankful for them and obedient, you are 100 per cent American seaman, a credit to your flag and to the United States.
>
> On the other hand, if you kick about such things, if you take part in "inciting to riot," join sit down strikes, and in that way interfere with the earnings of a run-down cargo steamer, you are a Communist. Living conditions, in brief, are the cause of much of the discontent and rioting we have had in the last two years along our waterfronts and on board ships of the United States merchant marine.[5]

In *Scholastic Magazine,* Senator Francis Maloney of Connecticut stated, ". . . that disorder among seamen resulted partly from bad ships and the fact that these men have been subjected to conditions . . . that amount to serfdom."[6]

However, with the increased involvement and consolidation of the maritime unions, conditions began to improve. The two major unions, the Sailors' Union of the Pacific (SUP) on the West Coast and the National Maritime Union of America (NMU) on the East Coast, even established training programs. The unions also began policing their problems of drunkenness and insubordination with fines and suspensions. An article in *The New Republic* described the small first steps:

> Until the advent of the National Maritime Union conditions on American ships were appalling. The union has shortened hours, raised wages, and made considerable improvements in living conditions. Considerable improvements mean nothing more than war on vermin, clean sheets, extra sinks, and fairly nourishing food. The average foc's'le is crowded, unlit and unventilated, and very little can be done for the crew on most American ships until the old tubs are replaced by modern craft.[7]

With the Merchant Marine Act of 1936, the means of building those modern craft was at hand. Joseph P. Kennedy, appointed Chairman of the United States Maritime Commission, gave a rousing speech before the Propeller Club in New York City on May 22, 1937. He said:

> Most of our ships are so old that, assuming twenty years as a conservative estimate for the life of a ship, eighty-five per cent of our fleet will be fit for retirement in five years.
>
> No eloquence is needed. That single statement shows clearly the crisis facing our merchant marine. What's the sense of talking about an adequate or a first class merchant marine in the face of such facts? For us an adequate merchant marine has to be a new merchant marine. The question comes — what are we going to do about it? The answer is BUILD SHIPS! — the best and most modern ships — and build them RIGHT AWAY.[8]

Along with the construction of new ships, the Maritime Commission would establish training facilities for merchant marine officers and seamen.

The stage was set. Thomas M. Woodward, a member of the U.S. Maritime Commission, writing in *Forum and Century* in May of 1939, pointed out that everything was in place for the U.S. to regain its maritime leadership role:

All the necessary factors for the re-establishment of a modern and efficient merchant marine are present today in this country. We are building the ships and, equally important, we have the man power which through training we hope to develop into a body of seamen second to none in technical skill and proficiency.

We have an act of Congress which, though far from perfect, is designed to enable the American operator to achieve a parity in cost with his foreign competitors. What we must have to make the project a success is the cooperation and support of the people of this country. Without that, the other factors are of but little importance. With that support, we can go forward and re-establish a merchant marine commensurate with the strength and dignity of this nation.[9]

Unfortunately, the negative attitude toward the merchant marine continued. Even during the war, the media and press corps played a major role in perpetrating the myth of seafarer as misfit. Felix Riesenberg in his monumental book *Sea War: The Story of the U.S. Merchant Marine In World War II*, wrote that the merchant mariner became associated with the photographs that were taken of him:

Gaunt men in borrowed clothing were posed unshaven and dirty for newspaper pictures. This was America's first sustained look at the merchant mariner and more strongly than ever in the popular mind he was viewed as tough, dirty-talking, devil-may-care sort of fellow . . . But he was a creature apart; the clean, wholesome and gentlemanly seafarer was identified with men who wore uniforms. This character was disturbingly at odds with the sea of white, glistening yachts and the stirring, rolling ocean seen in the movies when a battlewagon dipped her bows with a background of martial music.[10]

Two influential radio announcers were particularly tough on the merchant marine: Walter Winchell and Drew Pearson. The columnist Westbrook Pegler didn't endear himself to the merchant marine either. The National Maritime Union picketed the *World Telegram* building because of a critical article he wrote about merchant seamen earning more money than the Naval Armed Guard.

Perhaps the lowest, most biased and despicable journalistic act against the merchant marine was in an article run by *Time Magazine* dated December 21, 1942 entitled "Slackers & Suckers." Riesenberg cites from the article:

> 10,000 men between the ages of 17 and 35 who customarily greet each other as "Slacker," "Draftdodger" and "Profiteer," stood for one and a half hours in the icy offshore wind at the United States Maritime Training Station at Sheepshead Bay, N.Y., last week and heard themselves lauded by President Roosevelt (by letter) and a No. 2 company of lauders as potential gallant merchant seamen. To the undisguised relief of the station's 1,800 instructors, they uttered no boo, no Bronx cheer, and only a few rude mutterings . . .
>
> Rough and rambunctious, uniformed as sailors but fully aware that their civilian status permits nose-thumbing at MP's, the 13-week volunteer trainees sneer at their $50-a-month pay, wait for the day they sign on for double pay of $200 a month, or $250 for those qualifying for higher ratings . . .[11]

On that same page, Riesenberg cites a telegram that was immediately sent by Captain Edward Macauley, Deputy Administrator of the War Shipping Administration, on behalf of the WSA and merchant marine, to compare the facts in their article, which he branded "malicious." Part of the fiery message reads:

THESE "SLACKERS" ARE TRAINING FOR A SERVICE WHICH HAS SUFFERED A HIGHER PERCENTAGE OF CASUALTIES TO DATE THAN HAVE ANY OF THE ARMED SERVICES, AND THEY KNOW IT.

THESE "DRAFT DODGERS" ARE VOLUNTEERING FOR AS TEDIOUS, AS HAZARDOUS, AND AS ESSENTIAL A DUTY AS THERE IS IN THE WHOLE WAR PROGRAM. THOSE "PROFITEERS" COULD MAKE MORE MONEY IN DETROIT OR GARY OR CLEVELAND FROM THE BACKGROUND OF THEIR OWN HOMES WITH THE COMFORT AND PLEASURE OF PRIVATE LIFE THAN THEY WILL MAKE ON THE LONG COLD

VOYAGE TO THE ARCTIC OR RUNNING THE GANTLET OF
"BOMB ALLEY."

SOME OF THESE MEN WILL GIVE THEIR LIVES TO PROTECT
THOSE OF US WHO STAY AT HOME — INCLUDING THE
AUTHOR OF YOUR ATTACK.[12]

Meanwhile, the construction of ships continued at a breakneck pace.

Within a year and a half after the United States entered the war in 1941 the shipyards were building ships faster than the enemy was able to sink them. From 1942 through 1945 United States shipyards built 5,592 merchant ships, of which 2,701 were Liberty ships, 414 were the faster Victory type, 651 were tankers, 417 were standard cargo ships, and the remaining 1,409 were military or minor types.[13]

Throughout the war, the United States Merchant Marine paid an exorbitant price to uphold its part in the war plan.

At least 8,651 mariners were killed at sea, 11,000 wounded of whom at least 1,100 died from their wounds, and 604 men and women were taken prisoner.* Some were blown to death, some incinerated, some drowned, some froze and some starved. Sixty died in prison camps, and about 500 Americans were lost while serving on Allied ships. Of the 833 large ships sunk, 31 vanished without a trace to a watery grave. One in 32 mariners serving aboard merchant ships in World War II *died in the line of duty*, suffering a *greater percentage* of war-related deaths than all other U.S. services.[14]

How important was the U.S. Merchant Marine in winning the war? Commander in Chief of the United States Navy and Chief of Naval Operations, Fleet Admiral Ernest J. King, wrote to Admiral Land:

---

* The figure of 11,000 wounded is also low because members of the merchant marine weren't considered veterans and therefore records were not kept of their injuries.

During the past 3 1/2 years, the Navy has been dependent upon the Merchant Marine to supply our far-flung fleet and bases. Without this support, the Navy could not have accomplished its mission. Consequently, it is fitting that the Merchant Marine share in our success as it shared in our trials.

The Merchant Marine is a strong bulwark of national defense in peace and war, and a buttress to a sound national economy. A large Merchant Marine is not only an important national resource; it is, in being, an integral part of the country's armed might during time of crisis. During World War II, this precept has been proven.

As the Merchant Marine returns to its peacetime pursuits, I take great pleasure in expressing the Navy's heartfelt thanks to you and through you to the officers and men of the Merchant Marine for their magnificent support during World War II. All hands can feel a pride of accomplishment in a job well done.

We wish the Merchant Marine every success during the years ahead and sincerely hope that it remains strong and continues as a vital and integral part of our national economy and defense.[15]

This wish remained unfulfilled as, once again, Congress and the American people turned their backs on the merchant marine and the industrial strength gained in World War II through blood and sweat was left to crumble away. Worse was the nation's treatment of her merchant marine veterans.

These patriots and heroes did not receive veterans' benefits until 1988.

Perhaps this anthology will help educate the American public to what U.S. merchant mariners experienced and suffered during a war that would never have been won without their contributions.

FOREWORD

WHEN IS A VETERAN A VETERAN?

I began compiling this anthology in September of 1995. While researching and writing the biography of Rear Admiral John W. Wilcox, Jr., I met and became close friends with Matthew Loughran, historian of the North Atlantic Chapter of the American Merchant Marine Veterans. Matty gave me a great suggestion: "Now that you're finished with the Admiral Wilcox biography, why don't you write something about the merchant marine? No one ever writes about us!"

I quickly discovered he was right. So, for two years I collected stories involving mariner life in World War II. I wanted the men who created this history to record and document their thoughts so we could preserve them. These mariners and the role they played in World War II were indispensable. Without them, we would have lost the war. That was what this war was all about. That is what they have recorded.

My first touch with the history of these mariners came in a letter by Dr. Robert Colby, who was a dentist aboard the USS *Washington*, the ship on which Admiral Wilcox lost his life. A grand gentleman and friend, Bob helped me immeasurably with the Wilcox biography.

In September of 1995, Dr. Colby attended a local retired officers' shrimp broil and met Mary Parmelee. Mary lost her father, James L. Randall, on the liberty ship *Edward B. Dudley,* which was torpedoed and sunk on April 11, 1943. The *Edward B. Dudley* was part of Convoy HX-232 from Halifax to Liverpool. On April 4th, the freighter developed mechanical problems and fell behind the convoy. She was first sighted by the German submarine *U-615* on April 10th. Unsuccessful in sinking the ship on the 10th because of a malfunctioning torpedo, the submarine accomplished her goal the following day. Everyone on board was lost. Just over four months later the *U-615* was bombed and sunk south of Curaçao.

I contacted Mrs. Parmelee and she forwarded a packet of information about the ship and her father. The first document I saw was Casualty Form DD-1300. The remarks section stated:

Veteran was a member of the crew of the Liberty Ship SS EDWARD B DUDLEY, Official Number 242876, owned and operated by the Bulk Carriers Corporation of New York, New York. Vessel was torpedoed and sunk in the North Atlantic on 11 April 1943. Veteran was missing and presumed lost due to enemy action. In addition, the cause of death is presumed to have been in the performance of his duties.

The document elaborated on Randall's position of second assistant engineer on two previous voyages aboard the *West Texas* in October and December of 1942 and went on to list the decorations, medals, badges, citations and campaign ribbons he was entitled to: Atlantic War Zone Medal, Combat Bar, Mariners Medal, Merchant Marine Service Emblem, Honorable Service Button, Victory Medal, Presidential Testimonial Letter.[1]

Finally, the long-overdue recognition owed to every merchant mariner who served in World War II was paid to one fallen American hero.

Later, Mrs. Parmelee was advised by Admiral J.W. Kline of the U.S. Coast Guard that her father was eligible to receive a Soviet Commemorative medal for his participation in the convoy(s) to Murmansk. This award was dated October 11, 1994.

As I read the material, I was appalled by a letter dated June 21, 1994 from the U.S. Department of Transportation, Maritime Administration. The medals, emblem, and button could be obtained from the list of vendors provided! What an unconscionable and national disgrace that American veterans should have to pay for their medals.

Matty Loughran was so upset that he asked me to help him write an article for a Long Island, New York newspaper. Thus began my involvement.

I gladly wrote the article based on Mrs. Parmelee's documents and Matty's input. This is what *Newsday* published in their "Letters" column on Saturday, March 16, 1996:

A TRUE VETERAN

James L. Randall was too old to join the U.S. Navy in World War II, but rather than stay at home and work in a safe defense plant with higher wages, he volunteered as a merchant marine on a liberty ship, the *Edward B. Dudley*.

The ship was torpedoed on April 11, 1943. Aboard ship were 42 merchant mariners and 27 U.S. armed guards. There were no survivors. Randall, a second assistant engineer, was 57 years old.

Had he lived, Randall wouldn't have been eligible for veterans' benefits. If he had ever been employed by the federal government, his service time would not have counted toward his retirement, nor would any credit have been given toward civil service examinations. It wasn't until 1988 that Randall was posthumously granted veteran's status.

Randall's daughter was informed of the medals and awards due her father and where they could be purchased. Why is it that our merchant marine veterans have to purchase their medals and all other veterans do not? When is a veteran a veteran?[2]

There was no official response to the letter.

Second Assistant Engineer James Randall was fifty-seven years old; a beloved husband and father who volunteered and lost his life for his country and the free world. He was a true American hero.

The stories that follow depict men of the same caliber and are used with their permission. Their memories and experiences are now recorded for the world to remember.

Forgotten Men

No one bought a round of beer-
No well done or rousing cheer-
No one cared about their fear-
Just good ridence at the pier.

Out upon an angry sea-
Tankers, colliers, Libertys-
Cargoes keeping men free-
Forgotten men how can that be?

You could see them on a New York street-
Some had nothing just bare feet
Cold and weary, snow and sleet-
And not a soul would help or speak.

Exploding ships lit up the sky-
Only kin and shipmates cry-
Most didn't even question why-
The merchantmen sailed off to die.

Forgotten yes, these seamen be-
Who paid the price for liberty-
Yes, for the likes of you and me-
They traded life for liberty.[3]

Many of the poems in this anthology were contributed by Ian A. Millar from his book, *In Praise of Merchantmen*. In his book Ian says:

This collection of poetry is written as a reminder of those men who went down to the sea in ships, who came to the fore when their country called, who served, and who passed from view in the great sacrifice. Those who gave so much of themselves, only to be forgotten by the country they served. These poems cannot nor ever will take the place of the recognition these men deserve, they are truly the forgotten warriors of their nation's conflicts, they are the men who faced enemies' guns with little or no arms, they were the backbone of their country's war effort, without them there would have been no victory ...

These poems are ... given as a token of appreciation of those men of my father's (Adrian E. Millar) generation who followed the sea and who because of their following have a deeper sense of living.[4]

JAMES L. RANDALL

To you who answered the call of your country and served in its Merchant Marine to bring about the total defeat of the enemy, I extend the heartfelt thanks of the Nation. You undertook a most severe task—one which called for courage and fortitude. Because you demonstrated the resourcefulness and calm judgment necessary to carry out that task, we now look to you for leadership and example in further serving our country in peace.

Harry Truman

THE WHITE HOUSE

James Randall's efforts were recognized by President Truman. Courtesy Mary Parmelee.

EMBASSY OF THE RUSSIAN FEDERATION
1125 16TH STREET, N.W.
WASHINGTON, D. C. 20036

Mr. James L. RANDALL
c/o Mrs. Mary R. PARMELEE
1629 Maravilla Ave.
Fort Myers, FL 33901

October 11, 1994

Dear Sir:

On behalf of President Boris Yeltsin and entire Russian people I am pleased and honored to inform you that you have been awarded the Commemorative medal "The 40th Anniversary of the Victory in the Great Patriotic War (WW II)".

This award is a token of recognition of your outstanding courage and personal contribution to the Allied support of my country which fought for freedom against Nazi Germany.

Please, accept my heartfelt congratulations and wishes of good health, well-being and every success.

Most sincerely,

Vladimir I. CHKHIKVISHVILI
Charge d'Affaires a.i.

Enclosure: commemorative medal, certificate.

Letter from the Russian government recognizing the contribution of merchant mariner James Randall in World War II.

1

PRE-WAR

*T*he two stories in this chapter take place before the Second
World War started. One involves a World War I Navy
Veteran and the other describes an incident just before
the United States declared war in 1941.

The first story is about Lynn R. Fullington and was
printed in the Anderson Daily Bulletin.

~~~

Anderson Daily Bulletin
August 2, 1943

Responding to his country's call for service for the third time,
Lynn R. Fullington, Navy Veteran of World War I, has re-enlisted for
the service in the U.S. Merchant Marine and left yesterday for New
York to report for active sea duty. Mr. Fullington has a wife and 9
children . . .

Lynn Fullington, age 53, of W 13th, resident here for many years, who served two enlistments in the Navy in early life, including active duty in World War I, with his ship torpedoed at sea, has answered his country call for the 3rd time and enlisted in the U.S. Merchant Marine.

Fullington has been given the rating of Chief Mate on a merchant ship. . . . Chief Fullington, bade farewell yesterday to his family before departing for New York to be assigned to active duty on a merchant ship. He is expected to be 2nd in command of one of the government's newest vessels. Due to his long experience at sea, Fullington was entitled to a high rating. Enlisting May 15th, in response to appeals for experienced former Navy men to return to duty, Fullington reported to New London, Conn. for several weeks refresher course in training. He was granted his rating of Chief Mate and was home with his family here for a two week furlough before returning to active duty at sea.

Concerning his re-enlistment, Chief Fullington said yesterday, "I felt that my country needed me and decided to answer the call. I thought this was the best thing I could do to aid my nation." Chief Fullington spent 8 years in the U.S. Navy in his early life chiefly as a gunner. During an enlistment period from 1909 to 1913, he was on duty on the battleship New Jersey and other ships and travelled extensively in the North Atlantic and Mediterranean areas. He says that he covered approximately 250,000 miles at sea during this enlistment. Fullington's 2nd enlistment in the Navy was 1917 at the outset of U.S. entry into World War I.

One of his exacting experiences at sea, occurred early in 1918 when his ship, the City of Wilmington, a merchant vessel on which he was a gunner, had a battle with a German U-Boat near the Spanish coast. Later while the boat was enroute back to this country, it became stranded at sea for 35 days and was finally towed to Bermuda. The local man says that the water stood in the hull of the boat for some time and the matter of providing adequate food for the long period brought hardship.

Chief Fullington says that it was on the return trip on the City of Wilmington to Europe with a cargo, that the vessel was torpedoed and sunk.

Describing his experience, Fullington said, "We were about 800 miles east of Newfoundland, when the German U-Boat attacked us at sunset. The torpedo hit our oil tanks and set fire the vessel afire. We had no warning, but the 55 men in the crew of the 3,000 ton freighter got into lifeboats in 18 minutes. The Germans did not shoot at our small boats, but we had to float for about 2 1/2 days before rescue by another vessel."

Fullington says that after his boat was sunk he was assigned to duty training gunners for convoy duty. He was discharged after the war, but re-entered service on a commercial ship for two more years. Leaving the sea in 1920, he went to Dayton in 1921, and was married. The family moved here 15 years ago. Mr Fullington ran an electric repair shop here for several years. Mrs. Fullington and her children plan to continue to make their home here with Chief Fullington returning here for frequent visits when he is on leave from sea duty.[1]

~~~~

The following story was sent by Captain L. Roy Murray, Jr., in July of 1996. Captain Murray wrote the story in 1995 and had a portion of it published in the June-July 1997 issue of Professional Mariner *under the title "Rescue of British Sailors Is A Difficult But Rewarding Task." Capt. Murray graduated from high school in 1937 and shortly after that entered the U.S. Maritime Commission Officer Training Program as a deck cadet. In December of 1940, he graduated from the U.S. Merchant Marine Cadet Corps, now at Kings Point. Most of those three and-a-half years were spent on board merchant ships in regular service. On graduation he received a third mate's license and an ensign's commission in the U.S. Navy. It took him several months into 1941 to get a berth sailing due to the reduction in the number of ships in the U.S. Merchant Marine because of the war in Europe. He finally got a third mate's job on the Lykes Brothers steamship* Nishmaha.

The Sinking Of HMS *Dunedin*

In late November 1941 the British cruiser, HMS *Dunedin*, was casually patrolling in the Atlantic, just north of the equator and about seven hundred miles off the coast of Africa. The *Dunedin* was a light cruiser and carried a crew of 491, including officers and enlisted men. The mission of the "Deadly Dun," as her crew called her, was to find and destroy German surface raiders operating in the Southern Atlantic. These surface raiders, called "Q-ships," were heavily armed merchant ships usually disguised as neutral ships. The *Dunedin* was working a triangle area with another British cruiser and with an American cruiser holding the western corner of the triangle, although the United States was not yet involved in the war.

When I say the *Dunedin* was "casually patrolling," it was because the commander apparently felt that he had little to fear. Sort of like the lion on the African Veldt. At this point in the war none of the German capital ships that had escaped into the open sea were known to be in the South Atlantic. The surface raiders were a formidable opponent for the average lightly armed merchant ship, but they were no match for a cruiser like the *Dunedin* and perhaps the commander believed that there were no German submarines this far south in the Atlantic.

On the afternoon of November 24th, 1941 the weather was fine and clear with a light breeze, (almost like the doldrums) and there was a fairly heavy swell. The lookout in the crow's nest of the *Dunedin* reported a small craft with one mast, bearing two points on the starboard bow. The bridge watch altered the course to the direction of the reported sighting and continued in that direction to investigate. The submarine submerged and no doubt that the captain of the U-boat could not believe his eyes when the *Dunedin* came cruising into his sights, taking no precautions. The bridge watch on the *Dunedin* did not even sound general quarters. The lookout was criticized for giving a false report.

When the *Dunedin* came into range, the captain of the U-boat fired two torpedoes. Both hit the *Dunedin* on the starboard side, one hit the fore part of the ship and the other near the stern. The *Dunedin* immediately began listing to starboard and settling in the stern. Within ten minutes the *Dunedin* slid stern first below the surface and went to the bottom of the Atlantic.

More than half of the officers and crew were killed outright or trapped below deck as the stricken ship went to the bottom. Only those on deck and those able to make it to the open deck were able to jump into the water and swim away from the sinking ship. About two hundred men survived the sinking and many of them were badly injured.

There were very few officers among the survivors. The torpedo that hit forward apparently hit near the officers' quarters. The commanding officer did not survive the sinking. One of the ship's whalers and seven life rafts floated off the ship. The survivors made their way to the rafts, but the whaler was badly damaged and soon sank. The survivors were left with very little food and water.

The German U-boat surfaced among the survivors and spoke with some of them. From the conning tower of the U-boat the survivors were told that their position would be reported to the British. But the submarine did not make a report and after a few minutes turned and left the horrible scene.

The Submarine

The German submarine *U-124* was put in service in June of 1940 and for nearly a year and-a-half had been wreaking havoc with British and other Allied shipping in the North and South Atlantic and in the Caribbean Sea. The *U-124* made numerous patrols, returning frequently to bases in Germany for refitting and fresh stores. In August of 1941, Kapitan Jochen Mohr took command. In November Kapitan Mohr took the *U-124* into the South Atlantic looking for unescorted British or Allied ships.

On the afternoon of November 24th, 1941 the *U-124* was patrolling on the surface just three degrees north of the equator and about 26 degrees west longitude. The day was fine and clear. It became partly cloudy with a light breeze and a moderate swell. At about 1:00 PM the watch on the conning tower saw the British Cruiser HMS *Dunedin* on the horizon. It is most likely that the watch on the *U-124* saw the much larger *Dunedin* a good many minutes before the lookout on the *Dunedin* reported the sighting. By the time that the lookout on the cruiser reported the sighting the *U-124* was probably in the process of diving. After a few minutes Kapitan Mohr cautiously raised the periscope, fearfully, because he had come upon a formidable man-o-war instead of some hapless merchant ship. He was aware that his vessel would be under attack soon if the lookout on the *Dunedin* was able to identify what he had sighted as a submarine.

As Kapitan Mohr watched through his periscope the *Dunedin* changed course and headed in his direction. However the cruiser was not approaching in an aggressive manner; in fact it was not even maneuvering in a defensive way. As the *Dunedin* came into range, Kapitan Mohr aimed his torpedo tubes at the cruiser and fired both of the forward torpedo tubes at fairly close range. In just moments the explosions were felt by those on the submarine as both torpedoes hit their mark.

For another year and-a-half the *U-124* continued to take its toll on Allied shipping, now including American ships.

Kapitan Mohr would sink nine ships and be awarded the Knights Cross with Oak Leaves for his prowess. He wrote a poem about his success.

> The new-moon is black as ink,
> Off Hatteras the tankers sink
> While sadly Roosevelt counts the score
> Some 50,000 tons by Mohr.[2]

Captain Murray continues:
By 1943 anti-submarine warfare had evolved to the point where the hunters became the hunted. Most of the Atlantic Ocean was covered by shore-based aircraft and small aircraft carriers, called "Baby Flat-tops," covered the rest. Newly developed sophisticated submarine detection equipment was widely in use by Allied navies. By 1943 German submarine crews leaving on patrol had less than a fifty percent chance of returning.

The Rescue Ship

The American Steamship *Nishmaha* was owned and operated by Lykes Brothers Steamship Company of New

In early 1942, Kapitan Jochen Mohr received the Knight's Cross for sinking more than 100,000 tons of Allied shipping. Here he smiles over a "Knight's Cross" cake presented by his crew before the official ceremony. Bundesarchiv, Koblenz.

Orleans, Louisiana. The *Nishmaha* was a dry cargo ship of some 5,000 gross tons and could carry a cargo of up to 10,000 tons, deadweight. She was a World War I vintage freighter built in 1919, but that war was over by the time that she was put in service. A steam reciprocating engine gave the ship a speed of ten knots. The name was believed to be of American Indian origin, but no one seemed to know what it meant. Although a strange sounding name it is not hard to pronounce; just "Nish-ma-ha." It is, however, difficult to read when being transmitted by blinker light due to the sequence of the dots and dashes. Almost invariably when sending the name it had to be repeated at least once.

In the late 1930's the *Nishmaha* was used in the trade between United States Gulf of Mexico ports and Europe, the United Kingdom and the Mediterranean. In September of 1939 war broke out in Europe and in 1940 the United States government defined the European War Zone and ordered all American flag ships to stay out of that area. The *Nishmaha* was put in service between the United States Gulf of Mexico ports and Southern Africa.

I was lucky enough to be assigned as junior third mate on the *Nishmaha*. I was twenty-one years old. I put my brand new third mate's license in the frame on the chart room wall along with four master's licenses. These were the licenses of the captain, chief mate, second, and third mate. All much older and experienced officers — an indication of how scarce jobs were for licensed officers.

In August of 1941 the *Nishmaha* loaded general cargo at various Gulf ports. The cargoes were destined for South and East African ports. Since the United States was not yet in the war and since the *Nishmaha* was sailing in hostile waters there was an American flag painted on each side and a large American flag painted on the white tarpaulin on the number three hatch to be visible to aircraft. The flags on the ship's side were illuminated by flood lights at night. She carried a crew of thirty-seven officers and men. Captain H. S. Olsen was the master. I was assigned to the eight-to-twelve watch when underway.

The *Nishmaha* sailed from New Orleans on August 27, 1941, bound for South Africa. She stopped at Port of Spain, Trinidad on the way to take on fuel. The first discharge port was Cape Town, South Africa. From there she went around the Cape of Good Hope and continued up the East Coast of Africa, discharging cargo at Port Elizabeth, East London and Durban. Thence, farther up the East African Coast to Portuguese East Africa, (now Mozambique) to Ports of Lourenço Marques and Beira. The last cargo was discharged at the Port of Beira and the *Nishmaha* returned, in ballast, to Durban. There, she took on a full load of coal for the Belgian Congo (now Zaire). Leaving Durban, the *Nishmaha* headed south, back around the Cape of Good Hope and back into the Atlantic Ocean. She headed north along the West African Coast to the Congo River where she took on a local pilot for the one hundred mile trip up the river to the Port of Matadi. When the cargo of coal was discharged the *Nishmaha* headed back down the Congo River, back into the Atlantic and again headed north, bound for the Port of Takoradi on the African Gold Coast (now Ghana). At Takoradi the *Nishmaha* took on a full cargo of chrome ore destined for Philadelphia.

On November 24th, 1941, the *Nishmaha* sailed from Takoradi, homeward bound, now some three months since leaving the United States. November 24th was the same day that the *Dunedin* was torpedoed. Captain Olsen had read his instructions carefully before sailing. He was ordered to steam due south from Takoradi for twelve hours, then make a ninety degree turn to the right and steam due west until he reached a neutral zone. This neutral zone extended 300 miles from the eastern seaboards of North and South America. Captain Olsen was under orders to keep well within the neutral zone.

Captain Olsen reasoned that with most of the Old World already at war, it was only a matter of time before the United States got involved. If he wanted to spend another Christmas at home, he decided, it had better be the one coming up in five weeks. So he sailed due south for twelve hours and turned westward as instructed. But when he cleared the bulge of West Africa he laid a straight course for Philadelphia. Heading north northwesterly the *Nishmaha* plodded homeward at a steady ten knots.

On Wednesday, November 26th a small mechanical defect in the ship's reciprocating engine forced a stop for repairs. For eight hours the *Nishmaha* drifted westward in the Benguela current before resuming her course.

The next day, November 27th, Thanksgiving, dawned bright and clear. There were scattered clouds and the heavily loaded *Nishmaha* rolled easily in the moderate ocean swell. The steward's department had prepared a traditional Thanksgiving dinner with turkey and dressing, cranberry sauce, pumpkin pie, and all the other trimmings which was enjoyed by everyone. In another two weeks the ship would be in Philadelphia and with a cargo to discharge and another load there was a good chance that the ship would still be in the States for Christmas.

The Rescue

At twelve noon on November 27th, I came off watch and went directly to the officers' saloon, had Thanksgiving dinner and visited with the captain and other officers present. After dinner I read for a while and took an afternoon nap. Just before five PM I went to the bridge to relieve the other third mate so that he could go to supper, just as I did every day that we were at sea.

Only a few minutes after the other third officer left the bridge I was on the port wing of the bridge deck and thought I saw an object on the top of a swell about three points on the port bow. I got the binoculars and it seemed to be men in a small craft of some sort. I gave the helmsman a left rudder order and brought the ship thirty degrees to port and steadied up. I blew my pocket whistle for the standby man to come to the bridge to summon the captain.

Captain Olsen either heard a whistle or stepped out on the boat deck and saw the course change and came immediately to the bridge. I told him I thought that I saw some men in the water. As I handed him the binoculars he answered me with a long "Well," as if to say, "We'll see about that." The sighting now close on the port bow appeared again and Captain Olsen got a good look with the binoculars. His hands shook visibly and he told me to ring standby on the engine telegraph. The amidships house on the *Nishmaha* is directly over the engine room and the engine telegraph can be heard throughout the quarters. As I rang the engine telegraph nearly all of the crew were in the crew mess and officers' saloon and both rooms emptied in seconds as everyone headed for the deck. The engine telegraph sounding off at sea is unusual enough, but with war raging all around it is especially alarming to all on board.

As we approached the sighting it turned out to be a liferaft with three men in it. By this time a seaman had climbed the foremast to the crosstrees and was pointing out several more rafts at different bearings farther ahead. The engines were put full astern and the ship stopped near the raft, but it was not possible to maneuver the ship to the raft and the captain ordered the chief mate, Robert Auster, to lower a lifeboat and pick up the men from the raft. None of the four lifeboats on the *Nishmaha* had a motor and the chief mate took four seamen with him to man the oars. The raft was about a hundred yards from the ship and our lifeboat rowed out and picked up the three men and brought them back to the ship. After the survivors were on board, the ship towed the lifeboat to the next raft. There were two at this location. The lifeboat set out to pick up these survivors, but by this time it was getting near sunset and as darkness comes quickly near the equator, the captain decided to leave that lifeboat and go to the next sighting while we could still see to find them.

When the *Nishmaha* reached the rafts, there were two more. Captain Olsen ordered the other third mate to take a lifeboat and pick up the occupants of these two rafts. I went to the boat deck to help with the launching of the boat. Looking over the side I could see several ten to twelve foot sharks lazily swimming along the ship's side.

As my boat was being lowered the captain shouted from the bridge that there were two rafts last seen before it got dark and that they should be straight abeam from the ship. I stood in the stern of the boat with a sweep oar to steer with and we rowed away from the ship. When we were about a quarter mile from the ship we could hear the shouts of the men in the first raft. When we could see it, there were six men and we took them into the lifeboat. As we rowed farther out we could hear the calls of the other raft. When we came upon the second raft I was shocked to see that it contained some two dozen men. I was afraid that they would rush into my boat and overcrowd it. However they were well disciplined and there was a chief petty officer in charge. I told him that we could not take all of the men into our boat, but that they should pass over any that were injured or bad off. About six were taken into our boat and we gave the rest a rope to make fast to their raft and we towed the raft back to the ship. When back alongside the ship, the lifeboat was riding up and down the side of ship, about eight or ten feet, as the ship rolled in the swell. A short pilot ladder was rigged over the side on the after deck. As the lifeboat came up on the swell each time one, of the survivors was passed up to the crew members on deck that pulled them aboard. When all of the survivors were safely on the ship, we moved up under the boat davits and attached the falls, no easy task, and the crew on deck hoisted the lifeboat back on board. In the meantime, the other two boats had arrived back at the ship, after rowing several miles, and were brought on board after discharging their survivors.

It was 10:30 PM when all of the boats were secure and it was apparent that all of the sighted survivors had been picked up. A quick count indicated that we had picked up seventy-two survivors. After securing my boat I reported back to the bridge to finish what was left of my 8-to-12 watch. Captain Olsen informed me that he had changed our destination and had set course for Port of Spain, Trinidad, some twenty-five hundred miles away, but out of the war zone and the closest British Naval base.

For the rest of the night the crewmen off watch and the stewards' department worked at getting the survivors fed and bedded down and caring for the sick and injured. The survivors were bedded down in the ship's hospital, spare rooms, recreation areas, and in the rooms with officers and crew members. Five of the survivors died during the night. We were told that some of the five had drank salt water just before being rescued. The five deceased were given a seaman's burial that same afternoon. The ship's bosun sewed each into white canvas shrouds. The engines were stopped and the ship's bell was tolled. Captain Olsen read a burial prayer and the British flag was placed over each man, one at a time, and their bodies were committed to the deep.

The loss of the five rescued survivors was upsetting to the crew of the *Nishmaha*. It was sad to think that these five had survived the sinking of their ship and even more sad that they had survived nearly four grueling days in the ocean without food and water only to die after reaching safety. The other exhausted and

Nishmaha *picks up survivors on rafts from the British cruiser HMS* Dunedin. *Lykes Fleet Flashes.*

wounded survivors were hardly aware of their passing and having just witnessed the death of more than four hundred of their shipmates were not as affected as they might have been. Of the remaining sixty-seven survivors about fifteen were bedridden and had to be attended as if they were hospital patients.

As the *Nishmaha* plodded westward with its new human cargo the stewards' department had the task of feeding nearly three times the normal number of people. Food supplies had to be stretched. The survivors were issued cigarettes and clothing from the ship's store, called the "Slop Chest."* The "Slop Chest," on the *Nishmaha* was well stocked and it was where the crew could buy cigarettes, dungarees, warm clothing, work gloves, shoes, and other supplies that they might need. It was nearly cleaned out after supplying the survivors with clothing and other necessities.

The chief mate fell into the routine of making daily rounds attending to the sick and injured survivors, assisted by the ship's purser and carrying medicine and supplies from the ship's medicine chest. The survivors got to looking forward to his visits and treatment and began calling him "Doctor."

Ten days after picking up the survivors the *Nishmaha* steamed through the "Dragon's Mouth," the entrance to the Gulf of Paria and anchored off Port of Spain. The *Nishmaha* anchored about a quarter mile from the anchored U.S. Cruiser *Indianapolis*.

Discharging the Survivors

For security reasons Captain Olsen did not send out any radio reports of the rescue so the first the British knew of the survivors was when a British Navy officer boarded the *Nishmaha* on arrival at Port of Spain. The British Navy sent a converted trawler flying the British Navy white ensign to take the survivors

---

* The word "Slop" derives from the Old English word *sloppe*, which means breeches and at first referred to that garment which was carried aboard ship and sold by the purser to the crew. It later came to mean all commodities, such as tobacco, candy, etc. carried by the purser in his chest and sold to the crew.

ashore. As the trawler pulled away from the *Nishmaha* the survivors gave three cheers for the captain, officers, and crew of the S.S. *Nishmaha*.

Before leaving the S.S. *Nishmaha* the survivors composed a letter of thanks addressed to Captain H.S. Olsen, and signed by all sixty-seven of them:

> We whose names appear below, having been rescued from the ocean on November 27th, 1941, by the S.S. *Nishmaha*, wish to place on record our deep appreciation of the skillful seamanship by which we were picked up from our rafts; and our heartfelt gratitude for the constant care and attention which have been lavished upon us during the subsequent ten days passage.
>
> In caring for 67 men, a large number of whom were injured and helpless, the task so willingly undertaken by the 36 members of your ship's company was one whose magnitude we fully realize, and we find no words adequately to express our thanks for all they have done for us. The generosity and kindness which we have experienced under the United States Flag, and the skillful care by which so many have been nursed back to health by yourself, your officers and your crew will never be forgotten by us.

The admiral in charge of the British Naval Base at Port of Spain sent a letter to Captain Olsen as follows:

> Dear Captain Olsen:
>
> Since seeing the survivors landed here, I have learned of the exceptional kindness shown to them on board your vessel. Will you please accept on behalf of the Admiralty my warmest thanks to you and your officers and men. Your humane action has I am informed been the means of saving many of those who would not have otherwise recovered from the terrible ordeal that they had been through. I shall have the greatest pleasure in informing the Admiralty of what we owe to all on board the *Nishmaha*.
>
> Yours Sincerely,
> W.T. Hodges
> Admiral

On December 17, 1941, the day that the *Nishmaha* arrived at Philadelphia to discharge her cargo the British Government issued a short press release announcing the loss of the HMS *Dunedin*. The release was carried by the Philadelphia newspapers. No mention was made of the S.S. *Nishmaha's* part in the rescue of the survivors. Despite Admiral Hodges' promise in the last sentence of his letter, the British Government never gave any recognition or accommodation to the captain, officers, and crew of the *Nishmaha*.

To this day I am proud of the professionalism shown by the officers and crew of the *Nishmaha*. They were just normal merchant seamen going about their daily work when they came upon the survivors of the *Dunedin*. The boat equipment that they had to work with was antiquated. The boats had no motors. The boat davits were the quadrant type that had to be cranked out by hand. The boat falls were wooden blocks and manila rope. Just block and tackle and the boats had to be lowered and raised by manpower. There were no power winches. Except for being larger the boat equipment didn't represent a lot of improvement over what Christopher Columbus had on his ships. Despite the crude equipment the crew of the *Nishmaha* launched three boats in moderate seas, picked up seventy-two exhausted survivors from seven rafts scattered over several miles of the South Atlantic Ocean. The survivors were brought aboard the ship and the three boats recovered, all done without a mishap of any kind, not so much as a smashed finger. Most of it done in the dark.

On April 3, 1943 West of Oporto, Portugal, HMS Stonecrop *and HMS* Black Swan *destroyed the* U-124 *and all hands aboard including Kapitan Mohr. As for the S.S.* Nishmaha, *an angel sat on her bow for the remainder of her war-time journey. Captain Murray wrote:*

> The *Nishmaha* was a gallant old ship and a lucky ship. She served the war effort well, operating in all theaters of the war. She was in the war from the beginning to the end and finished the war without a scratch from enemy action. I last saw the *Nishmaha* at a cargo dock in Houston in 1949. She was under foreign flag and I went on board, for old times sake and visited with the Greek officers.[3]

2

DETERMINATION

*D*ick Burton lives in Lexington, Kentucky. His daughter, Trina Burton, wrote down his story in 1996. Dick was one of eighteen children. Four brothers served in the Armed Forces in World War II and four other brothers served our country after the war. Dick, like most merchant mariners, performed an act of patriotism and heroism by volunteering to go in harm's way. He could have sat out the war and earned good money ashore but kept trying, despite his disability, to serve his country and finally, by sheer persistence, found a way to serve as a volunteer in the merchant marine including service in the dangerous waters of the Mediterranean, North Africa and the North Sea. The irony was that when he got home, merchant mariners weren't acknowledged as "being in the service" — a situation that continued for fifty years!*

~~~

I was born at home, on September 26, 1924, in the eastern Kentucky hills of Morgan County. I was my mother's ninth child. My parents went on to have a total of eighteen children — a dozen boys and a half dozen girls.

When I was just a toddler, around eighteen months old, I wandered out to the wood yard and picked up an axe. I was curiously trying my hand at chopping wood, as I had seen all my elders do. I dropped the axe and it landed on my foot, cutting my ankle. The cut became infected, and I developed blood poisoning. Gangrene damaged the tissue in my foot, and the doctor and others doubted that I would ever walk again. Most remarked that I would be probably crippled for the rest of my life. Although I had to crawl or was carried until I was five years old, I never believed that I was a cripple. So, with all the determination that I could muster, I overcame and walked again. The permanent damage of the injury prevents me from setting my left heel all the way down, flat. Eventually, the only visible sign remaining was the "bounce," in my step. From then on, I've tried to prove that I wasn't a cripple. So, with something to "prove," I used every opportunity to "take on all comers," that challenged me. I was a real scrapper!

My oldest brother, Marvin, age thirty-one, joined the Navy in 1942. He had been a policeman before, so they assigned him to shore patrol. He served in Norfolk, New York, and Boston. Two other brothers, Oral, age twenty-six, and Osie, age twenty, joined the Army in 1942. They trained at Fort Hood in Texas. Oral went on to serve in General Patton's 3rd Army in the European Theatre. Osie signed up with the paratroopers and was assigned to the 101st Airborne. He jumped at Normandy on D-Day, also in Holland and Bastone, at the Battle of the Bulge. He jumped once more, fifty years later, in 1994 in Richmond, Kentucky, in commemoration of the Normandy invasion.

Younger brother, Rusty, at age seventeen, begged our Mom and Dad, until he finally convinced them to sign for him to join the Navy, in early 1943. On Christmas Day, 1943, Rusty was injured during the invasion of New Britain Island, in the South Pacific. He lay on the deck, near death, for most of the day. When he was found, they took him for dead and placed him under the

Flag with the other bodies for a burial at sea. Luckily, someone saw some movement and they removed him to the sick bay. Four days later, his right leg was amputated above the knee. We didn't hear about it until early 1944 when we received a message from the War Department, stating that he was Missing In Action. After this, I was determined to join the service, but my mother urged me to wait until my number came up from the draft.

When my draft number came up, in early 1943, I was very excited. I went to the Induction Center in Detroit. When I went for the physical exam, the doctor remarked how "the Marine Corps could use healthy, strong guys like you . . ." But, when my exam was completed, the doctor continued writing on my form. When I reached the final inspection, a Lieutenant stamped the form "Rejected." When I saw that, I went nuts and grabbed the stamp out of his hand, and yelled, "What do you think you're doing?" He said, "We find you unfit for military duty." It was due to the foot injury I had suffered as a baby. Once again, I had something to prove. I was worthy to serve! I said, "You want men to fight, don't you? Bring on three or four of your best men, and I'll prove that I'm physically fit to fight!" I was out of control, so he sent someone upstairs to get the captain in charge. Captain Bebe was a level-headed man. He diplomatically got me out of there, and took me to lunch. I calmed down and sadly accepted the outcome. When I went back to work as a 4-F, things just weren't the same. I felt like my chance to serve was gone.

After that, I had a real chip on my shoulder. Every able-bodied man was serving their country . . . and here I was. There was a popular song of the time, "The gravy's in the Navy, the rest is in the Army, and what's left will never harm you — they're either too gray or too grassy green." I hated that song!

Every week, I went to the local draft board to see if they would change my status, but there was nothing they could do. Soon thereafter, I read in the newspaper where the Army Corps of Engineers was accepting 4-F's. Once again, I went to Detroit to sign up. After going through the physical again, no one said anything about my physical condition. But, after I was finished, my papers were on top of a stack, and one of the doctors, leaning over the table, noticed mine and took a closer look. He said, "Who's this man? We need to check him again." They called me and checked me again . . . and, once again, rejected me. I was devastated. But I had learned it would do no good to protest, so I went back to Battle Creek, very discouraged.

Once again, I read where 4-F's were being activated, this time by the merchant marine, hiring men to serve on ships. I headed out for Detroit, again. It was June 6, 1944, the date of the Normandy invasion. I spent that night in Ypsilanti, Michigan, with my brother, Osie. I signed up with the merchant marine the next day. One week later, I entered the Maritime Training Base at Sheepshead Bay, New York. I was finally accepted!

My first trip was to Cuba and Jamaica. We shipped out of Brooklyn, New York on August 30, 1944. We were on an Army transport ship named U.S.A.T. *General George S. Simonds*. That tour lasted two months. We were transporting men back to the U.S.A. to work in defense plants. While anchored in Jamaica Bay, the captain made an announcement over the loudspeaker for no one to go swimming, because the waters were shark-infested. The chief electrician said, "Dick, let's dive off the ship!"

I said, "Didn't you hear the captain's announcement?"

He said, "What's the matter? You chicken?"

So, we stripped off to the waist and went to top deck, climbed on the lifeboats and jumped. It was about sixty feet to the water. As we were swimming back, the sharks started coming in . . . and we barely made it! We had huge red spots and bruises on our bodies from hitting debris in the water. And the captain chewed us out, good!

My first rank in the merchant marine was messman. That meant peeling a lot of potatoes and breaking a lot of eggs. I had to sign a waiver stating that I would enter the merchant marine under the Stewards' Department, due to my 4-F status. But I worked my way up through the ranks to Ordinary Seaman then Able Seaman, where I served as a Carpenter's Mate and Bos'n's Mate. That meant I worked on deck instead of down in the galley. The different types of ships I served on were: Army Transport ships, one tanker, and one hospital ship. Many of our trips were to deliver fresh troops, and to pick up wounded. The tanker was, obviously, delivering fuel.

The dangerous waters of the Mediterranean, which had many explosive mines, made our missions very treacherous. While in the Mediterranean Sea, we dropped depth charges, due to submarines in our area. Once, our ship hit one of the charges and damaged us so badly, we had to go to dry dock for repairs. We traveled to the ports of Oran, Algeria, on the coast of North Africa, and Marseilles, France, in the Mediterranean Sea. We went to LeHarve and Cherbourg, France, in the English Channel. We went to Swansea, Wales, and on up to Liverpool, in the Irish Sea. I remember making seven trips to Bremerhaven, Germany. To get there, we traveled north, through the English Channel and the Straits of Dover, to the North Sea. I passed the White Cliffs of Dover fourteen times.

While serving on the *Charles A. Stafford* hospital ship, coming back from Europe, we received an SOS from a cargo ship in our area. This ship was transporting, among other things, mules for UNRS (United Nations Relief Service). They had a fellow on who had been kicked by one of the mules and was suffering from a ruptured appendix. He needed to be removed to our ship for treatment or he would probably die.

I was among the men chosen to accompany the first mate as we were lowered in a life boat, down the side. The waters were very high and choppy. One of the doctors on board, Major McGraw, had a movie camera and filmed the rescue operation. The life boat was lowered by pulleys. When they were disconnected, they were swinging wildly, as the boat pitched about in the choppy water. One of the pulleys was about to hit the first mate, but I shoved him out of

Lifeboat lowered off the hospital ship Charles A. Stafford *to retrieve patient from cargo ship. Dick Burton.*

the way. At the time he didn't know what happened, but later he saw the film, and was very grateful to me.

As we approached the cargo ship, we threw them a line, but they missed it. Our little boat drifted in back of the cargo ship. A big wave caused the rudder to come up, high out of the water. At which time, we drifted underneath the rudder! I remember looking up at the massive prop and thought we were "goners." But when the ship came back down, the force of it coming down pushed us back out from underneath the ship. Whew! That was close! Then they tossed us a line, and we pulled beside the cargo ship. They then lowered the patient, we took him back to our ship, and he was successfully operated on.

When we made it back to New York, it was fun to be in the "Big Apple." There was so much to see and do. I would go to the

In 1996 Dick's daughter, Trina, painted her father standing on the Charles A. Stafford's *life rafts, from a photo taken while he was aboard. Dick Burton*

Pepsi Canteen, in Times Square. They let servicemen record messages on 45 rpms to send home. Once, I recorded myself singing the merchant marine song and sent it home. Many years later around 1960, my daughter found it. It became her favorite record. She still remembers the tune!

I also went to the Merchant Marine Service Club. It was sponsored by the American Theatre Wing. They provided discount tickets to all the shows,

Dick Burton, left, and two unidentified shipmates aboard the hospital ship. Dick Burton.

ballgames, etc. A serviceman could even get reduced fare home. The problem was that merchant mariners weren't acknowledged there as "being in service." So, our uniform wasn't recognized. I would have to ask other servicemen to get the tickets I needed.

I am proud to have served my country in the merchant marine, which was made up of all volunteers. The danger was every bit as real for us as it was for the other branches of the service. I am extremely proud to see the merchant marine is finally being recognized for their great and necessary contribution to the war effort.

And, I am very glad to see them gaining the much deserved recognition as veterans. I am now an active member of the Ohio Valley Chapter of the Merchant Marine Veterans.[1]

Ashore in New York in 1945 in Army Transport Service uniform. Dick Burton

Dick Burton as a professional boxer in Lexington, Kentucky in 1948. Dick Burton.

3

ENLISTMENT AND TRAINING

*W*hen the United States entered the war in December 1941, only "about 55,000,"[1] merchant seamen and officers were sailing. It became vital to train as many men in as rapid a manner as possible. Available manpower that volunteered and enlisted was at a premium throughout the war. The merchant marine did not have the luxury of a Selective Service pool to choose from.

The Maritime Service was in desperate need of men and, with parental consent, those as young as sixteen could join the merchant marine. After six weeks of training an applicant could get a job in the steward's department as a messman or utilityman. If the lad was sharp enough, he qualified for thirteen more weeks of training and could work on deck or in the engine room.

Early in the war, the lack of crews caused many merchant ships not to sail. "In the spring of 1942, ship delays from the lack of crews reached a critical point with an average of about 45 a month."[2]

The initial responsibility for training belonged to the United States Maritime Service, which was charged with this task by the Merchant Marine Act of 1936. Because of the large numbers needed, the War Shipping Administration Training Organization, took over this responsibility early in the war. Training was accomplished through three means:

1. The United States Merchant Marine Cadet Corps at Kings Point, which trained Deck and Engine Department officers. Schools in San Mateo, California and Pass Christian, Mississippi supported the U.S. Merchant Marine Academy by sending their graduates to the Academy after basic training.

2. The United States Maritime Service, which operated training stations for unlicensed seamen to be trained as stewards, deck or engine personnel. These schools were located in Avalon, California, St. Petersburg, Florida and the largest, Sheepshead Bay, in New York. Additional training was given to trainees selected for purser-hospital duties or as radio operators. Radio schools were established in Cold Spring Hills, New York, Gallup's Island, Boston Harbor, Massachusetts, and at Hoffman Island in New York Harbor. Upgrading schools for officers were established in Fort Trumbull, New London, Connecticut and Alameda, California. Other upgrading schools for bakers, cooks, officers and seamen were established in Wilmington, California, San Francisco, Seattle, New Orleans, Baltimore and Boston.

3. And, finally, there were five State Maritime Academies that trained officers: New York, California, Maine, Massachusetts and Pennsylvania. Together, "these schools trained a total of 270,000 seamen and 10,000 officers. Another 23,000 received refresher training, along with 7,500 radio officers and 5,300 pursers."[3]

Glen Trimble, who went for radio training at the Otto Kahn estate in Cold Spring Hills, recalled, "Each class of radio officers that were gathered up from the various boot camps were first sent here for a 'weed-out' session. The rumor was only the top fifty percent of any group were to be sent on to the six month school at Gallup's Island. I know we did not lose fifty percent of our class, but closer to fifteen percent."[4]

In the introduction to the training manual, This Is Sheepshead Bay*, the superintendent of the school wrote:*

> The discerning reader, however, will see beyond this description of a training unit geared for wartime emergency. The aim, to train men well for service on American ships, will have perhaps even greater purpose and importance in post-war years.
>
> Today, the United States is the greatest maritime nation in the world. Maintenance of this position after the war will have a major effect upon the permanence of peace and the effectiveness of security measures.[5]

~~~

The following story, and especially the letters, will bring back vivid memories of the early training days for many merchant mariners. It was sent to me by William Kellett of Lafayette, Colorado. Bill was the only boy in the family and his mother was a widow trying to raise three children at home. Their father was tragically killed in a mining accident on Bill's tenth birthday. He graduated from high school in 1942 and had to go to work to help support the family. He began work as an aircraft mechanic under the civil service in Denver, Colorado. His first assignment was to Peterson Air Force Base in Colorado Springs. In 1943 he was transferred to Lowry AFB in Denver, where he was injured in March of 1943. He was called for a physical by the draft board on June 4, 1943 and rejected for military service based on his injury. Herein are some of his memories along with portions of letters he sent to his mother.

Religion has always played a strong part in my life. In 1944, I went to Fort Worth, Texas and enrolled in the Baptist Seminary. Three events occurred there that changed my goal in life. If I had been able to go to college, I would have been a history teacher. That is what I wanted to be. In the seminary, one of the courses was church history and that was down my line. So I studied hard on this subject. I finished the summer semester and returned home.

Another event was the requirement to go down on the city streets of Fort Worth and preach. A group would go with a portable organ and set up on a street corner and sing to get a crowd and then preach. I felt uncomfortable doing this; I enjoyed speaking before people in school and church, but not on the street.

The third event was the guilty feeling of not being in the service. When I went to the barber shop to have my hair cut, the topic of students at the seminary was raised, and the barber's comment was that they were a bunch of men trying to avoid military service. That hurt, as I felt his remarks were aimed at me. It made me all the more determined to do something to get into the service. I requested a new physical, but was turned down by the draft board.

There was a radio broadcast "We Deliver The Goods" every weekend concerning the merchant marine, urging young men to join. I would listen to that and I made up my mind I would try to join. I made out an application and passed the physical, but was restricted to steward training only. That was working in the galley as a cook or helper. They would not allow me to be in the engine room or the deck gang where heavy work was required.

I enlisted in January 1945 and we boarded a train for the training station at Catalina Island in California on 10 February 1945. We were on the train for two nights and two days. We were confined to the cars and not allowed to get off at any of the stops. We were under supervision all of the time.

We arrived in Long Beach, California and were put up for the night at the YMCA and the next day taken to the waterfront to await the ship that would take us to Catalina Island.

A short explanation of what the United States Maritime Service was and what our training facility was like on Catalina Island is necessary. The United States has always neglected its merchant fleet. The demand for ships to transport goods to two war fronts required training facilities to turn out large numbers to man these ships.

The peace time merchant seamen were looked on as the dregs of society. Most of them went to sea because they could not adjust to everyday jobs. They were heavy drinkers and, in many cases, trouble makers. This pool of men was used up early in the war and the new ships had to have new crews. Thus the need for training facilities.

Catalina Island was owned by the Wrigley family and they were in the process of developing it into a resort. The island, about twenty miles off the coast of California, is about four miles wide, twenty-five miles long, and is mountainous. Avalon is the only city on the island. When the war started, all commerce between the island and mainland ended. The ships were taken over by the government and the establishment of a training station helped the civilian population and business.

Our parade ground was the former Chicago Cub's baseball diamond. The country club was our hospital. The hotels were used for different stages of recruit training and housing. The casino was used for shows, dances, and church services. The two ships that carried tourists to the island in peacetime were used to train deck and engine crews.

On our arrival at Catalina Island, we were assigned our quarters. There were small cabins about 8 x 10 laid out on streets like city blocks. Each of these cabins had four men assigned to them in two sets of bunk beds. There was a wash basin in the units with only cold water. That was to be our living quarters through basic training. It was run like any military training area. We were issued our clothes (twenty-seven items — value $49.78 all of which had to have our name stenciled on them) and then training began.

We had a specific routine that would begin at 6 AM and carry through all day. We had classes, drills, physical training, etc. The only difference between our training and the Navy's, was that we weren't allowed to carry rifles. Merchant seamen were supposed to be treated as civilians. In war, that does not happen. We would be subject to attack by submarines more than naval vessels. We were assigned to gun crews and had to train in that area, but no small arms.

Part of the training involved swimming, boat drill, and jumping into the water from a tower, using our pants as life jackets, ways to hold on to floating objects, etc. They were concerned with teaching us how to survive if our ship was torpedoed and sunk.

William Kellett was eventually assigned to the T-2 Tanker, S.S. Fort George *and sailed from San Pedro to Ulithi, the Admiralty Islands, Australia, Persian Gulf, New Guinea, Hawaii, and back to San Pedro. Following are some excerpts from the letters he sent home to his mother telling her what training was like. They all begin with "Dear Mom" . . . and end with "Love, Bill."*

February 15, 1945

We have been up since 6 this morning and on the go ever since. We had swell meals today and a class on boat nomenclature. We had a couple lectures and had tests all afternoon. How is everything at home . . . I haven't written to anyone yet, but hope to over the weekend. We have guard duty Saturday. Tomorrow we are going to go out on the parade ground and drill.

I've sure been lucky. All the boys in our cabin are protestant; 3 methodists and me. We are going to sign up with the choir as soon as we can.

We've been to the shower and washed our clothes, polished our shoes, and now it is about time to shave for tomorrow. The only bad thing about it is we have to shave in cold water.

We sure have a swell section leader, but he can be rough too. He warned us today that if we disobeyed his order, he would put us on the beach with full sea pack and march for an hour. The only thing I hate is the 7 more shots we have to take . . .

February 17

. . . We took our fourth shot yesterday and my small pox vaccination has taken again. We still have 5 shots to take, but they aren't too bad. (In a letter dated February 18 to an aunt and uncle, Bill jokes, 'Some of the boys ask if they will receive the purple heart for all their wounds.') Everyday now we are rowing in our lifeboats. We have to wear life preservers at all times. Our first day of rowing, our boat hit the steering oar on another boat and knocked a man overboard. It sure was funny, but he was soaked when we pulled him aboard.

It is foggy out here most of the time, but the sun does break through once and awhile. If we continue to stay in the honor section we will get Island liberty in two weeks and in four weeks we get 23 hours leave on the mainland. My bunkmate has an aunt or cousin in Long Beach, so we are going there together. Next week we will get into routine. We can't go to church in the morning, but in the afternoon we will. I guess we will go to the show also. I have to go to the dentist when we get on maintenance duty.

I am going to try to go to Cook and Baker school for 10 weeks. I think it will be interesting. It has a future after the war too, if you are a good baker. The food has been very good so far. Breakfast today consisted of shredded wheat, milk, coffee, eggs, toast. Dinner: Rolls, butter, coffee, potatoes, gravy, beef, corn and pie. Not bad is it . . .

February 19

Here it is, the end of another day and it has been a rather tough one. We were up late last night and had to roll out early this morning. We have been assigned our routine for the week. It covers; ship nomenclature, first aid, rowing, marching, elementary seamanship, and physical training. Each class lasts an hour. In physical training, we have to run an obstacle course, climb a mountain, calisthenics, boxing, football, volley ball, relay races and other games. It is rough to start with, but I think everything will get easier as we go along. We will be in first aid for a week and also tieing ropes, etc.

Today our section didn't fare very well in inspection. We got 6 demerits so some of the fellows are assigned extra duty. We are trying for the honor section, which means extra liberty.

Last night we went to the Casino and saw a C.B.S. radio broadcast. It was "We Carry The Goods." It can be heard there about 10:30 over KLZ. You can find it in the radio section of the paper. We are all assembled there every Sunday night, so you never know. I might get to speak to you over the radio.

I have been writing a letter every day, but still haven't received any mail. A fellow sure feels lonely when everyone else gets mail and you don't ...

Mom, if you can spare any of the money I send home, pay it on my account at Montgomery Ward. A person don't need much money out here. I still have five dollars left from what you gave me when I left home. If a guy goes on liberty though, he has to have some money. I don't even know if I'll go ashore though. I don't have anyone to go see and the other kids all have quite a bit of money to spend ...

It sure has been a funny day. First the sun was shining, then it rained awhile, then the sun came through, and it ended up cloudy and rather cool. You feel the cold more out here on account of the dampness. It takes 2 days for clothes to dry because it is so damp ...

Tell D to keep in school because it will do her plenty of good. If I had bookkeeping and typing I could go to purser school and become an officer. As it is, I'll have to stay here.

I am feeling fine, eating like a horse, and sleeping like a log. I haven't had a cold at all since I left, but some of the other fellows aren't quite as fortunate.

February 23

... We have Captain's inspection tomorrow and it will be really rough. We have to roll all our clothes and lay them out on the bunk. Everything has to be just so.

Today we had our first exams. I got 100 in Elementary Seamanship, 94 in First Aid and I don't know my grade on the other test. They were easy and I should have had a perfect in all of them. This afternoon we had to climb the mountain and boy was I tired. I was the fifth one up and stayed well up coming down.

I guess we aren't going to be paid until the 5th. It's going to make us skimp to cover it. We may get Island liberty next weekend. I think we are the honor section and that entitles us to extra liberty. I guess there are lots of places to go if you want too. There is a bird farm here with many varieties of birds, so that ought to be interesting. I might even try my hand at sea fishing. There seems to be a lot of fish out here. They just swim in schools.

February 24

… Today has been busy, exciting and something new. We had to lay out for the Captain's inspection first. That includes cleaning the cabin from top to bottom, rolling all your clothes, and laying them out just so on the bunk. It was the first we've had and the whole section passed 100%. If we passed our marching test we will be well on our way to being honor section. It means extra liberty for the section next Saturday and Sunday.

We marched in our first review and it is really something to see. There is a band and drum and bugle corps. They are dressed in blues. The advanced trainees are all dressed in whites, and we were in dungarees or overalls to you. It sure makes a beautiful sight with 8 men abreast marching by the reviewing stand.

On the reviewing stand were high ranking officers of the Merchant Marine and Navy. It sure gives you a thrill to be part of it and know that you are playing an important part in the war. We are all volunteers and most men have more respect for us than the draftees. I hope we have some pictures taken of our section . . . Maybe you'd like to know what one of our obstacle courses is like. Well here it is: 100 yard run with 6 - 30" hurdles, crawl through a pen that is 18" high without touching your stomach, climb a "Jacob ladder," (rope ladder), climb down a cargo net, up a 16 ft. ladder and lower yourself hand over hand by rope, walk with your hand on 2 x 4's, go hand over hand 30 feet, swing across a 14 ft. pit on a rope, walk up and down a 2 x 4, climb over 6 ft., 8 ft., and 5 ft. wall and that about completes it. I can do all but walk with my hands on a 2 x 4. I can't do that because both elbows have to be locked straight and I can't lock my crooked one. I haven't had anything that I couldn't do yet …

I went over this afternoon for male chorus tryouts and I made it. I am singing baritone in the chorus which gives me an Island liberty privilege every Sunday. That chorus is really something to hear. There is no accompaniment, it is all harmony. I have a part that I can sing for the first time, it isn't too high or too low …

… I only received two letters this past week. Hope more arrives next week. If you don't have anything to write, fill an envelope with clippings from the Post or Rocky Mountain News. We are all hungry for news from the outside.

February 26

... I weighed myself this morning and am up to 149 pounds already, so I guess the work isn't hurting me. I'm so full now that I am going to lay down for awhile. I no sooner got my shoes off and lay down when they called the show party. We assembled and marched over to the Casino. The show was good. It was funny and still had a good plot to it. The name of it was "This Man's Navy." There was a dance after the show, but we couldn't go without having our blues which we haven't. I am writing this from time to time so it may sound funny ...

Here it is Sunday again. We were allowed to sleep until 7 o'clock before we had to get up and we didn't have to clean our cabin unless we wanted to. I made my bunk and mopped out the cabin just the same. If you saw me eat breakfast now, you'd think I was a pig or kick me in the seat of the pants. Guess what I ate for breakfast; a large bowl of cornmeal mush, 3 pancakes, ham and rolls. I sure was full when I finished. That's one thing about here, we get plenty to eat. I came back from breakfast and took my nice cold shave in cold water. I had to change my dungarees and shirt before I went to choir practice. I think I will really like singing in the choir. They had a fine selection of hymns and an interesting sermon ...

I think I might be a sailor now. We received our dress uniforms today so as soon as I can, I'll send you some pictures. I don't know how expensive they will be and I may have to wait till payday. But I'll get them as soon as I can. Time is sure going fast out here. They keep us busy in our studies and I guess this is the reason why. I sure hope I can keep up my average. It is about 97 now and I'm going to try and get 100's in the rest of my exams ...

They sure are shipping the boys out fast. If things keep up, we may have to go in two or three weeks if they need seamen too bad. A lot of boys are moving out of the Villa into the hotels to make room for new recruits tomorrow. The Merchant Marine is like the Army. The clothes are either too big or too small ...

March 1, 1945

… I'm so tired tonight that I won't write much. We are down in the dump. We have extra duty again tonight. Someone put cookie crumbs on the floor after we left. We were just called in and had to swab out all the heads. It isn't bad though. It is raining cats and dogs out here now … Did my government check come through all right? I'll send most of my pay home next week. We're supposed to be paid the 5th. We haven't been swimming yet, but will be next week. My shots are ok now. Ask Dee if you would want a knife or a black wool sweater. I think I can buy them at the lucky bag …

March 5

… About those checks Mom. Take them up to Davis's and he will cash them. At least he said he would. You have my permission to sign them. I am sending $20.00 home to you. Use them for whatever you have to. If Dolores needs anything for school you can buy it for her. I don't need much money here and I don't know if we will go to the mainland or not. I've just finished two days of Island liberty so I have to get used to marching again.

I won't be able to write much tonight because I have an awful lot of studying to do. Friday is our finals and if we don't pass it means 6 months to a year at sea before we can take them again. I sure hope I can make the grade on them.

There are 600 recruits coming in tomorrow so we had to move tonight. I sure am disappointed with our new quarters. You have to get a pass to do anything and it is crowded. Only two wash basins to a floor for about 60 men.

We sure have some interesting and important classes this week. We are studying for our lifeboat certificate, practicing abandon in lifeboats, etc. We also have poison gas this week, emergency equipment, signals and rescue. We start drilling tomorrow on our guns. We are to man 20mm anti-aircraft guns. It is really going to keep us busy with all the studying and work on the side …

March 7

 … We've been busy this week. We had to leave this villa Monday night and went to the Boos Brother Hotel. It isn't as nice as the Villa though. There must be 150 men here. There are only 6 toilets and 6 wash basins, and 3 bathtubs for all to use. So you can see how crowded it is and it is not very convenient. We had a wash basin in every cabin in the Villa and most of them had wash tubs. There were also public showers to go to if you didn't have a tub. Here we don't have anything. No canteen, no place to wash our clothes, and no recreation. It is just like being penned up in a chicken coop.

 Tuesday night we had guard duty again, but I was lucky. I was a standby in case anyone got sick or had to leave his post. I was able to sleep all night long and wasn't called out. I also did my laundry. It took and hour and a half to do it. Most of the time being spent waiting for a bucket to wash in.

 Tonight, I want to study so I'm staying here in the room. I went to the counselor and made an application for advanced training. I sure hope I get it. It means a better job and more pay when I go to sea …

 I did write to Betty, but I don't care if I do anymore or not. Her and Francis are getting awful thick and you know how I feel about her. I only wrote to her, so I'd have mail coming. I think a lot more of Dorothy, but you don't need to worry. As long as the war is on, I'm not even going to consider going steady or marrying. Dorothy is a swell girl, but that's about as far as it goes. I've been jolted so many times mom, that I don't trust any of them. If all I had to worry about was women, I wouldn't have any worries at all. It's nice to have them write to you and all that but, I don't have any ideas at all …

 Well today I had my first swim in the ocean and boy was it cold. They wanted some pictures of lifeboats so we went out and turned one of them over. Then we had to turn it right side up. It was cold, but fun. One of the boys cramped so we had to put him in a launch and take him to shore. We all had to wear life preservers, so there wasn't any danger of drowning. That gives you an idea of the training we get. They do all they can to teach men to save their lives. If it's at all possible to get away from a ship, we'll know how. Everything protects us in all ways.

… We had a light supper tonight so I went through the line twice. I ended up eating 7 buns, jam, cup of pineapple juice, quart of milk and salad. They had fish and I wouldn't eat that. Well mom guess I had better sign off for tonight and start to study. I have a lot to do tomorrow night, stage and screen stars are coming from Hollywood to entertain us … (In a letter to his aunt and uncle, Bill wrote that the performers were from the Hollywood Canteen. The Mills sisters, who perform with Spike Jones, sang along with Christy Martin and Gloria Hughs.) I sure would like to have a cheap pen to write with. Out here they don't have any at all … I'll send as much home each pay as I possibly can. You only spend it foolishly here; candy, magazines, and cocoa …

P.S. Write as often as you can. A letter from home means a lot. It's going to be a tough pull and I'll need all the encouragement I can get.

Tell Mr. Mayfield I send my regards and pray that his father may remain with him a little longer. If he does pass away, give him my sympathy.

March 12

… We are still on mess detail and will be until Wednesday. I am working in the bake shop and I am learning a little I guess. We bake bread in the morning and pastry in the afternoon. It isn't like baking at home though. We use 2 lbs. of yeast, 1 lb of sugar, 50 #'s of flour, etc. That gives you an idea. I had to crack my first eggs today. I'm awfully slow, but maybe I'll learn …

I had to spend two hours in the dentist chair today. They saved all my teeth and filled three of them today. I have to go back the 21st and have the rest of them taken care of. I sure hate it, but I don't want to go to sea and then have tooth aches all the time.

I received a notice to report Wednesday for an interview about Cook and Baker training, so I should know before too long if I will be in advanced. I kind of hope to go to school, and then I would like to go to sea and get some money coming in . . .

March 29

I received your letter yesterday and was very glad to hear from you. It's at this point when a fellow needs a lot of mail from home. After being here eight weeks, a man begins to get restless. There is nothing to do but march and go to class. Our Island liberties are so limited and there is no place to go. I used to think that the U.S.O. was the bunk, but I've changed my mind. We can come here and write letters, read the latest news, and get a good cup of coffee or milk. If I have a lot of spare time, I work puzzles. All of this helps take your mind off of things. You would be surprised to see how long some of the days can be. It just seems like they will never end. I've been to chorus this afternoon and now am down at the U.S.O. Tonight I guess I'll take in a couple of shows and call it a day. We were supposed to go to the mainland, but were forced out of it. I would have liked to go just to get away from the Island.

… Monday we moved from our old barrack to the Saint Catherine Hotel. We also started our C.B. class. We've been busy cooking and Monday we start to butcher. Maybe I'll know a little when I get out …

We've been busy rowing everyday and I can say that I'm getting better at handling a boat each day. We had a practice rescue and landings and I passed them all ok. All a person needs is confidence. After you gain that you can do anything. While we were out rowing a navy flying boat came in and made a landing. That's the first time I ever saw an airplane land and take off out of water. They do it so graceful and really throw back a spray. While standing on the dock we saw a school of fish come into the harbor, some would even jump out of the water. Then a flock of pelicans swooped in and began catching fish. Some of them would dive right into the water while others would barely skim the surface. They sure were fast and like a flock of hawks.

It's these little things that help change the monotony. Sometimes the fellows play records on the juke box that sure makes a guy feel blue. I guess some days are worse than others …

How is D and her school work coming along? I've sent another box of cigarettes so be on the lookout for them. I hope they get through all right. It will be the last I can send. They are getting very strict about it here. Too many kids are making a racket out of it. They can get 25-50 cents per package on the mainland and that's the truth. You can even buy gas without a stamp if you will get a carton of cig. So you can understand why I can't send anymore. I'll send a few if I can once in awhile.

March 31

… This is Saturday so we all had to march in review. It sure was hot and the glare was terrific with everyone dressed in whites. The biggest honor of the morning came when the commanding officer read a telegram from General Douglas McArthur citing the Merchant Marine for their heroic work in the Philippines Campaign.

The day is really beautiful and I guess I will stay out in it as much as possible. There is to be another U.S.O. dance tonight, but it will be the same old thing.

When I say I really like it, I mean it mom. If I hadn't of gotten into the service, I don't know what I would have done. I don't like the way they do some things, but that can't be helped. In this large organization you can't please everyone and you have to be strict or the men could get out of hand.

I had a chance to go on the ships personal and remain here on the Island. It payed $94.00 a month, room and board. If I did take it you could have come out and stayed also if you wanted too. It didn't appeal to me so I turned it down.

But I do have a surprise for you. I have been selected for Cook and Baker training. We start classes tomorrow morning. They choose 15 men out of 400 to take it. It is really swell that I have made it and it also has added advantages. I have a change in rating and in my pay. My rating now is stewards mate 2/c and my pay is $54.00 per mo. If shipping continues slow when we finish our ten weeks of advanced, we will get a 10 day leave home. I sure hope we get it. We will come out either 1st, 2nd, or 3rd cooks. I think I will really like it, especially the baking. It just appeals to me …

I'm writing from the U.S.O. for a change. Here we have a table to write anyway and free stationary. It's awfully hard to write on a book or a table. It gets awful tiresome and the writing is sloppy.

Since I've made advanced, I'll be with the other boys from town … We still have a few other classes but half of our time will be in cooking and baking. We will get our lifeboat tickets now and that's important. We will still get physical training and sea safety …

They are having sunrise services tomorrow and I want to be there. It will truly be an experience. I know how much it means to the kids back home and it means a lot more for us in the service. Things aren't over yet and a lot of the boys will fail to return, but we can carry this with us. We will meet again in a land where there will be no war and no sorrow or parting. We have an everlasting home to go to if we will believe and follow Christ.

I'll be praying for you on Easter morning Mom and I know you'll be doing the same. I send all my love to you and maybe my sisters will go to church on that day. I've said all I can for now so will close.

> Your Loving Son & Bud
> Bill[7]

~~~

Walter Luikart, who resides in Pennsylvania, contributed the following story. He was typical of many young men who patriotically and determinedly worked to get into the merchant marine to serve in the war however they could.

How I Got Into The Merchant Marine

After trying to enlist in every service in the military and being rejected because of my weight (97 lbs.), I finally enlisted in the merchant marine. I even got rejected there, but the kind doctor told me if I could gain ten pounds in the next thirty days all I would have to do was to get weighed again without taking the physical.

I went on a crash diet of milk shakes, bananas, spaghetti, and carrots for my eyes. I was in high school and got the nickname of Mr. Rabbit because I always had a bunch of carrots in my pocket.

My weight did not pick up appreciably so when the time came for me to get weighed I still was under the ten pounds. I went to the bank and got all the change I could handle and hid it in my clothing and shoes and proceeded to be weighed. I waited until the line was up for weighing in and then got on line fully clothed. I pestered the doctor telling him all I needed was to be weighed. He said get on the darn scale and hesitated for a heart stopping second or so and said O.K., go ahead you passed. I was lucky to get out of there without my pants falling down from all the change in my pockets.

From there I went to Hoffman Island and three months of training. During the time I was there a peculiar incident occurred. I was chosen to go to the YMCA to test those rubber suits that turned out to be a big joke. In fact, one of the guys almost drowned because his suit filled up with water. From there I went to my first ship, the *Berkshier*.[8]

Merchantmen All

They came from the plains of Kansas-
From the rolling fields of wheat-
To serve aboard the merchant ships-
Cold decks beneath their feet.

They came from the Blue Ridge mountians-
Where hunting was their game-
To serve aboard the merchant ships-
In the ice, the snow, and rain.

They came from their ranches in Texas-
And the potato fields of Maine-
To serve aboard the merchant ships-
They were lost in smoke and flame.

They came from banks of Hatteras-
The sea they so well knew-
To serve aboard the merchant ships-
In the hell of World War Two.

They came from all over our country-
To answer their country's call-
To serve aboard the merchant ships-
Their country's forgotten them all.[9]

Ian A. Millar

4

FIRST VOYAGE

*I*n life, certain events involving a career, family, sport, or some important activity remain etched in memory forever. What occurred in between is often lost in everyday existence. For me, it was the first and last baseball games that I pitched. The first voyage for most mariners remains etched in stone, never to be forgotten.

~~~

Alfred A. New of Pendleton, Indiana writes about the knowledge a mariner acquires on his first voyage. Names were changed to avoid hurt feelings. Al retired as a steam engineer with the rank of Lt. Commander in the U.S.M.S.

43

Maiden Voyage of the *Jonathan Trumbull*

I was born on a small farm in central Indiana, a long way from the sea, but I got to visit New Orleans and some other ports a few times. I had been interested in ships ever since I was a small boy, especially when my mother used to read to me the stories by Guy Gilpatric about Colin Glencannon, the Scottish engineer on the freighter *Inchcliffe Castle.* I had loved steam engines ever since my father gave me a nice old brass working model which my sons still have in their collection.

We were laying a new carpet in my folk's living room one Sunday in December, and our radio was playing some sweet swinging tune by Henry Busse and his orchestra. Suddenly this program was interrupted by a news commentator who announced the attack on Pearl Harbor by the Japanese. This was later followed by President Roosevelt's speech, and the announcement of our declarations of war on the Japanese Empire and the Axis Powers.

Before long I got to thinking I had better get my act together and decide what branch of the service I wanted to go in. I considered it a disgrace to get drafted, and I never liked to get in a position to be forced to do anything I didn't want to do. I did not really want to leave home, but then again, I did. I, and everyone else, were mad at the Japs, and what we heard on the news made us hate the Germans and Italians. I am sure they fully deserved our feelings towards them.

Soon I got my orders from the U.S. Maritime Commission to report to New Orleans. When I arrived, I was sent to the U.S. Merchant Marine Basic School at Bay Saint Louis, Mississippi.*

Time really went fast at this school with basics in boat drill, gunnery, steam and diesel engineering, and all our other activities including a couple of training cruises on the school's vessel which,

---

* Because of the high demand for officers, the U.S. Merchant Marine Academy maintained prep schools at Pass Christian (Bay Saint Louis), Mississippi and San Mateo, California. After serving at these schools the cadets transferred to Kings Point as upperclassmen.

Pendleton Zoo Is Out for Duration; Keeper Joins Merchant Marine

Pendleton, Ind., Dec. 26.—(Special) — Pendleton's "home-grown" zoo has disbanded for the duration, for its keeper has a job to do in the merchant marine.

He is Midshipman Alfred A. New, U.S.N.R., son of Mr. and Mrs. Arthur A. New of Pendleton.

Upon graduation from high school, young New began to collect and train animals from many parts of the world. They were kept at his home here to be seen by the public.

In the menagerie were lions, jaguars, monkeys, badgers, snakes, birds and domestic pets.

During the last summer, preparatory to entering cadet training, New sold all of his strange collection except for a lion cub which he had purchased from Clyde Beatty. Now a friend in Anderson has the cub.

He completed basic training at the Merchant Marine Cadet School at Pass Christian, Miss., and was assigned to sea duty for six months. He will finish his training at Kings Point, N.Y.

MIDSHIPMAN ALFRED A. NEW.

With Al's acceptance to the Merchant Marine Academy, his earlier interests in animal training and zookeeping were put aside. The animals were sold and the zoo closed. Al New

I am sorry to say, had a diesel engine instead of steam. It ran well and we learned a lot anyway.

There were a lot of ships along the wharves, more than I had ever seen in one place, but the *Trumbull* looked the best to me of any of them. Some people called them "Ugly Ducklings," and "Kaiser's Creeping Coffins," but I liked Liberty ships. To me they are kind of pretty, and they looked like they were built to go out and do something useful, and maybe get you there and back. Better looking than the old World War I Hog Islanders. The *Trumbull* had a fresh coat of gray paint, nice looking lifeboats and rafts, a three-inch fifty caliber deck gun mounted forward, a four-inch fifty aft, and twenty millimeter guns amidships. The nice eight-inch diameter Star Brass whistle mounted on her stack was painted black.

When you joined the U.S. Merchant Marine Cadet Corps as a Cadet-Midshipman, either deck or engine, you also joined the U.S. Naval Reserve, even though you had seaman's papers and a Seaman's Passport. So we had been trained when going aboard a ship to stand at attention at the top of the gangway and salute the quarter deck. Ward and I both did this. I noticed some seamen around the deck, and even one fellow who I thought was an officer, were all grinning and laughing at us when we did this. That is the last time I ever did that on a merchant ship.

Cadet-Midshipman Al New at USMS Basic School, Pass Christian, Mississippi, October 11, 1942. Al New.

We were introduced to the first assistant engineer. Mr. Rankin. He was a big fellow wearing khakis and an Army Transport Service cap. He seemed like a nice guy, and he showed us around the engine room and fire room.

Now, on a Liberty ship the engine room and fire room (boiler room) are connected. These ships have a single main engine and condenser in the engine room along with three dynamos, the main circulating pump, blower engine, auxiliary condenser, hot wells, evaporator, and all the necessary feed, fire, bilge, and transfer pumps, etc. The fire room consists of two boilers, two settling tanks, the heaters, fuel pumps, transfer pumps, etc. Really a nice simple design. This ship had pretty much standard equipment for Libertys. The main engine was a twenty-five hundred horsepower three cylinder triple expansion condensing engine made by Worthington with 24-½-inch, 37-inch, and 70-inch diameter cylinders, and a 48-inch stroke. The boilers were cross drum sectional header water tube units fitted with superheaters, and made by Babcock & Wilcox. These boilers were designed to burn around thirty tons of bunker C oil per day. They totalled 10,234 square feet of heating surface, and had a working pressure of 220 pounds per square inch at a temperature of 450 degrees F.

I was starting to learn a little about the ship. She was four hundred and forty some feet long and had a single four blade propeller, and she was rated at over ten thousand tons deadweight and had a designed speed of eleven knots. The government classified these ships as EC2* vessels. Rankin kind of took me under his wing and really showed me around good in the hole. He let me start and stop some of the steam pumps and a dynamo, and showed me how to maneuver the main engine. He said he had been aboard when she was launched sideways by the local shipyard that built her, and he thought she was going to turn over when she hit the water. This shipyard that built her specialized in side launchings and all welded ships.

I got to be in the engine room for her trial run down the river. Tugs took us away from the wharf and then turned us loose for the first time.

Now it was time to make some adjustments in the engine room and other areas and to start loading fuel and supplies for the voyage, and to take on cargo. They loaded a lot of boxed and crated cargo in the holds including tanks, jeeps, ammunition, clothing, dry rations, etc.; with airplanes and jeeps in the tween decks. On deck were railroad tank cars filled with gasoline. These cars had their trucks off and were painted olive drab and

---

* E stands for "Emergency," C for "Cargo" and 2 indicates a length between 400 and 450 feet.

marked with the number of imperial gallons each held and with the gauge of whatever railroad they were going to. These cars were chocked and lashed down and catwalks were built between them.

The gun crew finally came aboard. This was a thirty man crew including their commanding officer, a Lt. (j.g.). He was a ninety-day wonder, but was a good guy and took his job seriously. He told me that when he was going to O.C.S., the thing they dreaded most was being assigned as gun crew on a merchant ship. Just before graduation, they had a play in school that portrayed some guy hanging himself because he had been assigned to the Armed Guard.

So, down the Mississippi we sailed. We went out the Gulf through South Pass.

We were assigned gun stations to man when we were off watch, and I was given one of the twenty millimeter guns amidships. I enjoyed shooting this gun when we had gun drill. I liked to watch the colored tracers. We learned to fire at high targets and also learned to fire low and lead our targets in case of torpedo bombers coming in low to the horizon. The gun crew practiced with the four-inch fifty stern gun by flying a kite tied to the aft rail. This kite flew well behind the ship. They never did hit the kite, but one shell cut the rope holding the kite, so they lost it. I guess that was the only kite they had because I never saw them try that again.

I was told not to associate very much with the deck department people. Rankin called them "sea-going truck drivers." I was glad to learn the different whistle and bell signals for fire, boats, etc., and also the abandon ship signal of seven short blasts and one long blast on the ship's whistle.

We got into the Caribbean. When I was off watch I enjoyed watching the porpoises and flying fish playing around the ship. Some of the seamen rigged two light lines to the stern rail. They had shark hooks on them with white rags wired to the hooks. They let them float astern, and caught a pretty blue and yellow dolphin fish and a barracuda that was about five or six feet long. They cleaned these and put them in the freezer. They were trying to catch sharks, which they all hated.

We anchored off Colon waiting our turn to go through the Panama Canal. We got to go ashore in Cristobal. We green seamen had not got our sea legs yet, and we were stepping pretty high as we walked along the docks. We went to a few sucker joints and got to stay ashore all night. I went to a gift shop and got some pretty pictures and a serving tray. Some of these were made with parrot feathers and some with butterfly wings.

Some of us tried out our life jackets and survival suits. You get up on the rail, look up at the sky, hold your nose shut with one hand, and jump out as far as you can. I sank down, down, down and went pretty deep into some soft stuff on the bottom. I wondered if I would ever come back up, but I did. I was glad it was not under the ship. They helped us back on board.

The ship got cleared to start through the canal. We went through the Gatun Locks. I noticed they had barrage balloons rigged over the locks to help protect them from torpedo bombers. This was all very interesting to me, as I had never been through a big lock before. After the locks we got out into the lake. There sure were a lot of ships of ours and our allies moving there including aircraft carriers, submarines, and others. Then on to Culebra Cut and Gold Hill with the big bronze plaque bolted to the side, dedicated to the men who worked on it. When I was a junior in high school I had worked as a water boy and load checker on a steam shovel gang on one of my father's road building projects. The steam shovel operator had told me that he had operated a steam shovel on the Panama Canal project. He said so many people were dying of malaria and yellow fever that he quit and came home. I thought about all those men when I saw the plaque.

There was a U.S. Marine in the engine room with us. He had a portable telephone to check with the bridge and make sure we were getting the proper engine room telegraph signals. There were other marines stationed aboard to prevent accidents or sabotage in one of the locks that would tie up canal traffic. Now we tied up outside Balboa. I was down below when Mr. Deck, the second engineer was on watch. He told me, "This is not going to be a trip right back to the States."

We went south down along the west coast. There must have been some kind of action going on somewhere near us. A double bottom tank under the engine room had been emptied so Rankin and I took off the man hole plate and went down in it to check it out and see about flushing it out. We were back in there a good way when a depth charge went off somewhere pretty close. It really resounded and shook in that tank which is only four feet deep and right on the bottom of the ship. Naturally we were squatting down, and when the first charge went off I jumped up and bumped my head on the bottom of the tank top. Rankin laughed at me, but after some more charges went off, we got out.

On that ship another bad place to be trapped in during action was the shaft tunnel, as there was no door from it into the engine room. There always was one on any other ships I had been in later, including other Libertys. Therefore, on the *Trumbull*, to get from the engine room to the propeller shaft, spring bearings, tunnel well, and stern gland you had to go up on deck and crawl down a narrow pipe chase. Then you could check and oil the bearings, check the stern gland to see if the labyrinth packing was leaking properly to lubricate the tail shaft, and pump out the well. Then you could go up a ladder in the stern and come up in the steering engine room. In other words, on that ship in time of action, the shaft tunnel was a good place not to be in. The oiler on each watch had to make the tunnel on their regular rounds, and the engineer on each watch was supposed to check it out also.

Our main engine was beginning to knock some. The first indication was the low pressure crosshead running hot, so each watch it was flushed out with kerosene and hosed down with cold water, but that didn't help much. We kept on steaming down the west coast of South America. When I was off watch, I was told that the most beautiful sunsets in the world could be seen in this area. They were beautiful, but I could not tell much difference between these sunsets and the sunsets in central Indiana. Maybe I was not observant enough.

We were running so far from the South American coast that we could not see land. I wanted to see the Andes. I thought maybe if we could get close enough that I could see Aconcagua, so I offered the first mate two hundred dollars if he would run her in close enough so that we could see something. He told me that he could not do this and he advised me that an enemy submarine had been following us. Someone seems to have seen the periscope or part of the conning tower.

As we got closer to Cape Horn, the weather got worse and the sea was rougher. That engine sure was carrying on. We shut her down on Christmas Day and keyed up on the crossheads, crank pin bearings, and main bearings. I got so hot and worn out swinging a sledge on the knock wrenches that I passed out for a little while. I would have fallen in the crank pit if they had not caught me. You engage the jacking gear and put steam on the jacking engine when you are working on the main engine. This way you can move the main engine back and forth as needed and also the main engine cannot turn by the movement of the propeller in the sea while you are in there working. One time, when I was keying up, I got pretty hot, and someone relieved me so that I could get a drink of water. I was on the port side of the engine room near the hot well, and I passed out again and fell right in the hot well with the loofah sponges. Luckily, it was the third stage I fell in and it was not hot enough to scald me. They pulled me out and I went back to swinging the sledge. We got her back together and started off again. We had not helped her much on the knocking, but at least the low pressure crosshead was running cool. I was so tired that as far as I got towards my bunk was the grating by the cylinder heads. Maybe I passed out again. I do not know, but at least that was where I was laying when the oiler shook me awake when it was time to go on watch again. I was getting broke in.

Everyone had been apprehensive about stopping with that submarine that was supposed to be following us still around, because we were dead in the water for more than ten hours. However, the seas were so rough by then that he could not have hit us anyway. We were trying to round Cape Horn and then run east across the Atlantic. The reason they sent us on such an out-of-the-way route was because we were running alone and they thought we would be safer on this route and have a better chance of getting there. We had to shut down again a week later, on New Year's Day. This time we pulled the low pressure cylinder head to see if any of the rings were broken. They were o.k. Most of the noise seemed to be coming from the aft end of the engine. We got under way as soon as we could.

The sea got even rougher. Forty foot waves, they said. I know we took a little water down the stack. The deck was awash most of the time. It really messed up those tank cars on deck, turning some nearly over, and tearing up the catwalks. I got up one time to go on watch, and when I put my feet over the side of the bunk, the water was half way up to my knees. My foot locker was floating around. The water was up level with the bottom of our door, and these watertight doors were around eight or ten inches from the deck. I guess we should have had the door dogged shut. This was clear up on the boat deck, so you can imagine what it was like down in the hole. If you were going to stay on your feet you had to hold on to something. The fireman just slid back and forth across the floor plates tending his fires. This is when I learned to stand a butterfly watch ... When you are in a heavy sea and the propeller is raising out of the water, you have to shut off the steam immediately or she would tear herself off the bed plates. You stand with one hand on an engine column and feel the engine shake from it speeding up when the screw bites the water again and she begins to settle down and work, you open the butterfly again. Our engine was in bad enough shape anyway, so we had to keep it from tearing up and speeding. There are no governors on these engines.

The *Trumbull* was not too bad a pitching ship, but she was a dead roller. She would roll over to a pretty good degree and then hang there and shake and shudder before she decided to roll over the other way. If you slept in a fore and aft bunk like we had, it kind of rocked you asleep, but sometimes it woke you up when she was hanging there and shaking. You wondered if she was coming back or was going to turn completely over. I had heard stories of ships that rolled over, completely capsized and drowned everyone.

Cape Horn! This was summer down there. I wondered what it would be like in winter. The sky was the same color night or day, the only way you could tell the difference was by the ship's clocks. One night we ran into an especially heavy cross sea, and the ship plunged into it and groaned and made another loud noise of some kind, similar to a cracking sound. We thought it was more damage to the railroad cars on deck, or maybe to the lifeboats, as they had been messed up some also. When we finally got around old Horn and into calmer seas, they had a chance to look things over better. They found one of the welded deck seams had cracked across the deck forward of the deck house. This crack extended about four feet down both sides of the ship. So she was coming apart at the seams now, but nothing too serious. We never sighted any land while making the Horn. The chief mate said he saw what looked like some black rocks off our port bow one night. He thought it might have been something near the Falkland Islands, but he said we were actually out of sight of land for forty-two days that trip.

We continued on across the Atlantic, bound for the Dark Continent. This part of the trip was uneventful. They kept saying that a submarine was still following us. They also said we crossed the equator eight times while we were zig-zagging along.

One night when we were nearing the Cape of Good Hope, I heard the bow gun go off. I learned later that the gun crew had seen something and thought that it was the submarine that was supposedly following us, so they shot at it. We learned real soon that they had blown a chunk out of the bow of a British ship. There was some stink over this action … Actually we had pretty good defenses on that ship. We had a degaussing system (demagnetizes a ship) to protect us from mines. I had the job of going down in the hold and resetting the polarity on this every time we went to an opposite magnetic field on the other side of the equator. About the only things we lacked that any other Libertys had were paravanes (used to sever mine moorings) and torpedo nets to trail along our sides. Some Libertys had larger stern guns, five-inch 38's.

They told us we were going to Durban, and as we got close in, a plane came flying over. We manned the guns, but they told us it was a British plane so we did not shoot at it. It had some red markings, and it rocked back and forth to greet us. We had studied silhouettes of planes so we could identify them in the dark conditions as enemy or not, but I was not too familiar with what the different ones looked like in the daylight. We went on into Durban, South Africa, and tied up.

We ran on up through the Mozambique Channel. Some seamen called it the Straits of Madagascar. One night when I was off watch, I was standing by the rail looking down at the water. I could not believe my eyes. It looked like a carnival all lighted up down there, with all the lights of different sizes and colors. Rankin came up by me and he said that it was luminescent marine life, mainly jellyfish.

We were traveling in the Indian Ocean one afternoon when Sparks and I were in the cabin shooting the bull. All of a sudden there was a bump that shook the ship pretty good. I told Sparks, "I think we have taken a torpedo, better go send an S.O.S."

He ran out and went to the radio room and was getting started when the first mate stopped him and said, "What are you up to?" Sparks told the mate that I had told him I thought he should send an S.O.S. The mate about croaked and told Sparks he was not supposed to pay any attention to what an engine cadet said, but to take his orders from them. I heard we had hit a small whale and pretty well mangled it.

We soon docked at Suez. This was our destination, so we started unloading cargo.

We had all had a full line of inoculations for various diseases, including a small pox vaccination, before we left New Orleans. We had our shot records with us. The Egyptian officials ignored these and lined us all up on deck and did everything over again before we were allowed to go ashore. We started working on the engine and other things that needed attention, and we doubled the watches again so we could be on eight and off sixteen. Sparks and I would go ashore together a lot of the time.

We went to a picture show. I don't know what the show was, but a big part of the time was taken by alternately showing full screen still photos of Joseph Stalin, Winston Churchill, and President Roosevelt. They played a song to the tune of, "We

Three Are All Alone," and showed the words in English, Russian, French, and Arabian at the sides of the screen. We were supposed to stand at attention and sing as each picture was shown, to the effect of:

"We three will make the world
Safer for democracy
Joe Stalin, Win Churchill, and Me,"

… if President Roosevelt's picture was up, and so on, with different beginning lines through the three pictures.

I wanted to see ancient Egypt.

Sparks and I hired a car to take us to Giza. I was impressed by the lions carved on the nice bridge across the Nile. Then, there were the pyramids of Giza right in front of us. What a sight! I about burst. We went to the Great Sphinx first. He had sand bags piled from the ground up to his chin to keep his head from getting knocked off by a bomb. We rented camels (dromedaries) to ride.

The Great Sphinx as it appeared in March, 1943 with masonry work and sand bags under the chin to prevent bomb damage. Al New.

Al New is second from right on "Missouri." Third from right is the radio operator and the other two are cadets from a different ship. Al New.

When we got ready to sail there were several Egyptian feluccas with their fancy painted bows and lateen sails going in and out of the entrance to the Suez Canal. We sailed down the coast, and docked next at Port Sudan. We were running light, so we stopped here to take on enough ballast to cross the Atlantic. It was chrome ore, dirty looking brown and very dusty stuff. The dust from it floated everywhere. We had to cover the engine bearings and engine room ventilators while loading. When you got up from your bunk, you could see the place on your sheet where you had been laying.

I always enjoyed warming up the main engine and getting ready to sail. After you had things ready and the drains were open, you got to give the bridge your engine signals for a change, instead of getting the signals from them. Of course, all you did were dead slows and stops and dead aheads, but you signalled them what you were going to do. Then when you gave them Finished With Engine, they gave you the Stand By when they were ready to go. My most difficult time was when we tied up and shut down the main engine and condenser and switched over the plant by starting the auxiliary condenser and turning into it the auxiliary exhausts from dynamos, draft fan engine, etc. At first it was hard for me to remember all the valves.

There was a lot of gambling going on board our ship at this time in the voyage. Our purser, Frank Gear, was always in on it. He came to me one time and showed me some diamonds he wanted to sell, also a star sapphire. They seemed to be nice ones, but I told him I wasn't interested as this was out of my line. He had got the diamonds in South Africa, and the sapphire off of someone on that Indian ship tied up next to us. He said the sapphire came from Colombo, Ceylon (Sri Lanka). He was short of cash on his gambling and wanted to sell some of these to raise money. He showed them to a lot of the crew, trying to sell them, and he and Chapel got into a row about this.

It sure was hot down below during this part of the trip. We would send the oilers up on deck and have them turn the engine room ventilators in a direction to catch any breeze possible. We would loosen a manhole plate on the end of the main condenser and sit under it and let the sea water run down on us, but the sea water temperature was around ninety degrees. I have seen it one hundred and sixty degrees in the engine and fire rooms. If you try to work at these temperatures, you are pretty slow. I tried to key up on a dynamo bearing once, and I took a long time at it. You pick up a wrench and pull on a nut and then you lay it down so you can rest for a while, and so on. We had a two inch lever-operated steam injector bolted to a column. We used it with a fire hose to pick up water and wash down the floor plates and side skin ... We always ran blacked out at night, and it provoked me to see those Swedish neutral ships running with their lights on as if nothing was going on ... The Argentine ships also ran with their lights on.

Sometimes I would get a call from the bridge to work on the telemotor or fathometer, if they didn't think they were working right. I didn't know much about them, but was usually able to act like I did and satisfy the bridge watch. One time I got a call from the bridge saying that we were going in a circle. This time the chief engineer came and got me. A telemotor oil fitting in the steering engine was broken off so the telemotor oil was leaking out and not working the engine control valve. The rudder was hard over. I got the broken fitting out. It was a three-quarter inch brass nipple. I had a hard time getting the new one started with Stokeman breathing down the back of my neck, but I finally made it and got it back together. We straightened out on course again.

We got the engine revolution orders at the beginning of each watch, sent down from the bridge for whatever speed they wanted us to make. I took pride in keeping her steady on the speed required. At the end of the watch you would figure the engine miles, and then get the sea miles covered and from this you could figure the slippage. Other information such as the various pressure and temperature readings and other important information on the engine and boiler room operation are recorded every hour in the engine room log, averaged at the end of each watch, and kept on record. We ran across the Atlantic alone, running pretty steady from seventy-two to seventy-five revolutions per minute. I thought I was getting so good at this that I named our watch "The Revolution Kids." This included my oiler, fireman, and myself.

We all wore blue dungarees on watch. We had an extra dynamo piston hung by a rope from one of the air pump arms, and down into an open drum on the floor plates. I rigged a water supply line to this drum, also a drain, and a steam coil to heat the water. When you put some soap in the drum, the up and down motion of the piston did a great job of washing clothes. I got three white caps from enlisted men in the gun crew. My fireman, oiler, and I threw our dirty dungarees in the wash barrel, along with the white caps. This colored the caps blue. We wore these on watch. "The Revolution Kids" were the only watch that had uniforms like this. I made up a song about our watch, and took my guitar down on watch two or three times. We would sing the song between rounds while I twanged away on the old guitar. One time when we were putting on one of our concerts, I looked up and saw the chief engineer standing on the crosshead grating and looking down at us. He just shook his head and left. He never said anything because we kept everything under control. I thought we had the best watch on the ship. We pulled into Bahia, Brazil for fuel, water and supplies.

I had a bad pain in my right side just as we got in. Everyone told me I had appendicitis, and I went ashore to a doctor. He examined me and a translator told me the doctor said I had colitis. This doctor spoke and wrote only Portuguese, so I could not understand him or the writing on the medicine he gave me to take back to the ship. It consisted of six small glass vials of something. You broke the tops off of them and drank them, which I did. It knocked me out for a while. When I woke up, I barely made it to the head. It cured me and I felt fine. I learned that I was supposed to take one vial a day instead of all six the same day. Chief Engineer Stokeman gave me some extra time off to recuperate, so I went ashore again. He sure was good to me.

We left Bahia with a convoy and headed north, up the coast of South America, running at seventy-two revolutions per minute. We had two Canadian corvettes for escort. About a day out, early on my day watch, there were a lot of explosions that reverberated on the sides of the ship, some real loud. The bridge phone rang, and they told me to give it all the speed I had. I told the fireman to play a tune on those pop valves, and I started the reversing engine and ran the links out all the way. The throttle was wide open. That triple Worthington really made her screw dig in and went puffing along for all she was worth. The explosions continued for a while. Some time later the bridge phone rang again, and they told me to cut it down to sixty revolutions. Basoa and his men relieved us at twelve. They told us that the convoy had been attacked by two or three submarines, and some ships had been hit. He said Chief Engineer Stokeman, First Engineer Hempsey, and the purser were sitting in a lifeboat. What bravery. They said the purser had taken a case of cigarettes into the boat with him. I suppose he had his precious stones with him too.

I went up on deck and saw oil and debris all over the water. They told me a tanker aft of us named the *Florida* had got hit in the machinery spaces and had upended and sank with all hands. A ship on our port side had got one somewhere near amidships, but they had been able to beach her. I could see her back over on the beach, heeled over and burning some. One torpedo had come at us from aft on our port side and had just missed our stern and had angled across and blown the bow off a freighter on our starboard side. This freighter was still afloat and running, and I could see it limping along. That was the reason for the reduced speed of the convoy.

Acting third engineer Al New, left and the oiler from his watch on rented bicycles at Georgetown. Al New.

They said they were going to try to go on to Mobile with it. I don't know whether they made it or not, as we left the convoy long before then. The two corvettes were still with us. I was told that they had got the Kraut submarines. Hempsey had always called me a fool when I went below when I was off watch and we were under attack, but I considered that was the duty of every engineer, and I still do. He evidently did not believe this. I guess some of the older hands had been through this before, and they were more spooked by this than we green hands, but that still didn't make it right in my book. We left this convoy at Georgetown, British Guiana, (Guyana) where we were to load bauxite.

I needed a haircut, so I found a barber shop at the edge of the jungle. It was a log narrow building with a sloped roof made of corrugated sheet iron. All along the comb of the roof were perched a row of big black vultures. It felt kind of funny to go in the building and have all those big buzzards staring down at you, but I got my haircut.

We sailed in and went up what they called the Demmerrara River. They said we were going up the river sixty miles to a place called McKenzie where there was a Canadian-owned bauxite mine.

When we tied up at the mine, the docks were being patrolled by soldiers. We all stayed on board while we loaded. Bauxite is very dusty also, but is a lighter or more reddish color than chrome. We had to cover the engine bearings and other things again. We could only load so much, as they told me there was a sandbar at the mouth of the river going out, and we could not clear this bar if we were fully loaded. We had an uneventful cruise back down the river.

Chief Engineer Stokeman had been cautioning me about the sandbar. He said that if we were too low in the water that we would drag on the sand and plug up the main sea water injection to the condenser and also stop up the main circulating pump, causing us to lose vacuum on the main engine, and messing it up. These engines run with vacuum on the pressure exhaust, and we always kept as near twenty-six inches as we could.

It was on my watch that we went out of the river and across the bar. I did feel her drag a little as we crossed. All of a sudden the main engine started to slow down and hammer. I thought the main injection was stopped up by us dragging, so I ran over and checked the main circulator. It was completely stopped. I checked the main steam valve on it, and found it was closed. I wondered how this could be, and I eased the valve open. The circulator took right off, and we got our vacuum back. The main engine settled down and got back up to speed. I was still over by the circulator when I saw the reach rod from deck turning and closing the valve again. There were emergency reach rods from several valves in the engine room, running clear up to hand wheels on the main deck. I yelled for Oiler Walls to come help me. As the wheel was still turning, we grabbed hold of it and gave it a hard pull, and opened it. I heard soon that we threw Chief Engineer Stokeman flat on the deck above. He was just testing me out. Actually, everything was all right. We sailed smoothly out of the harbor and on up the coast.

The captain came down on this watch and was checking the main injection to see if the detonating and explosive charge there would be the quickest way to scuttle the ship. There was an easier way to scuttle (sink) the ship, but I was suspicious that he might be trying to sabotage something, so I would not give him any information. I learned later that he was checking this for security reasons in case we had to scuttle.

We passed through a big school of salt water catfish, jumping and flopping all around. They must have averaged around two feet long. I had always heard they were poisonous to eat. A crew's messman fished off the rail and caught some of them. He cleaned some and cooked them and ate them. I saw them carrying him off on a stretcher at Port of Spain, Trinidad, our next port. I do not know whether he was alive or not. His face was all blotchy and he was not moving.

We pulled into Port of Spain to top the ship off with a full load of bauxite. More dust. They kept bauxite stockpiled there to load the ships. We went down to San Fernando to take fuel oil. We got some shore leave. I bought a nice burro from a fellow for a dollar. I rode it out on the pier and was going to take it on board, but a grinning apologetic policeman stopped and said I could not do this. I argued with this guy some, but could not change him, so I turned the burro loose and went on board. I think that policeman was probably in cahoots with the man who sold the burro to me. That guy probably knew that I couldn't get the burro on my ship, and he was probably hiding somewhere nearby so that he could catch the burro again and sell it to some other dumb seaman. So I was out a dollar. I always was a sucker when it came to animals.

We sailed on up into the Caribbean and towards the Atlantic. We caught glimpses of land a couple of times. They told me one was Puerto Rico and the other Hispaniola. Some seamen call this whole island Haiti, just because it is part of it. There had been some talk that we might have gone to Mobile, but we did not … We went smoothly up the coast, now that we were carrying a full load again. It was a little choppy off Cape Hatteras, but the *Trumbull* rolled right along like a good girl, back in the good U.S. of A.

We pulled into New York Harbor, past the Statue of Liberty. We had been gone seven and-a-half months.

I got to help the boiler inspector set the safety valves on the steam drums and superheaters. He connected his test gauge down on the instrument panel and he would watch this gauge while you go up and loosen the lock nuts on the safety valves and set them for him. This can be cheated on a little by someone wanting to be tricky if, when he yells for you to lock it down, that you could pull on the adjusting nut wrench and the lock wrench at the same time, thus gaining a few pounds on him. Probably a good boiler inspector would allow for this if he suspected the engineer doing the setting. The port engineer came on board to look things over, and we all recommended that, before the next voyage, there should be a doorway cut from the engine room into the shaft tunnel, and that it be equipped with a water tight door that could be dogged shut in case of emergency. This would permit easier access for the engineers and oilers to the tunnel to take care of things, and would keep it from being such a death trap back in the tunnel. All other Liberty Ships I have been below on had this door.

Customs people searched the ship and found some hashish the wipers had hid in the tunnel. I don't know what they did to those sneaky wipers. They took the dope.

We signed off the ship's articles and were paid off for the voyage. Mr. Gear, the purser, walked down the gangway wearing his whites and started walking nonchalantly down along the dock. He went to the customs guard and showed him his pass, continuing on. The customs guard yelled at him and he took off running down the railroad track. Another customs man joined the first one, and they ran after him. Gear tripped on something and fell down and got tar and grease all over his clean white clothes. The guards searched him and found the diamonds and sapphire in his pocket. If he had not shown his stones to so many people and made the saloon messman and some others mad at him, maybe he could have sneaked the stones ashore.

Half of my raise in pay for being Third Engineer came to something a little over two hundred dollars. I would not have to give it up, but Chief Engineer Stokeman and First Engineer Hempsey thought that they should have it, and they had both been pretty good to me and let me do pretty much as I pleased during the voyage, so I took it to Stokeman's cabin and gave it to him just before I left the ship. Hempsey saw me going down the gangway and he yelled at me and wanted to know where his money was. I told him I had given it all to Stokeman and that he could get his share from him. As I was walking on down, I could hear them yelling and cussing at each other through the port hole.[1]

5

THE
ATLANTIC OCEAN

*T*he Battle of the Atlantic began on September 3, 1939 with the torpedoing of the British liner Althenia. It continued for five and-a-half years, making it the longest battle of World War II.

Of the total merchant tonnage in the world in the year 1939, ". . . more than half of this was destroyed, largely by submarine or air attack, in the course of the next five years."[1] It was almost three and-a-half years before the pendulum of victory would begin to swing in the Allies' favor.

Naval warfare strategy at the beginning of World War II was basically a continuation of that developed during World War I. Control of the seas was essential for victory. Great Britain set up a naval blockade of German ports but this did little to stem the German submarine menace. A memorandum from the German war staff read:

Maritime Requirements For
The Decisive Struggle Against Britain

Germany's principal enemy in this war is Britain. Her most vulnerable spot is her maritime trade ... The principal target of our naval strategy is the merchant ship, not only the enemy's but every merchantman which sails the seas in order to supply the enemy's war interests ... [2]

When France fell in June 1940, it gave Germany direct access to the Atlantic. The German Navy moved into the French naval ports and submarine pens. This forced Great Britain to reposition a major portion of its surface fleet to protect the isle from invasion, which, in turn, provided the opportunity for the U-boat force, using wolf-pack tactics, to move into the Atlantic and wreak havoc upon the ships transporting goods to Britain.

By declaring war against Germany in 1941, the U.S. opened its east coast to increased U-boat activity. The Germans launched a submarine offensive called Operation Kettledrum Beat in January 1942 which was a full scale attack on merchant shipping in the Western Hemisphere. That year the U-boats were incredibly successful. "During the first months of 1942, losses of the American Merchant Marine from enemy action already surpassed those suffered during the entire course of World War I."[3]

"Before the war ended, the count of American merchant ships sunk in the wide-ranging battle of the Atlantic reached 141 in the North Atlantic, 78 along the American coasts, 27 off the Normandy beachhead. An additional 122 were lost in the Caribbean area."[4] The critical goal became to build more ships than were being lost in what became known as the Atlantic graveyard.

The year 1943 was the turning point in the Battle of the Atlantic. Adapting an old British ship design, the United States produced over 2,700 Liberty ships. These became the backbone of the supply line to Britain, Russia, and the other Allies.

~~~

The first story is a letter that was written by a shipmate to Leslie Vail's parents describing the torpedoing and subsequent sinking of his ship. Vail, the radio operator of the S.S. Illinois, was lost at sea June 1, 1942. Peter Dykovitz, of East Marion, New York, a member of the Peconic Bay AMMV, sent me the letter. He had become interested in Leslie Vail after veterans' status was granted to merchant mariners in 1988. Leslie Vail's name is on the war memorial plaque that is fastened to a stone on museum property in the village of Orient, New York.

Dear Mr. and Mrs. Vail:

Your letter of August 27th finally caught up with me here in Golden. I have been travelling steadily since August 1st and so mail is rather late in reaching me. I hope that what little I can tell you concerning your son and the trip of the S.S. *Illinois* will give you peace of mind.

On the night of June 1st we were 24 degrees 20' N. of the equator and 58 degrees 30' Long. about 1300 miles East of Miami. I had just come off watch (4-8). Stopped in the crews' mess for a few minutes then back aft to the crews' quarters in the stern of the ship. The Bo'sun and Tommy (an 18 yr. old kid we picked up in Capetown — he had missed his ship) told me that Gypo (a dog we had picked up in Egypt) had a fit. It seems that the dog was excited and barked and whined, wouldn't let anyone touch him. This was 8:30 in the evening and it was almost dark. I went on in to my quarters, took off my clothes and laid down on the bunk to read. About five minutes to nine the little dog started in again, yelling and whining. Three minutes later a torpedo hit the port side amidships. Immediately the ship's stern went up at a 15 degree [angle]. She started to go down at once. I ran out the companionway and up onto the poop deck awning (stern of the ship). This took about 15 seconds, then another torpedo hit the ship and when I picked myself up and looked amidships she was almost underwater. It was up at about 45 degrees at the stern and a wall of water was crashing over the radio shack, I turned and ran with the list of the ship, diving off and swimming away from the suction. Looking back I saw her sink under the water.

I swam around in the dark (the sea was calm and very warm). Wreckage came up and clinging to this I waited for something to happen. A flare went up about 200 yards away, then a signal light started to blink out a message, another blinker light answered back on the other side — two subs. Then they disappeared. All this took about two minutes. Some men started to come up and yell. I found a small rubber raft that had been lying on the Poop deck. Climbing in I paddled over to where the voices were and found five men. Some badly injured from shrapnel and one with a broken leg. We hollered but received no answers.

Paddling back to the wreckage we laid the injured men on it. I went back again but could find no one. It was very dark. Returning to the wreckage I found the rest sitting on top of a capsized lifeboat. The blast from the torpedo had blown a lifeboat off. We sat up all night — four of us were naked. It was very cold. We talked about the sinking and managed to piece together where everyone was at the time. The 2nd Engineer, the only officer to escape, said that he ran to the starboard lifeboat which was next to the radio shack. He said that he saw Les at the transmitter trying to get a message off, but it was useless as the radio shack was under water in about twenty seconds. Burns, an O.S. was at the wheel and the only man forward to escape. After talking it over, we arrived at these conclusions. The first torpedo broke the ship in two. (Burns was on the other half which sank in

The SS Illinois *was launched in 1920 and operated by States Steamship Co.*
William F. Hultgren

about ten to fifteen seconds). The ship sank in about thirty to thirty-five seconds. This was due to our cargo, manganese ore. The two torpedoes hit the engine room killing everyone below. I was the only one to get free of the ship before she sank; the rest went down with her and were blown back up by air bubbles about two minutes later. In short, it was a miracle that any of us escaped.

The next day we started to work on turning the lifeboat over. We could work only at it a few minutes at a time as the sharks were a constant menace. We had to beat them off with pieces of wreckage. Late that afternoon we got her over and bailed out. She leaked and we had to bail constantly. We set sail in a S.W. direction. It was very cold at night and very hot during the day. Most of us were burned badly. The injured men suffered badly. Fortunately we were picked up by a tanker seven days later and landed in Trinidad three days later. Two of the men were delirious. However, the six of us survived and we flew back to Miami two weeks later.

Concerning your son, I feel that I knew him better than anyone else on the ship, as I spent a great deal of time in his quarters while at sea. We talked of his home and Orient. His little girl was his constant thought all during the trip. As far as the crew was concerned he was thought a bit odd as he was the only one onboard ship that didn't drink or smoke. However he was well liked as he invited everyone who wanted to listen to the news up to the radio shack. As we were anxious for news, his place was packed from 7 to 8 every night, and from 12 to 1 a.m. It was the one thing we all looked forward to every day of the trip. This was against the law for seamen to be in the radio room, and we all had a soft spot for Sparks because of what he did.

Naturally, he was in for a good deal of kidding as it was his first trip at sea; he took it good-naturedly and soon became one of us. He wasn't seasick going around the Cape of Good Hope. The only time he was sick was coming back from India, and then we all were because of bad water. The only thing I know of that worried Les was his wife and child. He talked about them often to me and perhaps I believe he was just homesick. We all were; it was such a long trip.

We had seven or eight days to go yet before reaching Baltimore. None of us expected to get it where we did as we were so far out. In fact we all expected to arrive safely as we were so lucky during the trip. The last day and night in close to the coast we knew would be bad, but out there — well it was all so unexpected. I do know that Les could have saved himself if he had run out of the radio room to the starboard lifeboat. It would have taken him only a few seconds. That was where the 2nd Eng. went. But apparently he chose to stay by the radio and tried to get a message off before the ship went under.

I wish I could tell you more about your son but this is about all I know. I do know that I will never forget Les and I know none of the other five survivors will.

I expect to leave for San Francisco within the next ten days for another ship. This time Australia. The work your son gave his life for is the most important work in the war. None of us want to die, but we don't want any American soldier to die either because he didn't have that bullet to fire, or that plane to fly, or that oil or gasoline. So we all go back, knowing it has to be done, and then we carry food and goods to build instead of destroy — safely.

Goodbye and our deepest sympathy,

> Merton S. Barrus
> Golden, Colorado
> Oct. 18, 1942[5]

The S.S. Illinois *was torpedoed by the* U-172 *(Capt. Emmermann). Of the crew of eight officers and thirty men, only one officer and five men managed to jump into the water and right a capsized lifeboat. The* Esso Montpelier *picked them up six days after the attack and landed them at Port-of-Spain, Trinidad.[6] According to the German author Jurgen Rohwer, the second submarine that Merton Barrus mentioned was the* U-159.[7] *The* U-172 *(Capt. Hoffman) was sunk west of the Canary Islands on December 12, 1943 by the USS* Clemson *(DD-186); USS* Dupont

(DD-152); USS Badger *(DD-196); and USS* Ingram *(DD-255).*
There were some survivors.[8]

SPARKS

We were sailing two days out from Capetown-
And sailing all alone-
Crew thinking of their loved ones-
Who were waiting back at home.

And no one missed his family more-
Than Sparks, who all knew well-
Whose key might be our lifeline-
Across the rolling swell.

Then early in the morning-
In a great explosion's roar-
The torpedo ripped us open-
Two thousand miles from shore.

All was lost, the ship afire-
And settling by the bow-
Abandon ship the order came-
No time to tarry now.

We lost the first assistant-
And the bosun in the blast-
But up there sending signals-
Old Sparks was standing fast.

All around him raging fire-
The 88's came crashing in-
But still he keyed our lifeline-
Amid'st the battles din.

Old Sparks, he was our hero-
And no would deny-
No greater gift can one man give-
Than for his shipmates die.

Ian A. Millar[9]

~~~

This story was submitted by Lillard Waddle. It tells of the torpedoing and sinking of the John Carter Rose. *It is unusual in that the captain of the U-boat that torpedoed them also demonstrated some humanity and compassion toward his victims.*

We lay at anchor for five days in Trinidad awaiting a convoy. Why, I have no idea, as the ships heading north remained with the convoy, while our ship heading south to Freetown, Africa was turned loose to fend for itself.

On the evening of October 7th, 1942, we were at "GQ," and, as everyone knows, dusk and dawn were the most opportune times for attack. We were approximately five hundred miles off the South American shore and running at ten knots when out of the evening came this submarine from the direction we were heading. We did not see him and it was quite evident he did not spot us, until we were on top of each other.

The reaction of the submarine was to come about and shoot a torpedo at our starboard quarter, which missed, but the wake was very visible. The Navy gun crew fired about three shots, which did not hit the submarine. At this time, night was falling and our ship started zig-zagging and we lost him. All the next day we kept lookouts trained on the ocean and thought that we had escaped our deadly foe. By evening things had settled back to routine duties. The night was hot and muggy, so when I got off the four-to-eight watch, I decided to put my mattress on top of number four hatch and catch a few winks.

At 0030 GMT [Greenwich Mean Time] the noise and impact of the first torpedo hitting ahead of the midship house into the number three hold was like all hell breaking loose. Then torpedo number two slammed into the ship between number two and three hatches. The attack came from the starboard side. In these holds were stored 26,000 fifty-five gallon drums of high octane gasoline, which immediately caught fire and turned the forward part of the ship into an inferno. The men in the engine room, which was spared, shut down the engine. However, going at ten knots at the time of impact, it took the ship many minutes to lose steerage.

It took me a few minutes to clear my head and realize what had happened, then I headed for the boat deck. Soon, others joined in and we attempted to lower the lifeboats on the port side. At one of the boat stations, the men were lowering a boat with the falls when the captain jerked the rope from their hands and flipped it off the chock, causing the end of the lifeboat to fall vertically into the water.

After the boats were in the sea, the only two of us left on board were me and the bosun. As the ship was still in steerage, the lifeboats now were getting well astern of the ship. We headed for the stern and abandoned from there. The fire was now all around us.

It took us a number of hours to reach the lifeboats and my shoes were the first thing to go, then the pants which were dragging me down. The bosun who was a rather young fellow, told me he was going to remove his life jacket. It took a while but I convinced him to keep his life jacket on and that life was worth living. That we would make it to the boats and be rescued. When I finally climbed into the life boat, all I had on was a sleeveless shirt and my shorts, which I promptly lost over the side when rinsing them out.

In a disaster such as this, the mind plays tricks that sometimes you cannot overcome, such as the captain's folly. We had an officer aboard the lifeboat with us, and he became unstable. He curled up in the bow and stayed there just about all the time. Another mariner picked up this little ax that was part of our supplies and was threatening bodily harm to all. We told him to put it down, or we would throw him overboard, and we meant every word.

The next day the *John Carter Rose* was still afloat and the fires seemed to be going out so we decided to reboard her. As we drew near, a submarine *(U-201)* came from behind the ship. The sub then approached us and asked for the captain and the gunnery officer. Both were in our boat, but we didn't relate this to the Germans.

In our lifeboat we had some injured shipmates, one of whom was burned pretty badly. The captain of the submarine

(Gunther Rosenberg) asked if we had any injured aboard. He gave us salve and black bread sealed in gallon cans. They also told us to steer for the coast of South America. There were three lifeboats in all and we tied two of the boats together, but somehow we drifted apart. We rigged a sail and sailed 270 degrees compass course for South America, which was about 700 miles to our west. A ration of supplies was in order as we had no idea how long we would be alone at sea and drinking water was vital.

Our lifeboat spent five days on the open seas heading west, as best as we could determine. On the fifth day we spotted a ship and thank God it saw us. It turned out to be the Argentine Tanker, *Santa Cruz*, which picked us up on the 13th of October. The day before, it had picked up one of the other lifeboats from the ship. The third lifeboat was picked up by the SS *West Humhaw* and went on to Freetown, Africa.

The tanker brought us to Recife, Brazil, where the American Consul bought us two cheap suits and needed underwear. We stayed there for ten days until an English troop ship arrived. They put us on a cattle barge and took us out to a transport. The English wanted to put us in hammocks below deck like a bunch of stowaways. At this time we refused and raised a little hell. They then put us two to a cabin as the troop ship was empty and had enough space for all. I guess they got even for our outburst as they fed us mutton and boiled potatoes three times a day until we reached New York.[10]

The John Carter Rose was torpedoed by the U-201 (Rosenberg), on October 8, 1942. Five crew members and three Naval Armed Guard were lost. After the crew abandoned ship a third torpedo was fired into the ship and she was finally sunk by gunfire from the submarine. The U-201 with Rosenberg still in command met her fate on February 17, 1943 when she was sunk with all hands aboard off Newfoundland.

~~~

This story was submitted by James J. Fitzpatrick, U.S.M.M.A, Class of 1944. It tells of the torpedoing of the S.S.

Julia Ward Howe. *It is an amazing possibility that the* Howe'*s S.O.S. may have been one of two S.O.S.'s that were heard 600 miles away. See Burton Drew's January 28th Diary entry in Chapter 7.*

The Sinking of the S.S. *Julia Ward Howe*
January 27, 1943.

Early in the morning of January 13, 1943 the S.S. *Julia Ward Howe* steamed out of New York Harbor to join a convoy of fifty merchant vessels, tankers, and many foreign flagged vessels of all descriptions, as well as U.S. Navy escort vessels. We found out later the convoy was bound for Oran, Algeria to help Allied forces battle General Rommel's army in Africa.

The weather turned real bad by the second day and winds reached hurricane force. A number of ships reported difficulties maintaining convoy speed. The *Julia Ward Howe's* steering mechanism broke down, and a fire broke out in the #2 hold. Fire fighting efforts by the crew were able to contain the fire, but smoke filled the area and it was hard to breathe. Our captain, Andrew Hammond, and chief engineer, Thomas Foley, went into #2 hold to inspect the damages.

On January 27, 1943 I had just finished hanging my wash on the aft deck and with my shipmate and fellow Kings Pointer Thomas P. Brady went forward to see the damage the fire had caused. All of a sudden a huge explosion occurred and both Tom and I were blown in the air and came down on deck by the #2 hold.

Water was pouring in a huge hole by the #2 hatch and the ship started to list. Tom and I both ran to our cabin, got our life jackets and reported to our lifeboat. All boats and rafts on the starboard side where the torpedo hit were destroyed.

We jumped over the side and swam through the oil fire, and finally reached a life raft and lifeboat. Shortly thereafter, a second torpedo hit the *Julia Ward Howe* and she sank bow first. The last thing I saw was my shorts blowing in the breeze.

The German sub surfaced. I still can see the "Snorting Bull" on the conning tower. We were tied up to the sub for over

A rare photo of the crew of a torpedoed ship, the City of Flint, *being picked up in mid-Atlantic. James J. Fitzpatrick*

two hours. They interrogated several members of our crew, and finally set us free around dusk.

We drifted all night in heavy seas, but we were able to keep the life rafts and lifeboats close to one another. We spotted bright lights in the distance, and they turned out to be spot lights of the Portuguese Destroyer *Lima*. We all got on board and Chief Engineer Thomas Foley was taken to sick bay for first aid, but he later died from his wounds. The master, Andrew Hammond, also died in the torpedo attack. The captain and crew of the *Lima* conducted Burial At Sea Ceremonies which was attended by all hands.

Burial of the Julia Ward Howe's *chief engineer. Crews of the* City of Flint *and the* Howe *gather on the starboard side of the* Lima *as that vessel's master reads a prayer over the chief's body. James J. Fitzpatrick*

James Fitzpatrick after receiving new clothes from the American consul at Ponta Delgada, St. Michael, Azores. James J. Fitzpatrick

We later picked up the survivors of the *City of Flint*, an old Hog Islander which had slipped by the German blockade and joined the Allied course.

The weather was still very bad and while we were aboard the Destroyer *Lima,* she developed trouble with her rudder, and when hit by high seas she took a roll of sixty-seven degrees which threw Tom and I across the officers' mess and a radio console was pulled from the bulkhead and shot across the officer's mess. The leg with a steel tip went through my jacket pocket, missing my ribs by inches.

We finally reached the port of Ponta Delgada in the Azores, and were met by the U.S. Consul and were assigned housing, clothes and food. We remained in the Azores until a Prisoner of War exchange could be made. We finally sailed for home on a Portuguese passenger ship, the *City of Lima* which, in turn, was stopped by a German submarine, but released to continue to her destination. We arrived in Philadelphia on Easter morning and we thanked God for our blessings.[11]

Merchantmen Like Thee

Here's to thee, thy wandering heroes -
Roaming o'er the sea -
Gone are you from families loving -
To eternity.

Blazing sunshine... Frozen ocean -
Ocean winds blow free.
Here's a prayer for those departed -
Wandering o'er the sea.

Here's to thee, thy gallant heroes -
Brave boys of the sea -
Gone are you in battle's glory -
To eternity.

Man the deck guns... Launch the lifeboats -
In the raging sea.
Here's a prayer for those departed -
Heroes of the sea.

Here's to thee, thy fallen heroes -
Resting in the sea -
Gone are you in stormy tempest -
To eternity.

Blow the whistle... Bend the flags on -
Welcome home to thee.
Here's a prayer to those departed -
Sleeping in the sea.

Here's to thee, remembered heroes -
Spirits of the sea -
Missing yes but not forgotten -
Resting peacefully.

Slumber quiet... Sleep forever -
In the rolling sea.
Here's a prayer for those departed -
Merchantmen like thee.

Ian A. Millar[12]

The following inscription appears alongside this poem:
"For James J. Fitzpatrick, Remembering those who did not come
home. Best Wishes, Ian Millar, Kernersville, N.C."

~~~

This story was from George Paxton, the Purser on board
the Andrea F. Luckenbach.

I tried to join the Navy or Seabees, but could not pass the
eye examination. I walked across the street and joined the
merchant marine. I left home on Labor Day 1942 for New York
City. They put us up in an old seaman's home down in the
Bowery by the docks. What a sight for a bunch of young fellows
to see (old seaman lying around). The next day they took us to
Sheepshead Bay for our training. We were in the first 100 men to
start up the center. After three months we were sent to the Hotel
Chelsea in New York to wait for a call from a steamship
company. I left Sheepshead Bay with Fireman's papers, but
while I was on the waiting list, I was asked if I could type and I
could enough to get by, so working for the office in this hotel for
the War Shipping Administration, I got a ships clerk's papers and
that's how I shipped out.

My first job was to take a ship from New York to Boston
(Luckenbach S.S Co.). I left the ship in Boston and came back to
New York and was assigned another ship, the *Andrea F.
Luckenbach*. By the way, the ship I left in Boston left for
Murmansk and was never heard from again.

We sailed for England on January 29 and on March 10,
1943, we were hit by two torpedoes at around 6 P.M. Everything
happened so fast you didn't have time to be scared. I had my own
room and I was lying on my bunk reading when POW! everything
let go. I grabbed what I thought was my life jacket, but when I got
to my lifeboat I realized I had my peacoat in my hand. I hustled
back to get my life jacket and when I returned the lifeboat was
gone. By then the ship was tilting to the stern so I prayed and
jumped into the water.

The Andrea J. Luckenbach *was launched in 1919 at Quincy, Massachusetts.* Steamship Historical Society of America

Our one lifeboat was picked up by an English ship. I can remember looking up at this big ship along side of me. I was yelling Help! I started to drift around the stern and I can remember thinking the screws would pull me down, but they stopped the ship and the last thing I could remember was somebody tying a rope around me. My skipper and another seaman crawled down the net and got hold of me. We lost our whole gun crew and 15 merchant seaman (quite a loss).

We arrived in the northern part of Scotland five days later and were given clothing and whatever they could spare. The Scotch and English treated us like real heroes. In England they thought as much of their Merchant Navy as they did the regular Navy. Four of us were sent back to the States on a C-2. I came home for a few days and my skipper called me to get back because he had another ship, the *J.L. Luckenbach*. My first trip on her was eight months long. We sailed to the Far East and back by the way of the Straits of Magellan. After two and a half years on the *J.L. Luckenbach* I left and signed on a Victory Ship.[13]

The Andrea F. Luckenbach *sailed in Convoy HX-228. "...two torpedoes from the* U-221 *(Capt. Trojer) struck the freighter ... The master determined that the torpedoes had fatally damaged his ship, and he immediately ordered the ship abandoned. The freighter sank stern first in seven minutes, but the majority of the nine officers, forty-six men, twenty-eight armed guards, and one passenger got away in two lifeboats.*

Others jumped overboard and swam ... In just over an hour the oiler HMS Orangeleaf *rescued seventeen armed guards, nine officers, thirty-seven men, and the passenger ... The remaining twenty men died. Ten armed guards on the after gun platform perished when the ship's magazine exploded."*[14]

According to Arthur Moore, "The Armed Guard officer, who was on the bridge directing his gun crew, gave his life jacket to a seaman who did not have one. The officer could not swim and was unable to reach a lifeboat after jumping overboard. He was not seen again." The U-221 *(Capt. Trojer) was bombed and sunk Southwest of Ireland on September 29, 1943. There were no survivors.*[15]

~~~

This story was taken from the diary of Burton Drew and is an account of what occurred on board the S.S. Benjamin Harrison *on March 15 and 16, 1943.*

Mon. Mar. 15, 1943

At 6:50 last eve. a French ship in the column next to us on the Stbd. side was hit by two torpedoes. It sank in 10 minutes and just before she went down the skipper blew three short & one long blasts on the ship's whistle. V for victory. It was very dramatic! We learned later that all hands were saved. I had three pictures of it as it sank. The gunnery officer had all available men stand watch at the guns. We made several emergency turns to Port & Stbd. Some of them ninety degrees in order to throw off the subs from our course. I was on watch in the engine room from midnight till four in the morning. This is known as the dog watch[*] or graveyard watch. During this time, one depth charge was dropped awful close because we felt the concussion shake the ship. However, everything went along fine for a while.

---

[*] Technically, the dog watch is from 4-to-6 and 6-to-8 in the evening. The term comes from sailing ships when the crew stood watch on and watch off. The evening watch was "dogged" to two hours, instead of four, so the crew didn't have to stand the same watch all the time.

Tues. March 16th

After supper this evening, we decided to play cards in the saloon (officers' mess). We were playing about an hour when three depth charges were dropped. As I was sitting out the hand, I decided to go up on the flying bridge and investigate. When I reached there, the gunners were all excited because they saw the wake of a torpedo. I looked off to the Stbd. side and sure enough she was heading for us at a lazy speed of about 15 knots which is about 17 miles an hour. (One mile & an eighth for ea. knot.) It was reported and seeing that we could not fire on it, we ran to the smokestack & cuddled up against it on the deck like month old babies when they're sleeping — laying on our side & having our knees on our chest, our hands over our heads; trying to make us as small as possible. There must have been a dozen men lying against that stack. We heard the general alarm bell ring.

A few seconds later she hit in the # 4 hold aft of the bridge. The explosion blew off all shut doors and also collapsed the boilers. This forced condensate and water out of the stack along with the dirt and black soot inside the stack. It rained black water all the while we were launching the boats. I immediately ran down to my cabin for my life jacket & abandon ship kit, which I made up the night before. In this kit I had my important papers, camera, warm clothes, & a few other items. I proceeded to my boat station & in so doing had to climb over two doors which were blown off. My job was to help lower #3 boat.

In the meantime, the other ships in convoy began firing their machine guns & 5 inchers at the U-boat. It was getting darker now & you could hear & see the tracer bullets flying in the sky after they shined off the water. We were lucky no one was hit because they were close to us. I did hear someone say that one of the messboys had quite a burn on his cheek where a tracer bullet grazed him. It seemed as if all hell broke loose when they started shooting those 20 millimeters. That is when I was really scared. I didn't think I had a chance then. Wouldn't that be something, to be hit by bullets fired by your own men?

When the explosions occurred the engineer on watch stopped the engine. However, the ship was still coasting along when we lowered the lifeboats & consequently we lost two boats.

Although the men in the boats were in the water, they were finally picked up. My boat was one of the two that were lost & I & thirteen others were left on the ship, which was listing heavily to starboard. We noticed that one boat, although it was half full of water & banging up against the bulkhead of the ship, still had a line on it which held it to the ship. The fourteen of us worked furiously for thirty minutes and finally had it secure so we could man it. By this time the convoy was out of sight. I went back to my cabin, grabbed two cartons of cigs. as did the others, found some heavy jackets & a flashlight and threw them in the boat. We found a Jacob's ladder, threw it over the side & proceeded to man the boat. It was rather difficult because there was heavy ground swells. The boat would not stay still. Instead, it would float up & down with the tidal waves. We finally rowed away from the crippled ship, heading into the wind as we did so.

An hour or so later we sighted a destroyer and a little after that a freighter. We later found out that this freighter was the reserve ship for the convoy. We blinked furiously with our light an SOS, three dots, three dashes, three dots. We were in the lifeboat about three hrs. when we were finally picked up by this Panamanian ship.[16]

The U-boat responsible was none other than the U-172, which, as already mentioned, was sunk on December 12, 1943 with Eberhard Hoffman as captain.

After the first torpedo hit, the Benjamin Harrison's crew abandoned ship by jumping overboard. The # 4 lifeboat flipped over while being lowered, throwing the occupants into the sea. Three survivors were picked up by the USS Rowan (DD-782) and landed at Casablanca. The sixty-six other survivors were picked up by the SS Allan A. Dale, another ship in the convoy, and landed in Oran, Algeria on March 24, 1943.[17]

~~~

This story is from Ed Woods, who went to war when he was only sixteen years old.

It was August 1944, the height of World War II, and the Allies were fighting to strengthen and to expand their positions in Normandy, France. I was sixteen years old and on board a brand new oil tanker. On board with me was my childhood friend and neighbor, Vinnie McCarvill. It was to be my first trip as a merchant seaman. We were at anchor in New York Bay where the Verrazano Bridge now spans the Narrows between Brooklyn and Staten Island, New York. I could see the Statue of Liberty and the New York skyline in the near distance. Manhattan, my hometown, never looked so beautiful.

The week before we had been assigned to the ship, the SS *Horseshoe,* while she was loading up with high-test aviation gasoline at an oil refinery in Carteret, New Jersey. High-octane gas is not used much today with the advent of jet engines but it was the aviation fuel of World War II. It was extremely volatile and we worked aboard the ship under strict rules governing lighted cigarettes and any use of tools that could cause sparks on the open decks. A friendly old deckhand told us not to worry about any explosion, as we would never know what happened. He recalled that on one of his earlier ocean crossings a torpedo hit an oil tanker in front of him. All he saw was a bit of froth on the water for a few seconds and then all was gone. He added that if

*U.S. Maritime Service Training Station, Sheepshead Bay, New York, June —
July 1944. Ed Woods is second from right in the third row. Ed Woods*

he had to go, that was the way to do it. "One, two, three and goodbye."

From Carteret we sailed up the Hudson River and anchored midstream, dead center between New Jersey and New York, off the 79th Street marina in Manhattan. We were not allowed to tie up at a pier in New York City because of our dangerous cargo. There was concern about the possibility of fires or explosions close to heavily populated areas. Two years earlier, while at a pier in midtown Manhattan, the French luxury liner *Normandie* had caught fire and turned over on her side. It stayed there for eighteen months taking up valuable wartime dock space. Enemy sabotage was suspected. The authorities were thankful the famed liner wasn't carrying any explosive material.

During the war, tankers loaded with gasoline and ships loaded with explosives were anchored farther out in the bay away from the more populated areas. Since we couldn't tie up at a pier, barges were towed out to unload deck cargo for us to carry over our cargo tanks. A United States Army Sergeant, a pleasant older Irish-American, accompanied the cargo and was its official escort. He told me that underneath the heavy waterproof canvases were P51 Mustang airplane fuselages. The wooden crates next to him held all the parts necessary to get the planes assembled and into the air once we got to our destination.

When I was off duty, I was able to take a water taxi from our ship to the marina. From there it was a short walk to my home and family on West 84th Street. I remember the night I was told, "No more shore leave. We'll be shoving off in the morning." I was leaning on a ship's railing facing the New York shoreline and could see the lights along Riverside Drive and the auto traffic on the West Side Highway. In those days sixteen-year-old boys were not expected to show any emotion. Well, I didn't show any, but I certainly felt some. And it was mixed. I was happy to be sailing off, yet sad to be leaving the safety of home and family for the first time. Later, I learned that my feelings were not unique and were common to a lot of guys at the time.

I had no idea of where we were going. Our destination was a secret. All I knew was that I had signed Shipping Articles stating it was to be a "Foreign Voyage." The now well-known poster "A Slip of the Lips Can Sink a Ship," seemed to be everywhere. I believed it, too. I had seen the war time movies that showed the enemy spy listening to a sailor's every word in an attempt to learn his ship's destination and departure time. Well, he wouldn't hear it from me.

Unfortunately, this need for secrecy generated rumors, and I was relying on the old timers for whatever information I could get. I learned very quickly that these so-called "old salts" never hesitated to mix fact with fiction. I would have to decide for myself what was to be believed and what was to be discarded. The crew was making guesses as to our destination. It was said that if workmen came aboard and installed extra insulation on the bulkheads in our sleeping quarters, it would be to Murmansk, Russia. I gathered from the conversations that going to Russia was about the worst that could happen to us. Some of the crew had been in a convoy going to Russia that had lost more than half of its ships. Then, the few ships that got through to Archangel, the seaport for Murmansk, had been stuck there for over nine months because the German navy controlled the nearby area of the Barents Sea. Adding to the crews' misery were the freezing temperatures and the unfriendly Russian inhabitants.

Well, thankfully, we didn't get any special cold weather gear. So, if we didn't head south when we departed, it had to be North Africa or the British Isles. It didn't matter to me, I was anxious and eager to visit any foreign port. I had never been out of New York City in my life nor had I ever been aboard a ship. My seafaring experience had been limited to the Hudson River and Staten Island ferries.

After loading our deck cargo, we moved down the river and anchored just inside the submarine nets that protected New York harbor. From our position, I could look along the Long Island shore and see the Sheepshead Bay Maritime Training Station from which I had graduated just a few days before. I could also see little boats scurrying back and forth opening and closing the submarine nets to allow ships to pass through. They would soon be doing it for us. It was common knowledge that

German submarines had torpedoed ships close to the New York City shoreline. It was also known that a daring German U-boat captain had penetrated the British defenses at Scapa Flow, Scotland and played havoc with the British fleet. It was hoped that our nets and patrol boats would prevent that from happening in New York.

As far as the eye could see, the bay was filled with ships of different sizes and shapes; tankers, freighters and passenger liners. Many of them would be part of our convoy when we formed up outside the harbor. We were maintaining a partial blackout aboard ship with just the required mooring lights on. Once we left port, it would be a complete blackout at night for the entire voyage while at sea. The glass on the inside of the port holes was painted black to keep any light from shining through and heavy dark curtains covered the doorways.

The morning before we sailed, the Gunnery Officer, a Naval Ensign, held a muster in the crew's mess hall. He came to the point at once, and said, "I have X number of guns aboard this ship to maintain and use, and I am far short of the trained manpower to do the job efficiently without the help of volunteers from you, the merchant crew." He explained that the Articles of War offered some protection to his navy gunnery crew if they were taken captive, but legally we, the merchant crew, were considered civilians and did not have the same protection. He explained, "If you men are taken captive by the enemy and they thought you had used arms against them, you would be subject to immediate execution." He added, "For this reason, you have to volunteer; no one can order you to handle any guns."

I jumped at the opportunity, however, to be part of the fighting force and had visions, that only a teenager of the 1940's could have, of shooting down German planes and blowing U-boats out of the water. I was assigned as a "hot shell catcher" to our biggest gun, a 5-inch 38 located aft over the poop deck. This meant that each time the gun was fired it would be my job to get the spent shell off the deck as soon as it left the chamber and out of the way of the gun #7 crew. The shells were hot, and I was given heat resistant gloves to wear and told to put the spent shells in a nearby bin. (They had recycling, even then.) If we were ever engaged in enemy action, however, I was not to waste any time and to throw the spent shells overboard.

It wasn't until the next night that we weighed anchor and exited the harbor. I went out on deck through the blackout curtains and saw for the first time the bright and beautiful light from the bioluminescence created by the propeller as it beat through the water. It was an eerie sight against total darkness. The following morning we were among a group of ships off Montauk, Long Island. The convoy was forming and there was a feeling of expectation and excitement in the air as we were called to various boat drills. We had to memorize, if we hadn't learned them already, the various alarm sounds, and the locations of our fire, battle and lifeboats stations and what to do when we got to them. Adding to the excitement were United States Navy destroyers racing about through the line of ships with their horns blasting away and both light and flag signals being passed back and forth. Each ship had been assigned a position in the convoy formation and the escorts were directing them to it. It reminded me of the cowboys in a movie, shouting and yelling at round-up time, trying to get the cattle in line as the herd moved along.

Later, somewhere off Nova Scotia, we made rendezvous with more ships coming out of Canada and other northern ports. I was told that I was fortunate to be serving on a new tanker, a "T2" that could make good speed and keep up in a fast convoy. A fast convoy included troop ships, and troop ships meant additional protection. We could have more American and Canadian escort vessels with us than the regular and slower convoys, and possibly, though out of sight, a baby aircraft carrier in the vanguard.

At first, the Navy Armed Guard gunners were told not to fraternize with the merchant seamen. It was expected that we keep away from the gunners' sleeping quarters and they stay away from ours. We each had our own mess hall for eating and recreation. It took only a few days out to sea, however, before most of us became good friends and shipmates. We still respected each other's privacy, but we played checkers, chess and cards with each other. It was a gunner who taught me to play chess and, in addition to a lot of reading, that is what most of the crew did at sea.

The senior navy enlisted man was an old-timer, a bosun, who was put aboard to teach the young sailors some naval lore. He was a master at weaving and tying rope and would hold classes out on deck to teach the young sailors some basic seamanship. I think he was the only one in the Armed Guard crew that was over eighteen, and was like a father figure to everyone. The Navy sailors had to attend the sessions and we went by invitation. I thought that I knew how to tie a knot or two with some expertise until I met "Boats." He could, as the saying went, make a piece of line talk. Along with some other useful knots, he taught me the Navy's way to make a bowline, and to this day I can still throw one together and win bets with my speed and accuracy.

We didn't have any radar. In fact, we had never heard of it. One morning, an AB (able bodied seaman) said that during the night, while he was on the wheel, one of the escort ships signaled that we were to change position in the convoy by falling back a certain number of yards. He didn't know how they could tell our exact position in the complete darkness, but they could. It was then that I heard about radar for the first time. A gunner said that he had heard there was a "magic box" aboard one of the ships and the convoy commander could look into it and see the exact location of all the ships in the convoy, even at night. This technological marvel, together with the first P-38 twin fuselage airplanes that I saw flying by (awesome), convinced me that the enemy didn't have a chance. Not that I ever thought that they did. How could we lose?

The deck watch maintained a lookout on the bow and could warn the bridge by telephone if our ship got too close to the ship in front of us. This was not an enviable job, as the lookout was exposed to the elements. In addition, the Navy gunners stood a lookout from the twenty-millimeter gun positions. On foggy or moonless night, a "fog buoy" was laid out astern on a log cable. It was shaped so that when it cut through the water, it created a mountain of foam. If the lookout on the ship behind us sighted it from his post, he would know that the ship was getting close to us. I later heard that its resistance in the water cut down our speed and its use had to be kept at a minimum.

For the first few days out we saw some aircraft flying by and then the skies were empty until we got near Iceland and a few more planes flew over. The old-timers thought the aircraft were the answers to everyone's prayers and claimed the German U-boats would stay away from us when the planes were overhead. We didn't see any more planes until we got close to Northern Ireland.

The second mate, the officer in charge of navigation, was a real gentleman and an enthralling storyteller. He had been a history professor before the war and, if we met him on deck at the right time, he would tell us some great sea stories. It was from him that I first heard of the *Titanic* tragedy. One day he told us our ship was passing over the spot where it was believed the luxury liner had gone down. He added that before he migrated to the United States he had been a young deck hand on board the German liner *Amerika*. He went on to tell us that the *Amerika* had been the first ship on that fateful night to alert the *Titanic* to the ice field in its path. As we know now, the warning was ignored with deadly consequences. Well, they say it's a small world and I guess it is because, two years later, in 1946, I was working on the United States Army Transport the *E.B. Alexander* and learned she was the former German liner *Amerika*. She had been confiscated by the United States in World War I, converted into a troop carrier and renamed the *E.B. Alexander*.

After many wrong guesses, we arrived in Liverpool, England on the Mersey River and anchored midstream. Our pumps were connected to huge underwater pipes and our cargo of gasoline was pumped through them to the holding tanks on shore. Once the tanks were emptied we were allowed to tie up at a pier to unload our deck cargo.

Vinnie and I went ashore to see Liverpool, my first foreign city. We stopped at a few local pubs and I had my share of warm mild and bitter beer. While there, we heard all the jokes about the overpaid Yanks. I bragged to the locals that I was part

English as my great grandfather had been born in London. It didn't impress them. Their immediate goal was to get as many American cigarettes from us as possible, and they were willing to pay for them. We were only too willing to be the heroes of the day and to give cigarettes away. We were only paying fifty cents a carton for them aboard ship. So at five cents a pack we could easily afford to be generous.

The kids were a bit different. They looked, and often were, hungry. The older ones asked for gum "Any gum, chum," and the younger kids wanted chocolate. We gave what we could. Later, I stopped to listen to some street kids sing the words to "Maggie Mae," a song about an infamous hussy who frequented Liverpool's Lime Street, and an off-color song "Roll me over, Yankee Soldier." The next time we went ashore, we brought some oranges and bananas for the folks at the Seamen's Club. They claimed to have not seen or eaten any in years. I later heard that we could have sold the cigarettes and fruit on the "black market" and made some money. That never entered my mind and, while it may have been done, I never saw it in England. The city had been subjected to German bombing for a number of years and looked it. You had to feel sorry for the people and at the same time respect them for their "never give up" attitude.

On our way back to the States, I got assigned to assist the gunner on a twenty-millimeter aircraft machine gun. This was more to my liking. During gunnery practice, the gunner and I took turns firing the weapon and I loved every minute of it. We had lessons in one of the ammunition rooms and learned how to load magazines with the various shells that were available: incendiary, explosive and tracers. For practice, the big 5-inch 38 would fire a burst into the air and we would fire at the black clouds. While this was going on, the whole ship would be vibrating from the concussions of the big gun. Anything not tied down would be tossed about. The noise was ear-splitting, yet wonderful. It wasn't until later that I learned that if a U-boat attacked us while we were in a convoy we wouldn't be allowed to fire any guns without special permission from the Convoy Commander. Earlier in the war, the German submarine captains had been known to surface in the middle of a convoy to draw fire and in many cases Allied ships hit each other.

Our guns were limited in their field of fire. Behind the guns were iron stop bars that prevented the guns from swinging in a complete circle, and with good reason. When guns were first put on merchant vessels, the gunners would often continue firing as enemy planes flew over and around the ship. This, unfortunately, sometimes resulted in the gunners blowing away their own bridge and the men in it.

The crossing from New York to Liverpool had taken about nine days and the return voyage about the same. We were called to battle stations a few times both for practice and in response to alarms from the naval escorts that had picked up echoes on their sonar. Fortunately, we didn't encounter any U-boats or enemy aircraft and we arrived home safely.

Within a week, Vinnie and I were on another T2 tanker, the *SS Brandy Station,* and in convoy on our way to Casablanca, North Africa. We carried the same cargo, high octane aviation gasoline and P-51 Mustang airplanes. From Casablanca we were ordered to the Pacific Ocean by way of Curaçao in the Dutch West Indies and the Panama Canal. This time I didn't get back to the States for over a year. That, however, as they say, "is another story."[18]

~~~

The final story in this chapter is about Henry Miller. Miller was the First Engineer aboard the MS Atlantic Sun. *Henry changed his name from Moeller to Miller because of anti-German sentiment. The story tells of the heroism displayed by those who simply disappeared from the face of the earth. The story was sent to me by his son, Dr. Henry Moeller, who was five years old when his father died.*

On March 21, 1942, the MS *Atlantic Sun* en route from Beaumont, Texas to Marcus Hook, Pennsylvania was struck by a torpedo from a German submarine off Cape Lookout, North

Carolina. Capt. Mohr of *U-124* had observed the tanker but could not get into a favorable firing position because of the tanker's speed. As a last resort, Capt. Mohr fired a torpedo which struck the starboard side of the forward tank.

Capt. Richard Montague managed to get the vessel and its load of crude oil into Beaufort, North Carolina for temporary repairs. She then left North Carolina and arrived at Marcus Hook, Pennsylvania under her own power on April 5, 1942. None of the crew of eight officers, thirty-two men and five armed guards reported any serious injuries.

My father, Henry Miller, was first engineer on the *Atlantic Sun* for that cruise. When he arrived home, we hardly recognized him because of his dark tan skin. It appeared to me that he had been exposed to intense sunlight for a long period of time. He told my mother and me that many of his clothes had been used as dressings for crew members who had sustained burn injuries. I also remember Dad giving my brother, Richard, and me a can of pemmican. Pemmican was a concentrated food used by Native Americans and consisted of lean meat, dried, pounded fine, and mixed with melted fat. It was used in World War II as emergency rations aboard life rafts.

My father was home for Christmas in December of 1942. At the end of the Christmas holidays we went with him to New York City and he left New York aboard the *Atlantic Sun* on January 14, 1943 with a cargo of fuel oil bound for Iceland.

The *Atlantic Sun* *was launched in 1941 at Chester, Pennsylvania. Sun Refining & Marketing Co.*

During the crossing there was a severe winter storm at sea and the convoy was dispersed. Consequently, the *Atlantic Sun* arrived alone at Reykjavik, Iceland. Her cargo was promptly discharged and the ship joined convoy ON-165 on February 8, 1943 for the return trip home. During the end of the cruise the *Atlantic Sun* developed engine trouble and dropped out of the convoy. Captain Mergerson aboard *U-607* observed the vessel 150 miles off Cape Race, Newfoundland. He fired two torpedoes which struck the tanker on the port side. One split the ship in half and the other blew a hole in the bow. The bow section sank in twenty minutes. All who were in that portion of the ship were lost.

After the ship broke in two, twenty-two men abandoned the stern which had remained intact and on an even keel. William Golobich, a survivor of the sinking, said that the survivors hovered in a lifeboat near the stern of the ship for two hours. They concluded the vessel appeared safe and rowed back to it and reboarded. Soon they were below, changing into dry clothes and drinking hot coffee while my father and the other engineers were giving the engines a thorough going over.

A half hour later, with many of the crew still below decks, the *U-607* fired a third torpedo that struck fifteen feet forward of the stern post, causing the stern to sink thirty minutes later.

The surviving crew members went over the side and into the sea just before the ship turned over keel up and sank. One lifeboat was observed partly swamped from the stern section which had sank a few minutes earlier. Eight men including my father found their way to it and climbed aboard. There were no oars and it was filled with water so that the survivors were sitting in waist high cold water. The crew tried to make the lifeboat more buoyant by throwing overboard all loose objects.

After the stern section sank the sub surfaced. Four or five crew members and a Nazi officer emerged from the conning tower and pointed a machine gun at the lifeboat in case any of the men were armed or had a grenade ready to throw. The Germans asked for the name of the vessel and its destination which was provided to them by one of the lifeboat occupants. Then the crew members pleaded for oars and supplies. William Golobich jumped out of the lifeboat and swam for the sub. He was taken prisoner aboard the sub. The seven remaining crew members including my father were not permitted to board the submarine because it had a full crew. They probably died of exposure in the freezing cold waters of the North Atlantic. After the war, William Golobich was released as a prisoner of war and returned to the United States. At a memorial service provided by the Sun Oil Company, Mr. Golobich told the surviving family members about the incident. My mother and I were both present.

That was not my last experience with the Sun Oil Company. During my second semester of my senior year of college I had an outstanding bill of several hundred dollars and I did not know how I was going to raise the money. One day when I inquired about my bill, I learned that a Sun Oil Company person had paid the bill. I was free to graduate. I will be eternally grateful for that timely assistance.[19]

The Grey Wolves of the Morn

We've sailed in the north, where great icebergs are born-
And hid in the fog, so grim and forlorn-
And no one need ask of the terror we've born-
On meeting the deadly grey wolves of the morn.

We've sailed in the south, where the water is warm-
And witnessed our shipmates, all bloody and torn-
And no one need ask of the terror we've born-
On meeting the deadly grey wolves of the morn.

We've sailed in great convoys, in fair and in storm-
And many men wishing, they'd never been born-
And no one need ask of the terror we've born-
On meeting the deadly grey wolves of the morn.

Our nerves like our ships were brittle and worn-
From fear of the deadly grey wolves of the morn-
And for all of our dead there were few who would morn-
Who met the deadly grey wolves of the morn.

Ian A. Millar[20]

6

NORTHERN RUSSIA

*P*erhaps the most difficult — and most dangerous —
voyage a merchant mariner could make during World
War II was the trip to Northern Russia. Although it was
the shortest route, in distance and time, compared to going by
way of the Persian Gulf or Vladivostok, the Murmansk run was,
by far, the most treacherous. Weather conditions were
unforgiving and ships were exposed to the German Luftwaffe and
submarines. It was a nightmare fraught with fierce winter
storms, snow, ice, bombing attacks, strafing runs and torpedoes.
It was critically important, however, because Russia had to have
the goods to carry out her part of the war and hold the German
forces on the Eastern front.

Forty convoys, with a total of more than 800 ships, including
350 under the U.S. flag, started on the Murmansk run from 1941
through 1945. Ninety-seven of those ships were sunk by bombs,
torpedoes, mines, and the fury of the elements . . . They carried

more than 22,000 aircraft, 375,000 trucks, 8,700 tractors, 51,500 jeeps, 1,900 locomotives, 343,700 tons of explosives, a million miles of field-telephone cable, plus millions of shoes, rifles, machine guns, auto tires, radio sets, and other equipment.[1]

President Roosevelt promised aid to Russia after Germany declared war on her. The first shipments began in the fall of 1941. Historian Samuel Eliot Morison wrote, "This run from Iceland past Spitsbergen into the Barents Sea was one of the vital lifelines that provided Russia with the means to fight..."[2] Convoys were established to get the goods to Murmansk and Archangel; a run of often up to twelve days. The few convoys that sailed in 1941 were relatively successful.

Complicating matters was Hitler's determination to retain control over the waters leading to these ports.

...during the spring of 1942 the situation was profoundly changed. The Germans having failed to conquer Russia at the first dash, realized how important were Anglo-American supplies in stiffening Russian resistance, and they determined to do what they could do to stop them. A flotilla of submarines was sent north and soon rose to a strength of twenty. More aircraft were sent to northern Norway, particularly long range dive bombers and torpedo aircraft. Also the main strength of the German surface navy began to operate together in these waters.[3] It was a short trip for the Luftwaffe to bomb Murmansk. "The crew of the Yaka, at Murmansk, sweated out 156 air raids while off-loading cargo.[4]

Discharging cargo became a problem in these ports because of the number of vessels backed up awaiting a berth.

Without a doubt, the most devastating event on this run involved the disastrous Convoy PQ-17. Thirty-three well-escorted ships sailed in July 1942, and for some unexplainable reason were told to break formation. It had been proven there is safety in numbers and yet this axiom was cast aside. The Germans would sink twenty-three ships.

Soon after that the convoy commodore hoisted an astonishing signal: 'Scatter fanwise. Proceed to destination at utmost speed.'

Some of the captains could not believe the order and requested a repeat, but there had been no mistake. The escort had been ordered to abandon the merchant ships and their precious cargoes. Each vessel was to proceed independently and the devil take the hindmost. Long afterward, the mystified skippers learned the reason for their abandonment. The British Admiralty believed that the German battleship Tirpitz and battlecruiser Scheer had left their Norwegian bases to intercept PQ-17. Scattering the convoy was thought the best, but tragic, alternative to having the Germans pounce on all the ships in one compact group... [5]

Initially, the attitude of the Russian government left much to be desired.

The Russians, for all their splendid fighting qualities, were still highly suspicious of their 'capitalist' allies, forbade their people to fraternize with our bluejackets or merchant seamen, and made no public acknowledgment of the heroic efforts that they and the British were making to get the stuff through ...[6]

The Russian government, however, would eventually honor the American Merchant Mariners in 1985 with "The 40th Anniversary of the Victory in the Great Patriotic War Medal, for outstanding courage and personal contribution against Nazi Germany." The Russians also followed up with the 50th Commemoration by inviting forty mariners to their country's celebration.

~~~

The first story was submitted by John Brady who is treasurer of the Treasure Coast Chapter of the American Merchant Marine Veterans and quite an artist as well!

I signed on the S.S. *Beaconhill* in Staten Island, N.Y., and when I met the crew they did not know where the ship was going, but later on we were issued all kinds of winter gear; like felt boots, a rubber suit with a light on it, also a sheepskin coat and an aviator-style hat, fur-lined. So we all assumed that we were probably going to Russia, but we weren't sure. You never knew where you were going because they didn't tell you anything; they just issued you your clothes.

The ship left New York right after New Year and we went to Marcus Hook, Pennsylvania, where we picked up a cargo of aviation gas and then back to New York to await a convoy. Our ship had reciprocating engines and Scotch boilers generated the steam to run the engine so it was not a fast ship. Usually the slower ships made only about ten knots and the convoys were required to sail with the speed of the slower ships.

There were about thirty ships in the convoy and we had an escort taking us out. I'm not sure if they were made up of all British corvettes or whether there were some American escorts, but when we got out and were able to see what the convoy was made of, it seemed like we had quite a number of ships to protect us. We sailed up north, around the coast and went all around Halifax, Greenland, up along Iceland, the northern route, passed Bear Island and sailed along into Gourock, Scotland. We were there while they made up another convoy to head for Russia. We went to a place called Loch Ewe to get more supplies and once that was taken on board, we were on our way again.

We left there with a convoy of British corvettes and many vessels of different nationalities totaling about thirty ships. The further north we went, the more miserable the weather got. The days were sort of foggy and dreary, and then we were into ice floes, not real big ice, but cakes of ice. When we were up around North Cape, we spotted planes coming out from Norway. They were large planes, probably observation planes and they flew around the convoy. First there was one plane and later on that one was relieved and others joined in and continued to circle the convoy for the next three days. I believe it was on the third day that the bombers came over. I was down in the engine room and the engineer told me that we were going to be attacked and that we should change the tips on the burners to get more speed in the

U.S. Navy Armed Guard fends off Nazi air attack at North Cape off Norway.
John Brady

engines. Since I was in the engine room, I really didn't get up on deck to see what type of planes they were, but they bombed the ship and some of the bombs landed very close because the whole ship shook from the explosions. Our gun crew which was made up of about twenty-nine armed guard sailors and their officer, did an excellent job of keeping those planes off. From what I could remember, the bombings kept up for two days, and then the convoy split up; one half headed for Murmansk and the other half headed for Molotovsk. They split into fifteen ships each and we went on to Molotovsk.

When we got out into the White Sea, a big well-armed Russian ice-breaker accompanied us breaking the ice along the way. On the way we were attacked by bombers again, but this time the bombs didn't hit any of the ships and landed on the ice floes. The bombers also dropped incendiaries, long hexagonal cylinders about a foot or a little longer and some of them landed on our decks. The crew had to go around with sand to put them out when they started to light off. After the attack a Russian escort joined us and helped drive them off back to Norway.

Under attack in the White Sea. John Brady

When we arrived at Molotovsk on March 2, there was snow and ice around the dock area. At the docks we could see a number of men, some were guards and some were people very poorly dressed. We didn't know who they were, but they seemed to be under Russian guard. We were tied up at one dock where we could pump out the gasoline (high octane gas) into two ships that had been converted into tanks. We tied up after our cargo was unloaded and found out we wouldn't be able to leave to go back to Scotland or New York. We were sent to Archangel.

At Archangel, we anchored off the port, and when we wanted to go ashore we had to go on the ship's lifeboats. To make matters worse, we had to stay in this port until the month of May. We were then notified that we were to sail back to Molotovsk, where we loaded up with bunker oil and then proceeded with four Russian destroyers along the Russian coast to the Kola Inlet.

We were to take the place of a Norwegian tanker, S.S. *Marathon*, that was chartered to the Russians to refuel the Russian ships on the way to the Russian naval base on Kola Inlet. The *Marathon* had been heavily damaged and we were ordered to take her place. I believe we made sixteen trips during those six months; just back and forth, picking up oil and making the trip to

The Beacon Hill *refueling a Russian warship. John Brady*

Murmansk to the navy base and refueling British corvettes and Russian destroyers.

In the meantime, food supplies were getting low. We had hardly any American food left and the trips were getting on our nerves; going back and forth and the strain of not knowing if we would be torpedoed, and just not knowing what would happen in the few days, weeks, or months. The crew was getting very much on edge and some had arguments as the food didn't get any better and people complained. The cook went to the Chief Steward and demanded to know how he was going to feed a crew with no real supplies of American food on board. The cook was British and the Chief Steward was of Scandinavian origin. They got into an argument and the Chief Steward knocked the cook down and broke his leg. The cook, being an Englishman, was taken to one of the corvettes for treatment.

Later on we had other fights among the crew. We had one man who had to be taken off the ship because he tried to stab another seaman with a knife. They had to send to the Naval

The Panamanian-flag tanker Beacon Hill *refueling a Russian Navy ship. John Brady*

Marine Attache for an armed marine sergeant to take the man off the ship. He had locked himself up in his quarters with an axe and wouldn't come out. The marine sergeant told him that if he didn't come out he would have to go in and to get him and if he had to do that, possibly kill him. The man finally gave up, put down his axe, and came out. They brought him to an empty room where they handcuffed him to the pipes. The marine sergeant took him off the ship the next day.

Things of this nature went on for the months we were shuttling back and forth. The weather got warmer, of course. Whenever we had time off we would try to get over to the Intourist (Hotel), but we weren't there very long. As soon as the ship was loaded, we were back on our trip to Murmansk. We had the same Russian escorts taking us back and forth. Sometimes we had to go through mine fields. And several times we refueled the Russian naval ships at sea. We were there for nine long months.

One of the men on board ship went to a dance at the Intourist. He brought along his trombone thinking he could play it with the Russian band. When he tried to play his instrument, he was approached by a Russian officer who told him, "*Nyet dobriy,*" which meant, "Don't play it." The would-be trombone player had his brother along and they both got into a fight with the Russian officer. The trombone player hit the Russian and both he and his brother landed in prison. They weren't held long as they were returned to the ship before the next run to Murmansk. We all thought that was the end of that, but just before we were ready to sail back to England in a convoy, the Russian authorities came out in a small vessel and took the trombone player off the ship.

For years I never knew what had happened to him until recently. He was put in a prison camp and held there for six months. The people we had seen on the docks were prisoners. They did all the heavy work for fourteen hours a day with very little food. Most of them looked starved and were dressed in rags. These had been the people we were watching on the docks, and this is where he was sent.

After he was taken off, we joined a convoy and sailed out of Russia. When we got back to the lochs of Scotland where all the British warships were tied up, his brother went to one of the American embassies to find out about him. There was nothing they could tell or do because our ship was not flying an American flag. It was registered under a Panamanian flag even though we had an all-American gun crew and most of the crew were Americans.

Finally, we sailed from the loch, went back to sea, and sailed back to New York. We had left shortly after the 1943 New Year in early January and when we got back home it was around Christmas time.[7]

~~~

Carl L. Hammond of Waldeboro, Maine contributed the following story which involves three mariners, John Stanish, ex-Second Radio Officer, John F. Dunn, ex-U.S. Navy Armed Guard Signalman, and himself, ex-Chief Radio Operator, and their experiences aboard the Liberty John A. Quitman, *call sign KOTQ.*

We departed New York City on 14 November 1944 bound for the Clyde River with a general cargo of war material and foodstuffs below our decks. Our deck load was a locomotive and tender, boiler, condenser and generator cars forward and two 50-ton bridge girders stretched across the number 4 and 5 hatches. The ship was so deeply laden that we were able to step from the deck of the harbor tug onto the main deck when we returned from the convoy conference at Whitehall. We sailed into a storm that followed us across with high winds and quartering seas that gave us a horrible corkscrew roll making living, eating, and watch keeping a major effort. It was "rubber band on the Underwood typewriter carriage," weather for the entire run to Scotland.

This being John's first trip as RO, he had some problems acclimating himself to the miserable eastward progression of the ship.

We arrived in Greenock about two weeks later without anything more than the normal alarms inherent in every North Atlantic passage. I do not recall losing any of the convoy because of enemy activity. There was, of course, weather damage to most of the vessels.

While in the Clyde, we were fitted with a Marconi voice receiver operating in the 1600 kcs range. This set was installed in the shack with a remote gain-controlled speaker in the upper wheel house. It was intended to be an inter-convoy receive-only radio channel between the commodore, escorts, and merchant vessels supplementing the normal flag hoists and blinker. As a technical aside, this set had no squelch, so the noise was constantly loud and intrusive. The bridge watch and the RO's began to turn their speaker volume down, so there were excellent opportunities to miss traffic. The primary frequency guard was the bridge — we in the shack monitored at will. Two open storage batteries, one for filaments and the other for plate power, were arranged on a shelf in the battery room. That configuration lasted until we had our first deep roll and they fell back to the deck, destroying themselves. For the rest of the voyage the set ran off the ship's 110-volt DC main power whose noise added to that of the atmospherics, so you can imagine the racket. There was not much affection for this aid to navigation and it really never justified its existence.

We remained in Greenock for the remainder of November and December, after which we transited to Loch Ewe where we became part of convoy JW-63. While in Greenock, we had a grand Christmas dinner complete with drinks; a gift from Captain Meyers.

We left Loch Ewe 30 December and arrived at Kola Inlet 8 January 1945 after an uneventful trip. There was no air action — only the constant U-boat threats. The weather was typical of the northern latitudes at that time of the year. The high-frequency radio circuits used to copy BAMS (Broadcast Allied Merchant Ships) traffic was subject to the degrading influence of the aurora borealis. You could hear the atmospheric noise build in intensity and move up the band making the HF (High Frequency) spectrum useless. All of our CW (Continuous Wave) reception was from GBR (Radio Station), Rugby, England on 18khz, and that took some effort.

Together with seven other merchant ships we departed Murmansk, sailing through the White Sea to Molotovsk, somewhat west of Archangel. We went alongside, discharging cargo until early February. Molotovsk, now named Severodvinsk, was not much to write home about. Its main claim to fame appeared to be the prisoner-of-war camp that furnished the longshore gangs. The guards were convalescing Russian troops. The weather was very cold, several times getting to 40 below with strong winds. By this time the water in the harbor was beginning to freeze very quickly forcing us to pump hot water overboard to keep some free space around the hull.

My major concern was keeping the radio room storage batteries on charge. With the sub-freezing temperatures and non-insulated battery room, there was real danger of the electrolyte slushing unless a trickle charge ran constantly through them. The Russians wanted to seal the main switch on the Coke (Transmitter Assembly) machine. This would have disabled the battery charging circuits. A bilingual argument via a stunning blond interpreter led them to seal the transmitter switch instead, which saved all our faces.

Crew members, both merchant and armed guard, were allowed to visit only three places: the Intourist Hotel, a movie house, and the Young Communist League Hall. We got into town by bartering cigarettes for a jeep ride; you had to use Shanks Mare (you walked) to get back, a matter of several cold, cold miles. The hotel was two-pot: officers in a small room and the crews in a large room with no mingling. So much for Communist equality! For a few rubles, less than the going price of a pack of cigarettes, we could have vodka, spam, caviar, and black bread. It was customary for the Russians to give each merchant crew member a gift of 1000 rubles — just about the black market price for a pack of cigarettes.

The Armed Guard was presented with various gifts, but not locally. John Dunn and two other sailors traveled by train to Archangel to bring back the gift packages for all the gun crews in the harbor. John Stanish went along for the ride. Each of them carried goodies, such as cigarettes, matches, soap, and such for sale to the natives, thereby becoming instant capitalists. As it was later told to me, it did not take long for them to be stopped on the street by a militia member who spoke little English, and questioned them about their black market activities. Fortunately, an officer from the Port Director's Office who happened by, sized up the situation, and while shouting at the cop, told them to do a fast scram. They returned to Molotovsk forthwith with much fear and trembling.

In early February we were beginning to load sawed lumber as our return cargo. Because the White Sea was completely frozen over and we were now frozen to the dock, we had to wait for icebreakers to free us and the other vessels. While the icebreakers were working in the harbor and before undocking, the Russians had all of us, merchant and navy, lined up on the forward main deck while they searched the ship for stowaways. As we began undocking maneuvers several large and thick blocks of ice managed to become tangled with the turning propeller, bending two of the blades, thereby limiting our speed. A great start.

After leaving the harbor our eight-ship convoy very slowly followed the icebreakers for about three days until we reached open water where the British escorts met us and guided us into the Kola Inlet. While in the ice, a light ski plane landed and the pilot walked over the ice to one of the icebreakers presumably to report on conditions ahead. I must add that the crews of the icebreakers were women.

We experienced no enemy action while in Molotovsk or in the ice pack while returning to Kola. This calm soon evaporated. As we were doing slow knots in single file through the open submarine nets and streaming our own torpedo nets, the Liberty *Horace Gray* immediately astern of us was torpedoed as was also a Norwegian tanker farther astern.

The Horace Gray *was torpedoed by the German submarine* U-711 *(Capt. Lange) at 1210 GCT on February 14, 1945 at the entrance to Kola Inlet, Russia with a cargo of 7,500 tons of Potash in bulk. The ship filled with water on February 16 and was declared a total loss. There were no casualties. The U-711 was sunk May 4, 1945 off Harstad, Norway.[8] Coincidentally, the Allies called off their attacks upon Germany May 4, 1945.*

We took *Gray*'s gun crew aboard as passengers, quartering them in the lower wheelhouse.[*] Their living conditions were very cramped and uncomfortable. Having these extra people with us put a strain on our remaining food and water. Other vessels experienced the same problems when caring for survivors.

We left Kola Inlet 17 February 1945 as part of RA-64, a thirty-three ship convoy bound for the Clyde. The close escort was corvettes and sloops; the outer screen destroyers, cruisers and two aircraft carriers flying Wildcats. While exiting the inlet, the sloop *Lark* was torpedoed as was the freighter *Thomas Scott*.

---

[*] Liberty ships were not built with an upper wheelhouse. As launched, the upper navigation area (flying bridge or monkey bridge) was open to the elements. It was the practice on many Libertys to close in this area with temporary bulkheads, windows, doors and an overhead — especially if the ship was on the run to Northern Russia.

A second escort, the *Bluebell* was lost with all hands except one seaman who was blown into the sea and eventually rescued. This sinking was witnessed from the radio room with great interest as she was close by on our port beam and there was a strong feeling that we may be included in a periscope's view.

The Thomas Scott, *was torpedoed by the* U-968 *(Capt. Westphalen) at 1050 GCT on February 17, 1945 ... All were saved ... and the* U-968 *(Capt. Westphalen) surrendered at Narvik, Norway in May, 1945.*[9] *Meanwhile, the sloop* Bluebell *was sunk by the* U-711, *with only one survivor.*[10]

By this time the weather was beginning to deteriorate very quickly. Gale force winds and building seas began the next day, increasing to a whole gale over the next two days. Station keeping became more and more difficult for all vessels and the convoy began scattering. We fell farther and farther astern,

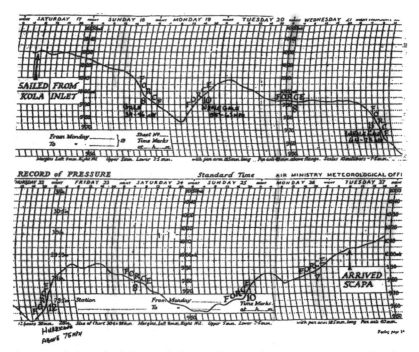

Barograph from the John A. Quitman *showing barometric pressure the ship experienced during the hurricane. Carl L. Hammond*

unable to maintain convoy speed given the sea state and our dicey propeller. We were not alone in becoming a laggard and it became apparent that there were now two groups of ships — the main body and us stragglers. This configuration lasted for about two days when the weather began moderating somewhat and the convoy attempted to reform. We were still astern in company with three other widely spaced ships and several escorts.

About this time a strong air attack was made by the Germans with several of them being shot down by the escorts and our fighter cover. There were no losses to us. How these pilots were able to fly off the carriers and then land in this terrible weather I will never know.

The weather began to deteriorate for the second time, increasing to hurricane force and again scattering the convoy for several days. After reforming in moderating weather, there was another aerial torpedo attack made on us stragglers. The freighter *Henry Bacon* astern of us was hit and commenced foundering. She was carrying Norwegian passengers rescued from Sovoy Island in addition to her normal crew and armed guard. There was not enough room in the lifeboats for everyone, so some of the crew and armed guards stayed behind, giving up their places in the boats. The survivors were picked up by the escorts …

On the 22nd, the master thought he had steamed ahead of the convoy and turned his vessel back. At 1400, while the ship was on a reverse course, lookouts spotted twenty-three enemy torpedo bombers. The armed guards skillfully protected the ship as the planes reportedly launched forty-six torpedoes. At 1420 a torpedo struck the starboard side at the # 5 hatch. The explosion blasted a large hole in the hull, blew off the hatch covers, damaged the rudder and propeller, and ruptured the steam lines, causing the ship to settle by the stern quickly … Seven armed guards died along with six merchant officers and nine men.[11]

All this time the commodore asked on 500kcs whether any merchant vessel knew the whereabouts of the JU-88's and our own fighters. Captain Meyers gave me the go-ahead to answer. It certainly was an uncomfortable moment for us to announce our presence. This instance, by the way, was the only time I transmitted during the war.

The weather began moderating over the next three days and we were able to'rejoin, a very comfortable feeling, I assure you. We reached the Clyde 1 March, worn out and very thankful.

The remainder of the voyage was an anticlimax. We discharged our passengers, took on fuel, water and some food, all in very short supply, joined a coastal convoy to Rouen, France where we discharged our lumber. We went into a graving dock in Port Talbot, Wales for propeller replacement and stern repairs. It was an experience to see the British dockyard workers beating on the red hot shell plating with sledge hammers — no pneumatic tools, thank you. Very noisy, also. We took on a load of general cargo for Gent, Belgium, returning to the UK to join a convoy to New York, arriving 22 May 1945.

The outstanding memory that I have of these events was that we were all very tired from the lack of sound sleep, the long hours of watch standing and being pounded by the constant rolling and pitching. Our meals were not Cordon Bleu; most were warm at best because of the difficulty in keeping the coal fires in the galley ranges. It was remarkable how well the cooks and stewards coped with the feeding of all of us. The engineers certainly had their hands full nursing the revolutions when the prop came out of the water during the storms. The deck gang and armed guard were exposed to all manner of abuse — biting winds, cold water, and cold bodies. Captain Meyers, a grandfather well into his sixties, was in the upper wheelhouse almost constantly. He was a remarkable example of endurance. It was good that most of us were in our twenties. I do not know if I could do it again now being in my seventies . . .

In an effort to amplify my sketch description of the continuing storms, I have included a British Air Ministry Meteorological Office Record of Pressure hand annotated with the wind strengths, but no directions.[12] The plot is more definite than my writings could ever be . . .[13]

The Liberty ship John A. Quitman *was sold to the Cleveland, Ohio ship breakers in January of 1973.*[14]

~~~

The following story was sent to me by Adolph G. Rutler.
Adolph passed away in 1998 and thankfully he was able to record
this first of two stories for this anthology.

The Difference Between "Doc" and the "Dock"

I sailed as FWT (Fireman Watertender) aboard the Liberty ship *Julien Poydras* in 1943. We started in a convoy for the Mediterranean, but part way over a large crack developed on the starboard side and went across the deck to a corner of # 2 cargo hatch. We pulled out of the convoy and headed for England. Part way there, another crack developed on the port side and spread to another corner of the same hatch cover. We did make it to Glasgow where we unloaded, went into dry dock at Govern Cross, and the ship was welded back together again. We reloaded and joined a convoy for Russia.

I had an Italian friend on board who lived in Passaic, New Jersey. He had a heavy black beard and he was completely bald. Naturally, we all called him Baldy. Well, Baldy developed a very bad cold, possibly pneumonia. After docking in Murmansk, the first thing Baldy and I did was to go in search of a doctor or medicine. At each place we visited, I had Baldy cough and I would say, "See sick, needs Doctor, you know Doc," but no one seemed to understand.

After about four more places, Baldy was tired of coughing and I of saying "Doc." Eventually we did find a place where a young girl seemed to understand what we wanted. She called someone on the telephone then handed it to Baldy who then told me all was o.k., and that we just had to wait there. After a short time two Russian soldiers came and pointed to us and asked "Doc?" We said yes and then went with them outside and got into an American-made jeep.

After a very short ride we pulled up to where our ship was tied up. They pointed to the pier and said "O.K., dock." We did not have the heart to tell them that this was not the "Doc" we were looking for. We thanked them and left. There was no way we would go through that again. One thing we did learn was how to get a ride back to the ship, but never again say "Doc" when you want a doctor.

We stayed in Murmansk while they outfitted the aft hold with bunks and equipment for 100 Russian sailors who were to take over a light cruiser. A number of ships were so equipped. After a couple of days out, I came off the 12-to-4 watch in the boiler room, and watched the Russians celebrate May Day on the aft deck. They were having a great time and at that moment I looked up to see the ship just astern hit with a torpedo. The ship's masts folded up like tooth picks in a big cloud of white smoke. By the time I got my life jacket and went to my battle station that ship had disappeared. That ship also had 100 Russians aboard.[15]

The Julien Poydras *was scrapped in Bilbao, Spain, May 1971.*[16]

~~~

The next two stories were written by John J. York of Fishkill, N.Y. who was the Chief Radio Officer on the S.S. Benjamin Schlesinger.

The Angel of Archangel

The sturdy Liberty ship S.S. *Benjamin Schlesinger* had safely crossed the North Atlantic, carrying a full load of war supplies to our hard-pressed ally, Russia. Our holds were full of Lend Lease supplies. Locomotives, large generators on railroad wheels, rails and fighter planes filled the decks. After safely dodging German planes and submarines, we arrived in the White Sea and the mouth of the Dvina River in early November of 1944. The cargo was unloaded near Molotovsk by slave labor. It was cold, snowy and icy.

For recreation some of us would leave the safe haven of our ship, take a small tug boat, acting as an ice breaker, to cross the river from our dock, heading for Archangel. (In a couple of weeks, the trolley tracks were laid across the frozen river for five months' duration). After leaving the tug, we would take a trolley into the city of Archangel. The trolley was unheated, rusty, missing windows, and doors. The Intourist Hotel was the only place Americans were allowed to stay. The meals were meager, borscht soup, boiled potatoes, turnips and other vegetables. The upper floors were used to house slave laborers in transit.

A propaganda movie against the Germans was being shown all over town. It depicted Tanya, a young woman who had been raped, stabbed, hung by the neck and left hanging in the winter wind by the German military. We went to see a play in a large opera house style building. Again, it was strictly anti-German. The large theater was unheated, so everyone sat with coat, hats and mittens on, then during intermission everyone walked in a large circle in the lobby in order to get warm.

On the night of the play, three of us headed back to the ships. It was later than our usual departure time. Of course the city was blacked out and because of a potential air raid, the trolley was not running. It was bitter cold, probably forty degrees below zero. The snow squeaked with each step. There was no moonlight, just the extra-bright northern lights and stars in the clear air. We walked for miles, stumbling along the trolley track bed. Where the tracks ended was where we should have caught the ice breaker to cross the river, but the tug was closed down for the night. What were we going to do? We had no place to stay, and even worse, no shelter from the extreme cold. At least my feet were warm because Uncle Sam in his thoughtfulness had issued farmer-style boots for this Russian run.

We stood shivering, wondering what to do. It was too tiring to walk back and there was no place else to go. After a few minutes we heard the trudging of many footsteps in cadence. A group of slave laborers was being marched from camp to work. A well bundled-up woman who was helping direct the march, saw our dilemma. We were not able to communicate except for sign language. She led us a short distance to a low building in the darkness which seemed to be made out of rough sawn lumber, like the imperfect slabs that are discarded when good boards are sawn from logs. She opened a door and we all stepped inside before she lit a candle. The unheated room was perhaps ten by twelve feet. There was a table in the center made out of rough lumber with no tablecloth. There was a bench on each side of the table, made of logs split in half with the flat side up. The legs had been shaped by an axe and inserted into the split logs. One unlit electric light bulb hung from the ceiling, directly over the table.

In one corner of the room was something that looked like a combination wood stove and oven that was covered with plaster-like material. The room's walls were of bare logs with an occasional newspaper clipping. Also on the walls were hand-carved wooden bowls and crudely carved wooden spoons for eating from the bowls.

The woman tried to offer us food, but we refused. Then she did something that to this day moves me deeply and rekindles my faith in people. As we stood wondering what to do, the woman went into the adjoining room and we heard voices of sleepy children who were being disturbed in their sleep. The woman came out of the room carrying three blankets still warm from the children's bodies! We kept telling her *"nyet, nyet,"* but she insisted. Shortly after, she left, leaving three strange men in her home with her children. She was an Angel with a capital A.

The Third Engineer wrapped himself up in a blanket and slept on the table top. The benches were narrow, but by laying on my hands, I was able to sleep on a bench. The Second Radio Officer, after putting the candle out, decided to sleep on the floor. While trying to fall asleep I felt something crawling on my face. I picked it off and threw it down beside me on the floor next to me. When the "something" started to bite, I guessed what they were — bedbugs!

About six a.m. the one overhead light bulb came on and I heard a rustling noise. Looking around I saw the walls and floor were alive with cockroaches scurrying for cover! What a situation — a woman with a heart of gold, having to live under conditions where she could not afford to buy, even if it was available during war time, the insecticides to protect herself and her children.

We left early that morning before the woman came home and before the children woke up. We left rubles, and what candy and gum we had in our pockets. Several days later when going to Archangel, we dropped off warm clothing, soap, towels, candy, food, and whatever else we could "requisition" from the Steward's department.[17]

The Benjamin Schlesinger *was scrapped in Veracruz, Mexico in July 1963.*[18]

The Non-Angels of Archangel

On my first convoy to Northern Russia, we carried a Russian Naval officer who had been in the States for training. Boris (what other name did you expect?) was distant and uncommunicative, though he could speak excellent English which he learned in Russia. There were many American engineers and teachers who had gone to Russia in the 1930's under five and ten year plans to teach there. Boris was deathly afraid of the North Atlantic and stayed in his room during the trip.

The first inkling that I got about the Russian obsession with secrecy was when they immediately sealed my radio shack to prevent the use of any equipment. We were also ordered not to take any newspapers, magazines, catalogs, and like materials ashore. The reason became obvious once ashore, because the people were living in abject poverty, with only Russian propaganda newspapers available. They had no radios for news, only street corner loud-speakers that blasted out slanted news and propaganda. We were not allowed to take American money ashore. In its place we were issued rubles.

The Russian military people did what they pleased. The first thing Boris did once he was ashore was to force an encounter on a teenage girl, acting though it was expected of her because he was a military officer.

Many things happened during the three short days that I was there. It was high noon, but it was barely light near the Arctic Circle. Three of our crew boarded a small tug which was used as a ferry to go through the ice which had formed in the river. It was bitter cold, snow on the ground, and the tug's deck was wet from the engine heat. A Russian woman stepped from the dock onto the slanted tug deck and went sprawling about twenty feet, ending up in the coiled tow lines. The Russian military men laughed uproariously and did not offer to help her up. So we Americans helped her up. She was injured somewhat, but not severely.

Several hours later, while taking a trolley to Archangel, we stopped in the countryside to pick up passengers. The trolley was fully loaded with standing room only. A Russian woman with a baby in her arms tried to stand on the first step leading up into the trolley. A Russian soldier, one among a group of many soldiers, raised his foot, and being higher than she was, kicked her in the chest, and she fell off. She and the baby rolled down the embankment in the snow. The soldiers had a good laugh. We three were outnumbered, so we decided "neutrality" was the better part of valor.

On the return trip back that night, a similar incident occurred. When the trolley tracks ended we were forced to walk along the track bed. There was a large group of Russian soldiers ahead of us. They were forced to slow down because of a woman who was carrying a large bundle of tree branches for firewood on her back. One of the soldiers tripped her and she ended up crying on the ground between the rails. This time, we Americans helped her up, dusted her off, and carried her load until she could find a side path off into the Arctic winter darkness and bitter cold.

Another example of Russian brutality occurred on my second convoy, to Murmansk this time. As we were getting ready to leave for Scotland, the Captain, the USN Armed Guard and myself as Chief Radio Officer went to the convoy conference, held by the Commodore and the escorting naval forces. While passing through the dock area, I saw a Russian armed guard arguing with one of the male slave laborers. The guard watched us cautiously as we passed by. I looked back and the guard, thinking that we were no longer looking, raised his rifle butt and hit the man between the eyes and knocked him down.

One more observation to show how rugged and fierce their military was. That was in the Murmansk Harbor area in late April 1945. There were a large number of flat open barges usually used for carrying bulk cargoes moved by tugs. These barges had horses and hay on one end of the barge and horse drawn cannon with ammunition on the opposite end. In the middle were the troops with fires in 55 gallon drums for heating and cooking. These barges were ready to make a beach head in the northern part of Norway in an attempt to attack Hitler on another front.

My observations and personal contacts showed that the common Russian people by themselves were quite open and friendly, but they were suspicious of others and would only talk to us when alone.[19]

~~~

In the preface of this chapter I mentioned that a contingent of American Merchant Marine Veterans was invited to Russia in 1995 to celebrate the 50th Anniversary of the victory against Germany. The following letter was submitted by Robert Gustin of Madeira Beach, Florida to MM&P (Masters, Mates and Pilots) Magazine, but was never published. It tells of the wonderful experience he had in Russia.

They Treated Us As Heroes

I recently returned from a trip to Russia, which included Moscow, Murmansk and St. Petersburg.

Our group included twenty-three veterans of the Murmansk run with twelve of their wives and one son. The group was led by Admiral William Thompson, of the Navy Memorial Foundation, and his wife. Also in the group was Robert Naser of the Foundation, and Franceline Rudd of Cultural Tours, Washington, D.C. Our group consisted of forty people. Included in the group were seven captains, one engineer, one purser, several AB's, some oilers and FWT's.

If anyone is in doubt about whether or not the Russian people appreciated what the merchant marine did to help defeat Hitler and help save the Soviet Union, they should have been with us. They treated us as heroes.

While in Murmansk, we toured the Russian Navy's northern fleet base, visiting places never before seen by Americans. Our tour bus was escorted by a police car and a television crew followed us taking a lot of video pictures of our group laying wreaths at monuments and gravesites. We were also interviewed for the evening news.

We also toured the Navy base at Kronshtadt, near St. Petersburg. The current Admiral of the Russian Navy sent his own boat to transport us from St. Petersburg to the base. That boat trip took about an hour and upon arrival we were greeted by their Navy band.

Other highlights of our trip were the Moscow Circus, the Kremlin and Red Square. There were a number of lunches and dinners along with speeches and numerous toasts, with vodka, so we were well fortified.

A very interesting part of one speech took place at a meeting between our group and Russian veterans including high ranking Russian Navy and Army officers. A Russian Admiral let it be known that the Russians were annoyed about not being invited to the recent D-Day ceremonies at Normandy.[*] Admiral Thompson acknowledged their complaint and informed them he "got the message," and would let the proper authorities know about it when he returned to Washington.

Next to speak at that meeting was another member of our group, Captain Louis Dorfmeister (eighty-three years old) and retired from MM&P in 1952. He told the Russians that he understood how they feel about being ignored at the D-Day ceremonies, because we, the U.S. Merchant Mariners were also

---

[*] In 1994 world attention was focused on the 50th Anniversary of D-Day. Veterans, ships and aircraft converged on Normandy, recreating the landings of June 6, 1944. Among the ships was the SS *Jeremiah O'Brien*, one of the Libertys that took part in the original landings.

ignored, by the U.S. Government, the press, and television networks, in spite of participating in all U.S. invasions during World War II.

I am told there will be other tours in the future. I urge any veteran of the Murmansk run to go if they possibly can. Some of our group plan on making the trip next year when there will be extensive celebrations in Russia, of the 50th anniversary of the end of World War II in Europe.[20]

On July 29, 1994, a Salutation was entered in to the U.S. House of Representatives by the Honorable Jack Fields on the behalf of Alfred J. Beauchamp.

NORTH RUSSIA

Young men in years the battle strain showin-
While the liberty's deck was pitchin and rollin-
The fog banks came on, then the Arctic gales blowin-
Ammo fire set deck plates a glowin.

Icebergs and U-boats make mighty tough goin-
The lifeboats they had were bastards for rowin-
And many a merchantman's frayed nerves were showin-
To the hell of north Russia their ships were goin.

There were many back then and today still not knowin-
Who called them draft dodgers, and the place they were goin-
Was far from the fronts the newsreels were showin-
Their gallantry screened by the Arctic snow blowin.

Some men sailed twice and again fully knowin-
The Condors and Heinkels and tracers a glowin-
The Stars and the Stripes from the fantail a blowin-
The merchantmen kept the war supplies flowin.

Ian A. Millar[21]

7

THE MEDITERRANEAN

*I*n November of 1942, U.S. and British forces landed in French Morocco and Algeria to begin the North African offensive. Complicating this massive offensive and the remaining objectives in the Mediterranean was the major logistical problem of how to supply two naval forces, American and British, with the materials and ammunition needed to conduct the campaigns.

Philosophical differences also developed on how to conduct the remainder of the war. Stalin, re-fortified with supplies and war materials, was holding his own on the western front but a new frontal attack was crucial in order to take some of the pressure off Russia. The British pushed for a southern offensive through the "soft-underbelly," of the Mediterranean while the Americans proposed an assault via the channel.

Early in 1943, the Allies turned the corner in the North African campaign. Meeting in Casablanca, Roosevelt and

Churchill plotted the next steps. Essentially, it was agreed that Germany must be defeated before Japan, and that a southern offensive was necessary since the cross channel invasion wasn't possible until 1944. The southern campaign would commence by crossing the Mediterranean and invading Sicily.

In May of 1943, the Mediterranean was considered relatively "safe" and the merchant ships could fulfill their function. "Helping to lift these great armies and their vast impediments were scores of Liberty ships that had assembled in African ports over a period of many weeks."[1]

The price the merchant marine paid for this support in men wounded or killed, and ships damaged or sunk, was enormous. "During the entire war period, a total of 413 merchant ships — 1,740,250 tons — were sunk in the Mediterranean by enemy action."[2]

To what effect and how important the merchant marine was to the entire Mediterranean campaign, was best defined by Admiral of the Fleet, Sir Andrew B. Cunningham, RN, Commander Western Allied naval forces in the Mediterranean: "the fine spirit, discipline and calm determination of the many officers and men of the Allied Merchant Navies. They were our real comrades in arms, undaunted by any difficulty or danger."[3]

~~~

Ernest S. Standridge of Fort Worth, Texas signed on as a wiper and ended up a licensed Assistant Engineer of Steam Vessels in March, 1945. He is a member of the S.S. Stephen Hopkins *Chapter of the American Merchant Marine Veterans.*

The adventure began for those of us aboard the Texas Company tanker Motor Vessel *Rhode Island*, during the latter days of October 1942. Our ship lay serenely at anchor in a ship-crowded New York City anchorage. She was a sleek and sturdy ship with a cruising speed of eighteen knots and was the undisputed queen of the Texas Company tanker fleet. She rode low in the water, her bowels filled to capacity with an explosive cargo of 100 octane gasoline.

Her topside bristled with weapons of war — her fantail deck was mounted with an artillery gun that fired 5½-inch diameter shells and on her bow was an artillery gun that fired 3½-inch diameter shells. Ten 20-millimeter antiaircraft guns were mounted in heavy gauge steel circular gun turrets, five to starboard and five to port. Twelve regular Navy gunners were assigned to our ship, one in charge of each gun. Off-watch ship personnel were assigned specific gun crew duties. Also, twelve disassembled and crated P-40 FS fighter planes were lashed to our cargo decks, six on each side of the catwalk. Everyone aboard ship was well aware that our cargo of gasoline transformed our ship into a gigantic floating super bomb — a super bomb which one spark in contact with gasoline or gasoline fumes could ignite and incinerate everyone on board. Nevertheless, the merchant marine all-volunteer crew of the M.V. *Rhode Island* was ready to begin the voyage.

Our ship, and many other predetermined ships in east coast ports proceeded as ordered to Hampton Roads where we were aligned into convoy formations complete with war ship escorts. During the next few days at sea we rendezvoused with other U.S. Naval warship units. The additional forces enlarged our convoy into a huge armada that covered a 550 square mile area of the Atlantic waters.

The force ran an easterly, zig-zag, fourteen knot course by day and a straight line course by night. During an evening hour of November 7 we arrived at a position several miles out to sea from Casablanca, French Morocco. Our secret mission was no longer secret. We learned our armada was officially "Western Task Force 34," which was one-third of "Operation Torch," commanded by Major General Dwight D. Eisenhower.

Soon after our arrival the "Naval Battle of Casablanca" ignited, and, to our surprise we received orders to sail. Our ship departed the convoy as American and French naval forces, plus French shore batteries and land-based planes, dueled in deadly combat.

The *Rhode Island* was destroyer-escorted on a coastwise course toward Gibraltar. There, we rendezvoused with the combined Eastern and Central Task Forces of Operation Torch, which had earlier departed from Britain. During morning twilight the combined Task Forces began passage through the fourteen-mile wide Strait of Gibraltar. Five-hundred merchant ships were escorted by three-hundred-fifty Royal Navy "Force H" warships reinforced by land-based planes from Britain, Gibraltar, and Malta. Once the entire procession entered Mediterranean waters, the combined Task Forces separated. The Eastern Task Force continued toward its target, the Algerian port city of Algiers. The Central Task Force, which included the *Rhode Island*, veered off toward the Algerian port city of Oran.

The Task Force went into a slow-ahead circular holding pattern just outside Oran Bay as its invasion units moved shoreward to troop-landing positions. Early morning Allied troop landings were made on three beaches in the Oran area. Although French (Vichy) forces defended fiercely, Allied encirclement maneuvers forced their surrender.

Soon after the surrender, convoy ships were ordered to proceed into the more protected waters of Oran Bay, while Force H warships patrolled the bay's open sea perimeter. Mine sweepers, however, still systematically searched for mines and sub chasers still searched for renegade submarines that might lay hidden in bay or harbor waters. The *Rhode Island* led convoy ships on a single file course into the deep water channel that led to the harbor.

The harbor ahead was indeed a welcome sight for those aboard our ship and for those aboard the British ammo ship S.S. *Browning*, which was second in line, perhaps five-hundred yards behind the *Rhode Island*. Seemingly, the most dangerous part of the voyage would soon be over.

The "all clear from battle stations" signal sounded as the *Rhode Island* continued her slow-ahead channel course. The A.B. seaman at the wheel steered a few degrees to starboard to gain a straight line entry into the harbor. Meanwhile, a seaman on the bow watch observed two streaking, straight line disturbances in the waters ahead. The tracts ran parallel to our portside, spaced only a few feet apart and one slightly ahead of the other. The disturbances resembled faint white capped wakes made by fast swimming large fish with dorsal fins slightly breaking the surface. They sliced past the stern of our ship and disappeared in our propeller wake.

Seconds later, the *Rhode Island* was slammed by a massive wave of pounding water and a deafening explosion. A huge swell thrust our ship upward and forward. Everyone on board believed we had either been torpedoed or had hit a mine. Battle station alarms clanged as all off-watch personnel rushed to their battle stations. A huge column of tar black smoke boiled upward above the place where the ammo ship S.S. *Browning* had been only moments before. Prevailing winds sheared off the smoke cloud's upper section, spreading the blackness and blotting out the sun. Small pieces of heavy gauge sheet metal and pieces of piping rained down from the sky. Minutes later, surface haze began to clear, revealing thousands of dead fish bobbing up and down in the turbulent waters. Floating debris was all that was left of the huge ammo ship and her brave crew. (*The S.S. Browning was torpedoed by the U-595, Lt. Jurgen Quaet-Faslem in command.*)[4]

Royal Naval vessels swarmed the area of destruction. The *Rhode Island* bow watch seaman's report provided warships with information for an immediate search area. Sonar devices located a silent submarine lying on the sea bottom outside of, but near the harbor entrance. Revengeful numbers of depth charges quickly destroyed the sub. We never learned if the submarine was German, French or Italian. (*The U-595 was damaged, beached, and scuttled by British Squadron 500 on Nov. 14[15?]*[5] The only matter of importance to us however, was that the remains of more than three-hundred of our fellow seaman lay on the muddy bottom of Oran Bay.

A routine turn of a few degrees to starboard had resulted in the torpedoes missing our ship and hitting the ammo ship. A quirk of fate had determined that those aboard the ammo ship would die and those aboard the *Rhode Island* would live.

The *Rhode Island* led the way on into Oran Harbor, which lay behind a native stone breakwater jetty. U.S. salvage crews worked within the harbor using hoisting cranes to clear scuttled ships from the passage lanes and docking areas. French forces had not only scuttled their own naval vessels, but also merchant ships and floating dry docks before surrendering to Allied forces.

The entire area adjacent to the Port of Oran was under a sundown to sunup total blackout, and descending darkness brought with it the first of German air attacks. Squadrons of Luftwaffe bombers, dive bombers and torpedo planes attacked ships in the sea lanes, bay and harbor waters. They also attacked airfields, ground force targets and dropped parachute mines in the bay and sea lane waters.

During a pre-midnight hour two acts of sabotage occurred within the harbor. One jarring, but muffled explosion was followed by another minutes later. Explosive devices had been detonated on the propeller shafts of two freighters. The explosions twisted propeller blades out of balance and blasted shafts out of alignment on both ships. Such damage caused the ships to be dead in the water until extensive repairs could be made. Investigators concluded that the saboteurs swam undetected across the dark harbor waters, attached time bombs to the shafts, then returned to shore.

Royal Navy vessels began a night schedule of dropping a series of depth charges in midwaters the length of the harbor. This would instantly crush any saboteurs in the water during a depth charge run. The *Rhode Island's* captain added a defensive procedure of his own. A sundown to sunup special two-man fantail deck watch was added to the regular watch schedule. Each seaman on special watch was armed with a 45-caliber pistol and standing orders to shoot anything that moved within waters adjacent to the stern of our ship. The depth charges dropped not only kept saboteurs out of the waters, but also provided another very unexpected benefit.

Soon after the first series of depth charges exploded, a huge barrel-shaped object surfaced in mid-harbor. It floated with about two-thirds of its rounded shape submerged. There was much speculation as to what the object might be. A patrol boat crew towed it carefully to a jetty side dock. It was inched up onto the wharf. Inspection of shipping labels and destination stamps revealed it to be one of a shipment of 250-gallon wooden barrels of Algerian wine. Depth charges had jarred it loose from securing lines on the deck of a sea going tug boat that French forces had scuttled in mid-harbor.

Perhaps ten minutes after a late night "all clear" signal sounded, battle station alarms clanged again. Every antiaircraft gun in Oran was fully loaded and pointed skyward with a gunner's finger on every trigger. We waited in darkened silence for the rumbling droning sounds of incoming formations of enemy bombers. Long minutes later, the faint sound of a lone, single engine plane was heard.

Searching beams of brilliant, high voltage lights revealed the intruder to be a British Spitfire. The small plane leisurely circled the nearby field. The pilot radioed a request to land. The request was granted. Runway lights were switched on and "all clear from battle stations" was sounded. The pilot began a descent as if to land on an outside runway. Recently unloaded P-40FS planes were lined up just beyond and parallel to that outside runway and in various stages of being reassembled. The descending Spitfire's engine roared in response to full throttle as it began a bombing and strafing run over the P-40's. Within a matter of seconds the Spitfire disappeared into the darkness beyond.

The German pilot of the captured Spitfire had flown into an incredible assortment and quantity of poised and ready antiaircraft weapons. He had accomplished his mission and escaped without having a single shot fired at him. Such a warrior had to be respected even by members of opposing tribes — not only for his skill and courage, but also for his luck.

Early morning twilight brought with it a quiet after the storm. We received orders to sail to Algiers where fuel storage facilities had been captured undamaged. Royal Navy warships escorted the *Rhode Island* on our 250-mile journey to what we dared to believe would be our actual port of discharge.

We docked at a tanker berth in Algiers Harbor, and the process of pumping our cargo into the port storage began soon thereafter. Hours later the process was completed. We flushed our cargo tanks with sea water, then partially refilled them with sea water for ballast. Only then could we breathe a sigh of relief that the extremely hazardous portion of our voyage was over at last. Other reinforcing and resupply convoys were on the way. Our mission had been completed and our homeward voyage would soon begin. We of the *Rhode Island* were proud of our British Allies, proud of our ship, proud of ourselves, and most of all proud of our country.[6]

~~~

Burton Drew's first trip in the merchant marine was to Mers El Kabir aboard the Benjamin Harrison. *The 5th day out he got so seasick that he literally turned green. He was never sick again. Burton had just turned eighteen in October of 1942. When they had to maintain machinery, a second engineer would send him to the tool room to get a certain size wrench. There were no markings (sizes) on them and he would bring the wrong sizes back. This happened about three times and the second engineer would carry on ferociously. His favorite expression was "Son of a whore," when the machinery acted up. This was his last trip. They said that he was going to buy a farm in Maine and raise potatoes.*

Burton Drew's diary describes this voyage to the Mediterranean. The voyage reflected the everyday workings and tension that were forever present while at sea.   It was on his second voyage aboard the Harrison *that Drew was torpedoed in the Atlantic. That story appears in Chapter 5 - The Atlantic Ocean.*

Dec. 12, Monday 12:30
Got through the night o.k. but couldn't sleep because the ship was rolling so much. This A.M. I went down to stand my watch 8:00 to 12:00. About 8:30 the first assistant said to lash the 55 gal. drums of engine oil again. We did a good job this time. The sun out this A.M. and we saw a beautiful rainbow for five minutes. I

can hardly write. Things are moving from one side to the other. You can hardly stand up. We lost convoy and are trying to locate it. Sea is a beautiful green color. The officers can't understand why the cadets are not seasick. Am feeling good but am a little tired. Will try to sleep this P.M. All the fellows are growing beards.

2:00 P.M.

Just came back from Slop Chest. Got 10 cartons of cigs. pr. gloves, oilers cap, and 10 packs of gum. Just sighted another Liberty ship off our starboard quarter. We can barely see her thru the glasses. Think we are near Bermuda. The engine cadet I bunk with slept in his rubber suit last nite.

Dec. 13, 1942 Sunday 3:15

Sea is very rough and choppy. Just lost # 1 lifeboat on starboard side. I am in # 3. All boats were swung out according to law, but after we lost one boat we swung the others in. #1 boat was hanging by the bow and the stern was in the water. The sea kept hitting it up against the side of the ship. The third mate grabbed a hatchet from the other lifeboat and cut the line holding the boat. We all hated to see it float away for we may need it later on. Before all this happened the captain ordered all hands to go on deck. We put our life jackets on went out and pulled in the other boats so they would be secure. The ship is rolling heavily and broken dishes are all over the galley. Things are clattering and breaking all over the ship.

7:00 P.M.

Managed to eat dinner and then alarm sounded for all hands on deck. The 55 gal. drums of engine oil broke loose. We had to lash them up again. They were skimming all over the boat deck. So were we. Some of the deck hands said they were sick, and stayed below in their fo'c'sle. But the cadets stuck it out and did the best we could. Many of us have bruised ankles. My feet are soaked but the water is warm 60 degrees. Just changed shoes, socks and pants for the third time. We are very lucky no one was washed overboard. All ships in the convoy are out of their station order.

We are near the gulf and think we are getting part of a hurricane. All are good spirits in spite of all the trouble we had. We left Thursday because of heavy fog. Two days ago, we had trouble with the fuel oil heater, and worked all night to get it fixed. Slop Chest was opened yesterday and we all got cartons of cigs. There is a rumor we are going past Bahamas, over to Canary Islands, up African Coast to Gibraltar and over to Oran in Algeria. Will let you know later if it's true.

Dec. 15th
Came off watch at noon, ate a roast beef dinner by holding my plate in my hand and then went out on deck. Weather is good and warm but the sea is green and a little rough. Engine room is very hot and will be worse in a few days. Thank God I saw some snow before I left. One of the crew has a puppy called Mike. He is very spoiled because everyone plays with him. Had very little sleep last night. Still haven't found convoy.

Dec. 16th
A patrol bomber found us this A.M. and circled us all morning. We all feel a lot better. Expect the plane to contact convoy and then tell us its position.

3:50P.M.
Spent afternoon on deck. Patrol bomber again sighted us and used blinker system to tell us course and bearing so we could reach convoy. We are nineteen miles away from it. Expect to catch up with it at 11:00 o'clock tonight. Engine running full speed which is about 70 rpm. Weather is warm and a little windy. The crew barber is cutting hair on deck. They are playing records on a phonograph. Everything else is calm.

Dec. 17th 12:30 P.M.
Got a good night's sleep. About 9:15 I felt sick and came up above, vomited, and then lay down for an hour. I ate a little just now and feel better, but am weak. Caught up with convoy last night. It is still very stormy out and the officers expect it to be that way all the way across. I hope and pray it isn't. We are doing our

best to keep up with the convoy. Ship is rolling badly as I write this. They told us at school to make an abandon ship kit. I am using my ditty bag. In it I have two suits of long underwear, sweater, fishing line, a few cartons of cigarettes, gum, and a few other things just in case. However, we do not have to fear U-boats in weather like this, I hope.

Dec. 18th 2:00 P.M.
Had fire and boat drill at 1:00 P.M. Right after it was over, the naval gunnery officer, Lt. (jg) Geisert gave his gun crew a lecture. We are on the flank of the convoy and there are two destroyers flanking us. The weather is warm, but breezy, at night the ship is very hot because all the hatches and port holes must be shut, so the ship will be entirely blacked out. The convoy is a fascinating sight to view, since all ships are in their correct station order. In it we have thirty ships. The commodore gets his orders from the six destroyers and sends them on to us. He is on a tanker in the front center of the convoy. Am starting to write letters to mail when I reach port. Nothing else of importance has happened yet.

9:45 P.M.
Just found out there are forty-five ships in the convoy. We set clocks ahead one hour tonight at 12:00. This P.M. at 4 o'clock, the gunnery Officer gave instructions to a few men in the crew about the guns, so if any of the gunners get knocked out, we can fill their places. I am the loader on the 20mm Oerlikon AA in No 5 turret. If anything happens to the trigger man, I take his place. In a few days we will have actual firing practice.

Dec. 19th 12:30 P.M.
This morning at 11:00, all the ships in the Convoy had gun practice. It was very exciting. I shot a few rounds on a 20mm. It is a swell day and the sun is shining brightly and warmly.

Dec. 20th. 8:00 P.M.
Nothing very exciting happened today. It was much different from last Sunday. We went out on deck this P.M. and slept in sun

on army cot. We change our course late every afternoon, and go back to our original course a few hours later, when it is dark in order to elude the subs. We expect to be home in early March. The trip is getting a little monotonous to me now.

Dec. 21st. 1:45 P.M.
The clerk, Richard Stanton Hammett, cut my hair yesterday, but it doesn't look any better. It is just like a summer day on deck. Just finished washing my clothes and hung them in the engine room to dry. The steward says he has a nice turkey dinner planned for Christmas Day. I certainly hope so, although it won't be anything like home.

9:00 P.M.
Destroyers sighted a sub at 3:20 P.M. and relayed the message to us. All gunners were called to their battle stations, but so far nothing has happened. We are now in dangerous waters, and must expect anything.

Dec. 22nd. 2:30 P.M.
Sea is very rough and ship is rolling like mad. Clocks were set ahead again last night. Nothing else of importance has happened.

Dec. 23rd. 9:30 P.M.
Very warm today, however, we had a rain squall for a little while and then saw a rainbow. Sea is rough tonight. Another full moon again which makes it bad. The "Sparks" (Radio Operator) heard a U-boat report this P.M. That's all for today.

Dec. 24th. 1:00 P.M.
We are a few hundred miles from the Azores. We all hope to be in port New Years. Sea is calm.

8:00 P.M.
No moon tonight, although sky is full of stars. Received word this P.M. that U-boat was trailing us. Had fire and boat drill today at 4:15.

Dec. 25th. 4:00 P.M.

Merry Christmas! We had a swell turkey dinner and everyone dressed for it. The cadets didn't have to stand watch today. Weather is nice but windy. Expect to be ashore in three or four days. Thought about all of you last night and today. Couldn't sleep last night. Just finished writing a few letters.

Dec. 26th 1:00 P.M.

Convoy is speeding up. Yesterday we were 2,847 miles from New York. Went to bed around midnight last night, because I worked on my studies. Set clock ahead another hour. Played some pinochle also.

Dec. 27th, 1:30 P.M.

We are a few hundred miles from shore. Sighted one of our patrol bombers this morning. Just took a shower and am about to clean my room a little. Had roast duck for dinner. Yesterday, we were 3, 054 miles from New York. "Sparks" heard over the radio that Admiral Darlan (Commander in Chief of Vichy French forces in North Africa.) was assassinated. Are heading into a little squall.

Dec. 28th, 2:30 A.M.

General alarm bell rang fifteen minutes ago. Everybody woke up, dressed and reported to emergency station and gunners to their battle stations. All got an awful scare. The mate on watch saw a flare presumably dropped by an aeroplane. It meant enemy sub. in vicinity. Everyone was very calm. We were dismissed fifteen minutes later. From now on I sleep in my rubber suit.

2:20 P.M.

Set clock ahead another hour today. Just got issued a gas mask and steel helmet. Only the ones assigned to the guns got the helmets. One of our aircraft circled the convoy again this morning at 8:30.

Dec. 29th, 1:30 P.M.

While we were eating dinner, we heard a depth charge go off. We all went up on deck immediately and gunners cocked and loaded their guns. All the ships with transport loading were ordered to move inside convoy. We were one of them. After the charge went off, we saw a destroyer take its opposite course and speed away. There are also a couple of planes flying around. We sighted land off the port bow. We can hardly see it with the naked eye. Gunners are still on alert.

Dec. 30th 1:00 P.M.
Now there are only eleven ships in the convoy for the rest anchored at Casablanca. We expect to go through Gibraltar. This morning the clerk made a list of the amount of money we wanted to draw. We will receive it in francs.

Dec. 31st, 12:30 P.M.
Just passed another convoy on the way out of Gibraltar. We can see the coast of Africa very plainly. Will probably reach Gibraltar tonight. We have travelled 3,850 miles.

7:00 P.M.
Are now passing the Rock. There is a small Spanish town on the coast. And another town on African coast is all lit up. Just like Manhattan. Mountains on both sides of us. They sure look good.

Jan. 1st. 1943
I was on deck and saw a huge orange flame from the ship in front of us. I hit the deck and little pieces of soot and such rained down on me. When I got up, the ship was gone. It was the S.S. *Arthur Middleton.*

The Arthur Middleton *was proceeding toward Oran and just prior to entering the harbor was hit by two torpedoes.*

... two separate explosions occurred in succession at the *Middleton*'s bow. ... The ship disintegrated from the # 5 hatch to the bow. The after part of the freighter remained afloat. Of the ship's complement of nine officers, thirty-five men, twenty-seven armed guards, and twelve passengers, only three of the armed guards survived ...[7]

Jan. 2nd., 7:00 P.M.

The engineering detachment is unloading the cargo. Went into Oran this afternoon. We are in the Port of Mers El Kebir, which is a few miles from Oran. Both towns are very poor and dirty. The streets are full of beggars. The children ask you for cigarettes and bon-bon. All the kids are in the shoeshine racket. We went to and from Oran in an army truck, which is the only means of transportation besides an old broken down bus and donkey carts. Soap is very valuable to the natives. We also saw a few Arabs. Practically all the populace are clothed in rags and go around barefooted. It is very windy and cold here at night. I will probably wear my new blue uniform all the while we are here. We heard that New Year's Day Casablanca was heavily bombed. Last night at midnight we had a blackout, too.

Jan. 8th, 1943 Friday 6:45 P.M.

Have been going into town every other night. Yesterday, I did not have to work so I had my hair cut, mailed some letters, saw an American movie, "China Passage," which was spoken in English, but had French words written underneath. Also tried to do a little shopping. While at Oran I met Ernie Larue, who was in my section at the Academy. It was certainly good to see him. We talked over old times. He is on a tanker, the *Esso Charleston*. I went aboard it that night and met another fellow from my section and another deck cadet that I knew. It was swell seeing them. I have been rather busy and have had to skip writing in my log for a week.

Jan. 10, Sunday. 4:30 P.M.

Went into town yesterday and ate dinner in a French restaurant. Sour red wine, sour rye bread, soup, artichokes, egg omelet and tangerines. It seemed more like an appetizer to us. We then went to the Floridax Club. Five of us bought a bottle of champagne for 600 francs; about $8.00. They had a small dance band there, that played American music. There were many American nurses there also. I slept all this morning, but if I am here next Sunday, I intend to go to church here at Mers El Kabir. Weather is nice today.

Jan. 13th, 12:30 P.M.
About an hour ago, part of a British Fleet came into dock here: two battleships, the *Rodney* and the *Nelson*, the aircraft carrier, *Formidable* and eight destroyers. They are here probably to refuel and make repairs. Went to the cinema last night and saw "Three Comrades"; it was spoken in French and was not the least enjoyable. The curfew was 10:00 but now is 7:30.

Jan. 16th Saturday.
Will leave here tomorrow noon probably. Shore leave stops at 8:00 A M. tomorrow. Went ashore last night to the Chantilly Club. Weather the last few days has been just like summer. I hear an English news report every night at 9:00. That's all the news we get.

5:10
A British sub came in here at Mers El Kabir a few minutes ago. Sure is a busy place.

Jan 18th Monday 12:30
Captain came back from a conference yesterday. Have a bad cold. This morning we moved out to Oran Harbor and will be on our way back in a few hours. Last night the fireman on watch had a heart attack; he fell down engine room stairs and broke his neck. He was killed instantly, leaving a wife and four daughters. The ambulance took him to Oran. One of the seaman and an oiler had a fight yesterday. The oiler has a broken finger and his arm is in a cast. Never a dull moment. We won't feel safe until after we pass Gibraltar. The crew is pretty well sobered up today and are outside taking sun baths. The ship is light and will roll very much, once we get on our way. Every night we were in port, depth charges were dropped. At least a hundred every night, outside the submarine nets. And the destroyers would scan the coast with powerful searchlights.

Jan. 19th, Tuesday, 1:00 P.M.
Last night I washed some clothes and then the oiler on the 8:00 to 12:00 watch said that the third (Assistant Engineer) wanted me

down below. A bearing and crankpin were getting very warm. I stood the watch till 12 mid. During that time numerous depth charges were going off. At this moment the Rock of Gibraltar is in sight. At 4:00 P.M. we are supposed to pick up a few more ships. There have been two fighters and a bomber with us since we left Oran. Weather is very nice, just like a summer day. Will probably see the Statue of Liberty around Feb.7th.

8:00 P M.
The sunsets here are very beautiful and outlined against the sky the convoy is a real spectacle. This P.M. at 4:00, we picked up nine ships. Eight of them are tankers. Tomorrow P.M. at Casablanca we will pick up 33 more ships. There are many destroyers out here patrolling back and forth.

Jan. 20th, Wed. 6:00 P.M.
Just had dinner — and what a dinner! Four of the officers blew their tops and really bawled out the steward. I hope they don't dump him overboard; all he does is read the bible. Well we picked up thirty ships at Casablanca; we now have forty-two in the convoy.

Jan. 21st. Thurs. 1:00 P.M.
Set clocks back an hour last night. Had a full moon since we left Oran. We have an excellent position in the convoy. This A.M. it was still raining, but now the sun is out.

Jan. 22nd. Fri. 1:00 P.M.
Just took a shower. All this A.M. I had to throttle the engine, because the sea is so rough, the screw goes out of the water half of the time.

Jan. 23rd, Sat. 4:00 P.M.
Another full moon last night and another beautiful day today. Laid out in the sun today and had a little burn. We are going farther south everyday. Every one seems to think we are going to New Orleans, La. If so, home will be quite a ways off. Set the clocks back another hour last night.

Jan 24th, Sun. 1:00 P.M.

This A.M. while I was on watch, in the engine room, we heard two shots. We thought it was in the engine room at first, but soon found out that our ship shot off two rocket flares. We were just told that they were testing them. It kept me thinking for a while. I intend to wash some clothes now. The sun isn't shining very bright. We had a little difficulty getting the news broadcast from England last night. The 'Sparks' said that in a few more days, we will be able to pick up the U.S.

Jan 27th, Wed. 3:00 P.M.

Two days ago, we were parallel with the tip of Florida. We have now stopped going south and are heading west. The clocks were turned back again last night. Now there is only two hours difference in our time and New York time. One of the deck cadets slept outside last night. It is very warm. I started last night to stand two watches. They are using the evaporator and someone has to watch it. A few days ago, they collected our gas helmets and tin hats. From the radio, we heard that President Roosevelt had a conference with Mr. Churchill off the coast of Casablanca. Have a long watch to do, but I am going out in the sun for a while now.

Jan. 28th, Thurs. 2:15 P.M.

The 8:00 to 12:00 oiler was sick last night and I had to oil the engine. I did a pretty good job, but not as fast as the oiler. This A.M. I felt a little sick myself. I think it is too much sun. I have been in bed up to now. We are over 2000 miles from Oran. Last night about 8:00 o'clock the radio operator heard an S.O.S. from the ship that was torpedoed 600 miles north of us. Today the destroyers are refueling from a Navy Tanker off of the Convoy.

Based on the facts that they were 2,000 miles from Oran, and information from Jurgen Rohwer's book, the S.O.S. could have come from one of two Liberty ships that were torpedoed on January 27th; the S.S. Pinckney *or the S.S.* Julia Ward Howe.[8] *According to Arthur Moore, both ships were stragglers. However, the* Julia Ward Howe's *"radio was completely destroyed along with the antenna"*[9] *so it was probably the* Pinkney.

Jan 29th, Fri. 1:40 P.M.
This A.M. while I was on watch, the general alarm bell rang. One of the navy gunners saw a ship in the convoy firing into the water and he sounded the alarm. However, the other ship was merely having gun practice. The skipper issued 38's (automatics) to all the deck and engine officers yesterday. Just had a small shower of rain. Last night was very dark, in fact, it was the darkest night we had since we've been out. We were afraid of being rammed. The ice-box is on the bum and our food isn't very good. Washed clothes last night and today am going to iron.

Jan. 30th, 2:45 Sat.
Turned clocks back last night again. Yesterday the commodore sent the following message to all ships: "Submarines in vicinity, Keep good station order, don't show light, no smoking." About half an hour ago a destroyer sent up a flare and all the other destroyers started shooting. There are a few black puffs of smoke in the air from A.A. fire. It is merely practice, but we did not know it, because the destroyers are so far away, we cannot read their flag hoists. Expect to be in Port about eight more days from now. I pray to God, we get there soon. The ice-box ran out of gas and isn't cool; all the meat is rotten.

Jan. 31st, Sun, 1:30 P.M.
Since noon, all the ships had gunnery practice again. I finally shot the 20 mm. Oerlikon and have a shell as a souvenir. All the officers shot their automatics. There was quite a bit of shell fire, since all of the forty-ships shot their guns at once. Well, they say a week from now, we should see the "Girl with the Torch." I will naturally have to make another trip and imagine this time it will be to Murmansk because it will be the spring of the year.

Feb. 1st, Mon. 1:00 P.M.
It is raining this P.M. Nothing of importance has happened. Mr. Doyle, the 3rd Engineer is helping me with my studies. I have

quite a bit done. The cadets are going to try to get a week off when we hit port.

Feb. 2nd, Tues. 1:30 P.M.
Sea is rougher than it was a few days ago and the weather is a little cooler. Last night around midnight, one of the ships in the convoy turned on a red light, which meant she broke down. It lost the convoy then, but this A.M. it caught up with us. We all felt very sorry for them last night, because they were sub. bait.

Feb. 3rd, Wed. 1:00 P.M.
We are going to Norfolk, Va.. I am a little disappointed, because I may not be able to get home. Sea is rough and it is very cold out. We aren't making much time, because of the weather. Last night I heard a rebroadcast of the "Bob Hope Show" from Puerto Rico; also heard Fred Waring. Set clocks back last night, so now we are on New York time. The Deck, Engine and Steward departments are all cleaning house. And getting the ship cleaned up for when we reach port. This A.M. we polished all the gauges and brasswork in the engine room.

Feb. 5th, Fri. 2:00 P.M.
We hit a storm last night about midnight and it is still going strong. The nine ships that are going to Norfolk just broke away from the convoy. A patrol bomber just circled overhead. It stopped raining a few minutes ago and the waves are running 40 feet high. The ship is rolling heavily — about 30 degrees. We have to throttle the engine because when the screw comes out of the water, it vibrates the whole ship. Hardly anyone slept last night because of the rolling.

Feb. 6th, Sat. 2:00 P.M.
Washing clothes today. The barometer is falling and it is getting stormy again. We are getting a few snow flurries. Can hear the States swell on the radio. Making good time — about 10 knots.

Feb. 7th, Sun. 2:30 P.M.
Expect to be at Hampton Roads, Norfolk around midnight. Real

cold today for the first time. At noon two depth charges went off and shook the whole ship. Last night at 6:30 a gunner sighted a sub. and turned on the battle station alarm. However, nothing at all happened. We are passing a red buoy, but I don't know what it means.[10]

~~~

Peter Dykovitz sent the next brief story of his Mediterranean experience. It is not very difficult to understand the fear and apprehension involved as your vessel sits dead in the water and the enemy is possibly lurking below.

S.S. *Evangeline*
January 1943 to August 1943

I was a watertender on this former passenger vessel that was converted to carry 1,000 soldiers. After two delays we sailed from New York at night. I was on duty the next morning when all the fires in the six boilers stopped burning. I dashed into the pump room thinking that the fuel oil pump had stopped. The junior engineer was there and said, "Water in the oil. I will change strainers and tanks, shut all the valves." He called out to stop the engines.

I called out to the fireman to shut all the valves. I lit a torch: the fireman got a light from mine. In the meantime, the first assistant and chief were in the fireroom watching us. The fireman would insert the torch and the water in the oil would blow it out and we would get another light. After a few minutes a fire would stay lit, then another and then all of them. We could feel the vessel rocking in the rough water. Steam was low by this time and I had to raise it to operating pressure. As the pressure built up I would signal the engineer to open the valves a little more and feel the ship going forward. When the boilers were at full pressure the engineer signalled the bridge on the telegraph, "Full speed ahead." The captain called down that he saw the convoy (twenty ships) and would soon catch up with them. These were 18-knot convoys.

At lunch I heard that a destroyer had been circling us and the convoy had slowed to half speed ahead zig-zagging across the ocean, through the Strait of Gibraltar and into the Port of Oran. We had a cruiser, the *Brooklyn*, with us and destroyers on both sides and another ahead. There were a number of depth charges dropped and we heard a dull thud.

The soldiers were taken to their camp site. I made four trips, saw two enemy subs blown to the surface and then sunk to the bottom. Our vessel brought German P.O.W.'s to the States twice. The *Evangeline* took part in the invasion of Sicily, landing troops at Gela. A week later, we were bombed along with two other ships in the port of Palermo. Fifteen bombers came over and one was shot down by our ship. An interesting point of this attack was that we were told to make dark smoke to confuse the incoming bombers. This was the first time we were allowed to make smoke.

After the last trip I had enough sea time to go to Officers' Training School at Fort Trumbull, New London, Connecticut, to be enrolled in the 24th class. I graduated as a third assistant engineer and an ensign in the Maritime Service.[11]

~~~

The disaster at Bari, Italy is one of the secrets of World War II. On the night of December 2, 1943, over one thousand Allied military personnel and Italian civilians died when one hundred tons of poison gas, stored on an American ship, were released in a Nazi bombing raid. It was mustard gas, the deadly chemical used by the Germans in World War I and regarded as the ultimate in hideous weaponry in an arsenal not yet containing the horrors of the atomic bomb.[12]

The disaster became known as "Little Pearl Harbor," because the Luftwaffe destroyed seventeen ships and damaged eight other ships.

In October of 1943, one hundred tons of unstable mustard gas were secretly loaded onto the Liberty Ship, S.S. John Harvey, supervised by six chemical warfare agents led by first Lieutenant

Howard D. Beckstrom. President Roosevelt had warned the Axis powers against the use of chemical weapons:

> I have been loathe to believe that any nation, even our present enemies, could or would be willing to loose upon mankind such terrible and inhumane weapons ... We promise to pay any perpetrators of such crimes full and swift retaliation in kind and I feel obliged now to warn the Axis armies and the Axis people in Europe and in Asia that the terrible consequences of any use of these inhuman methods on their part will be brought down swiftly upon their own heads.[13]

But the U.S. felt it was necessary to have some chemical warfare supplies available on a global basis. During World War II, the U.S. underwent extensive testing of mustard gas and lewisite.

> These testing programs involved the use of close to 60,000 military personnel, of whom 4,000 to 5,000 were involved in gas chamber field tests. Most subjects were told never to reveal their participation, and most did not, even to their families or private physicians.[14]

The Captain of the John Harvey, *Elwin Knowles, couldn't reveal his secret cargo upon entering the crowded harbor of Bari on November 28th and was forced to await his turn to unload at the pier. On the night of December 2nd, the* John Harvey *was still loaded with its death cargo when the harbor was attacked by thirty to forty JU-88 Luftwaffe bombers. In the attack that lasted less than thirty minutes, the* John Harvey *became a total mass of flames, finally blowing up and sinking with the loss of everyone (forty) on board. This was only the beginning, as the mustard gas began to drift in the water and float off into the air. "More than 600 serviceman were treated for mustard gas exposure ... The accident killed eighty-three [actually 123] serviceman and nearly 1,000 people from the town."[15]*

At the end of the war, set against just 7,500 tons of Japanese gases, the Americans had 135,000 tons: 20,000 tons more than the combined total used by every nation fighting in World War I.[16]

This introduction leads us to a story from Leroy C. Heinse of Vancouver, Washington. During a phone conversation he said, he had "Been to hell and back!" God was surely by Roy's side on the evening of December 2, 1943, in the Italian port of Bari.

My schooling was only high school as I wasn't encouraged to go to college, but I did have a strong technical mind. The war came along and I had to sign up for the draft. If I was going to serve my country, I wanted to serve it in an area that I was interested in. I initially tried to get in the Navy, and I was turned down there. I tried the Coast Guard next and was turned down. Any organization relative to the water, I was turned down. I wrote my senator and I explained that I had a lot of experience in water involving small boats and that I taught small boat handling and seamanship in the United States Power Squadron.

As the war progressed, there was a need for a Coast Guard auxiliary which I joined and volunteered my services. I was being rejected because of my six-foot, five-inch height and the standard uniform would not fit.

Then I learned that the Merchant Marine Cadet Corps had been formed and that it was patterned after the service academies. I applied there and was accepted. The uniform wasn't a problem with them. I left home and went to a place called Pass Christian, Mississippi, which was one of their training centers on the Gulf. I successfully completed the ten week course and then started the next ten month phase where I was assigned to the engineering staff as an engine cadet. You essentially worked for the company that owned the ship under the War Shipping Administration's facilities. You did all the things that are necessary to run a ship as far as the engine room was concerned and you stood your watches and worked closely with the people that were educated in the particular areas of the engine room and propulsion system.

I completed my ten weeks of basic and was assigned to a brand new ship, the *John Bascom*, built in Panama City, Florida. I made the initial voyage with an insignificant cargo to Ponce, Puerto Rico. We pulled into a sugar refinery where we loaded raw sugar and we took that up to New York. We made subsequent trips which were basically uneventful across the Atlantic to Great Britain. These trips were educational because I learned a lot about convoy operations and such. We never encountered any torpedoing or shooting at the members of the convoy. We had convoy escorts.

Two things come to mind regarding those trips. Oftentimes at night a German submarine would come up in the middle of the convoy at periscope level to recharge their batteries. One night somebody on one of the ships obviously spied it and they opened fire on it. The periscope and the submarine quickly submerged. It was kind of exciting to know that this was the first firing that any of the ships made to defend themselves. The other thing that made an impression was that the ships going over were very heavily loaded and on one of these trips, several of the ships actually lost their lifeboats while rolling in the heavy seas. We lost a boat because of this rolling action. When a ship lost a lifeboat, the escort vessels would sink it with the idea that they didn't want any of the ships to stop for it, thus endangering the convoy.

On the last trip, we knew nothing about where we were going. I also was in the ninth month of my schedule in training that I was supposed to be at sea. I had an excellent rapport with my crew members and they asked me whether I would approve of them getting me a variance so that I could sail with them again. I said it was O.K. with me because the extra experience would be helpful. Little did I know what was in store for us. They got the variance for me and I have to say again that I had a lot of respect for a lot of my crew members that ultimately died when we got to Bari.

We made the trip across the Atlantic and we were coming into Gibraltar where we were hounded by submarines. I remember that planes were going overhead and dropping depth charges ahead of the convoy. Ultimately we came into a little port called Augusta, Sicily. This is where our convoy and other ships were laying to be broken up into other convoys. We left Augusta and went up around the boot into the Adriatic Sea and came into the port of Bari. I had no idea of our destination. It was afternoon when we arrived and soon thereafter we heard anti-aircraft guns firing. They were firing at German reconnaissance planes that were flying over the port and looking at a target which ultimately was going to be theirs the following evening. That was a tip-off, so to speak, that something was going to happen, and I guess in view of the fact that I wasn't involved in any combat up to that time, it just never bothered me too much. It was understandable, but by the same token, it didn't put me on edge or anything.

At about 7:30 the next evening, bombs started to drop that were preceded by German parachute flares that just lit up the whole harbor. You could just sit there and read a book, so to speak, because of the brightness. My battle station was in the wheel house and I was supposed to be working with a first assistant engineer. He and I were supposed to reload these 20mm

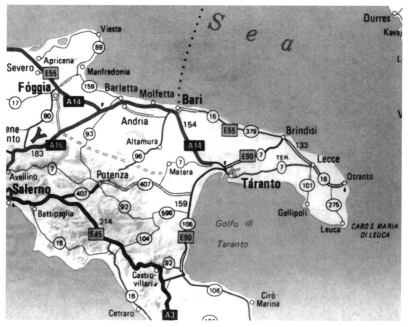

Bari, Italy, location of one of the worst disasters in World War II. American Automobile Association.

magazines which fitted onto a Oerlikon gun. We had ammunition for these reloading exercises in various places aboard the ship, some of which were actually in the cadets' quarters. I was in the process of bringing those containers that had these into the wheel house where the first engineer was going to reload the canisters.

From Disaster at Bari:

> Then without warning, a string of explosions ripped the *John Bascom* as the attacking planes renewed the strike. The ship was bombed from aft to forward. One bomb hit the forward end of number four hatch; one bomb went through the top bridge and the radio operator's room into the vessel; one bomb landed in the number three hatch; and one hit between numbers one and two hatches.[17]

There was a tremendous explosion. It was so great that it blew off all of my clothes. Shoes, everything. The only thing, to the best of my knowledge, was that I was left with my dogtag and silver identification bracelet on my right arm. My watch was blown off my left arm. When something like this happens to you, you're conscious and unconscious, so you have some recollection and at other times there's a big blank and you just don't know what happened. From all the accounts I got, somebody knew that I was injured and they tried to give me first aid, etc. I remember very distinctly them sitting me on the area of the ship adjacent to where my quarters were or the captain's quarters.

From Disaster at Bari:

> ... Heitmann (Captain) walked back toward his quarters. Outside his damaged quarters he found Cadet-Midshipman Leroy C. Heinse lying on the deck. The twenty-three-year-old cadet was covered with blood and all his clothes had been blown off. His stomach was covered with lacerations. Heitmann washed the wounds with water from a nearby bucket and then tried to pull the worst wounds together with adhesive tape. As he did, he recalled that a short time before the bombing he had seen Heinse at the

starboard forward top bridge gun reloading the magazines and, since the cadet had not been lying in this spot when Heitmann went to the hospital area earlier, he had apparently gotten there by walking. He wondered how he had gotten that far before he had collapsed.[18]

They wrapped me in a blanket and it wasn't too cold. That part I remember. I'm sitting there and I had two recollections, one of which I've never told anybody before in my life. When I was looking toward the stern of the ship, I saw two things. I saw an image of my mother who was looking at me, but not saying anything. I don't know if I said anything to her, but I've never mentioned this to anyone in my life. The other thing was that the flag of our ship was still flying on its mast. Why that wasn't blown away, I don't know, but I remember the stars and stripes were flying and of course there was no reason why I couldn't see the flag because the sky was continuously lit up by the parachute flares. I was obviously bleeding from numerous locations and that kept up for a long, long period until they got me to the hospital. I guess there was some first aid given to me, but I have no proof of that. I can only tell you that I've got the bracelet and the dogtag. The dogtag was made of stainless steel and showed no evidence of being hit. Yet, the bracelet shows numerous places where shrapnel struck the bracelet because it was made of sterling silver which is very soft. I believe all the portholes' housing glass were all shattered because I had tremendous amounts of glass removed from my body over a long period of time. (The average piece of shrapnel can be seen on an x-ray, but glass is transparent and can't be seen. At later dates, I'd have to say there's something in my arm and mark it. When the total would reach half a dozen, they'd go in and remove the pieces of glass from me.)

After the bombardment the planes flew away and people started picking up the pieces. I was told later that we had only one lifeboat left on our ship and the rest had been destroyed. There were people like myself that needed to be gotten ashore to receive medical attention. I can only speak of myself because I don't remember who else was in the boat with me. They put me in the lifeboat with other people. They lowered it over the side and took me over to the wall of a breakwater. (There were fifty-two men in it and Captain Heitmann ordered even more over the side to climb into the lifeboat or to get into the water and hang onto the seine floats).[19]

The breakwater was a large structure that encompassed the docking area where all these ships were located. There were rooms (shelters) up on the breakwater, I guess for people to get out of the weather. The rooms had steel doors on them. However, there was a problem because the breakwater was quite high relative to the tide. The problem was how to get me and the other injured up onto the breakwater. The bottom line was that they had to establish a human chain of people leaning over the breakwater and getting hold of people like myself and pulling them up and placing them into the shelters.

All the while, the whole area was heavily saturated with mustard gas, either in gas or liquid form, and was splashing onto various and sundry things that a person would come in contact with. I was awake and heard people saying, "That ship over there is loaded with bombs. We've got to get into these shelters right away or we're gonna be killed." I remember them taking and dragging me into the shelter and laying me on the floor. Someone said, "Get that door closed. Get that door closed, that ship is going to blow anytime." Some period of time after that it (the *John L. Motley*) blew. I remember the concussion that the thing caused. It blew off the door or slammed it open. The people that were standing around me were knocked on top of me.

I found out later that it created a tidal wave in the harbor whereby all this mustard gas that was on the surface of the water splashed up onto the breakwater and shelters. This is where I got clobbered with the mustard gas.

> The entire harbor seemed to empty as the tidal wave caused by the explosion of the *John L. Motley* washed over the breakwater.[20]
> The violent explosion that followed the blast of the *John L. Motley* was the worst detonation Heitmann had ever experienced... The *John Harvey* had blown up... the only men who could warn the

others present at Bari that a large amount of deadly mustard had
been released over the harbor were now dead.[21]

That was the last I remember of anything concerning the
harbor and the actual bombing. Anything that I later learned was
in some sort of makeshift hospital. It was operated by the British.
I was sort of startled when I found somebody saying to me that I'd
have to be taken to the theatre and I said to myself, "I'm obviously
all banged up here. What would somebody want to take me to a
theatre for? Did they want to get my mind off my problems or
what was going on?" I later found out that the British called the
operating room a theatre and their nurses were called sisters.

I have no recollection of ever going to an operating room.
I don't remember what the bed was like until another time when
we were told that we were under another bombing attack. I kept
saying to somebody, "Is this building marked with a red cross?"
They assured me that there was a red cross on the building and it
was also illuminated for night vision. They had been feeding us
at the time and I do remember that I was on a cot with the food
right below my chin. When the sirens went off they moved all the
beds to the center of the ward, away from any flying glass, so they
could cover our faces and be protected. A funny thing happened
during this situation. They just took the plate of food which I
think was spaghetti and meatballs and turned it right over on my
face.

A little about my treatment. The Navy authorities came
from Palermo, Sicily, where they had a hospital. They found that
the care we were getting, particularly those exposed to mustard
gas, was not in accordance with the treatment appropriate for
handling casualties that were exposed to mustard gas. Mustard
gas gets on your skin and it produces a tremendous burn. In my
case, I had a burn scar from the middle of the calf of my leg, all
the way up to the next section of my leg which goes up toward the
hip. I have about two feet of burn area that varies anywhere from
six inches to maybe eight or ten inches.

They flew us out to Palermo, Sicily. The main thing there
was that the Navy had all these injured Armed Guard that they

were immediately responsible for. The merchant seaman like myself were sort of secondary, but they did oversee that we were getting the same treatment that the Navy injured were. They also had the moral responsibility of treating us in the same manner that we were in the British hospital. I don't know how many days I was in the Bari hospital.

One of the first things they did was to tend to my badly burned right leg which had been put in a plaster cast. It began to smell pretty bad. Later I found out that what the British had done in their good intentions was incorrect. I was in great pain and I tended to bring my leg up to loosen the skin under my knee. If I had healed with the cast on, I wouldn't have been able to stretch my leg out. So, their first order of attack was to get that cast off. They took me to the operating room and began to peel off the cast. My flesh had become embedded in the gauze. I remember the horrible pain and just screaming while they were doing this procedure. Ultimately they put me into some sort of restraining device whereby I couldn't retract the leg anymore and put me laying face down in a bed. They treated the wound with hot saline dressings made up of saline pads soaked in salt water and on top of that they'd keep hot water bottles. This was the procedure that they used to treat people that were subject to the mustard gas material. I found out at a later date that on the right and front side of my body, I had many shrapnel and glass wounds; some of them were an inch to an inch and a half long. When they got me to the hospital in Bari, all they probably did was to put on butterflies because I've got all these scars on my body without stitch markings.

It was Christmas in Palermo and I had absolutely no personal possessions in the way of toothbrushes, razors, or anything like that. When my ship went down I lost all my possessions. As a merchant marine cadet, while you're at sea you perform what is known as a sea project. You have all these textbooks, outlined courses of study. All of these materials were lost. All I was left with was my dogtag and identification bracelet. I am indebted to and will always wave the flag for the Red Cross because they came to my rescue. They supplied me with a little ditty bag that had a razor, toothpaste, brushes, and numerous other things that you would need in the hospital. I'll never forget that. I hear a lot of people bad-mouthing the Red Cross, and what they did and so on and so forth, but that wasn't my experience.

I'll always remember a Roman Catholic priest named Redmond. He would come by and ask if there was anything he could do for me. I said to him, "Well, you could write my folks and tell them my relative condition. I'm sure they were notified that I was injured, but didn't know my condition." After that day, that gentleman would religiously come by and would always say, "Would you like me to write a letter to your folks?" and I'd say, "Yes."

In late January, I was flown to a U.S. Army Hospital in Algiers and spent the next month there. I was next moved to the U.S. Naval hospital in Casablanca. On 4 March, 1944 I was put aboard the USS *General Butmer*, bound for Norfolk, Virginia. I'll never forget the ship voyage because we had German POW's on board. The expression on their faces was that of self-defiance. Like how dare we put them in prison. When I reached the States I developed some respiratory problems and was soon transferred to the U.S. Public Health Hospital in Baltimore. I met a wonderful student nurse at this hospital and eventually we were married. While at the hospital, I underwent many operations to repair nerve damage in my fingers and arms. To this day, I still periodically develop fish-like scales on my leg where I was burned from the mustard gas.

After my stay at the hospital in Baltimore I was ready to return to the U.S. Merchant Marine Academy to pursue my studies toward the Cadet-Midshipman USNR — Inactive duty rating. This turned out to be a real catastrophe. After being through everything I had been through, I simply couldn't pursue my studies any longer. I had been away from it too long and my injuries simply prevented me from mentally and physically handling the regimen. I asked for a medical discharge. I left with a sour taste in my mouth because there was no one there that said, "I understand what you have been through." This was difficult to accept especially in light of the highly commendable letter that my skipper had written the War Shipping Administration, requesting that I be awarded the Mariner's Medal and to be considered for the award of the Distinguished Service Medal.[22]

Leroy C. Heinse was notified in a letter dated 22 July 1944 from E.S. Land, W.S.A. Administrator, that he had received the Mariner's Medal.[23]

~~~

Bari, Italy was also the setting for another tragedy that occurred later in the war. On March 9, 1945, the S.S. Charles Henderson *sailed from Norfolk, Virginia, in Convoy UGS-80. She arrived in Bari, Italy, on April 5. In the process of unloading her cargo of explosives on April 9 she blew up, killing,*

... her complement of forty-two crew members and thirteen Naval Armed Guard. The chief engineer, who was ashore at the time of the explosion, was the only survivor. The ship was completely destroyed. Two hundred sixty-seven Italians were killed and over 1600 wounded. An undetermined number of Allied Service personnel were killed also. The port installations near the ship were destroyed plus two berths. In addition, five ships in the harbor were damaged.[24]

On June 18, 1945, Lt. Comdr. R.H. Farinholt, of the United States Coast Guard, wrote Mrs. Ann Flaker stating:

We regret very much to advise that our records show Wendell George Flaker was aboard the S.S. *Charles Henderson* at the time the vessel was destroyed ... that the sole survivor of the merchant crew was Oscar Davis, who was the Chief Engineer ... Mrs. Flaker could contact Mr. Davis in New York City for any firsthand information he has...[25]

Ann Flaker wrote to Chief Engineer Davis. The reply, from Mrs. Davis, dated June 28, 1945, read:

Dear Mrs. Flaker:

My husband is out on the ocean some place so I will write all I can about the accident which destroyed the S.S. Charles Henderson. You do not say what position your husband held but my husband would probably know him. The company would be sure he was on the ship when it exploded if they informed you.

The S.S. Charles Henderson blew up with a load of aerial bombs in Bari, Italy harbor April 9, killing approximately 400 and injuring 1730 civilians. The explosion happened at lunch time and the men were all on board for lunch. Chf. Eng. Davis went ashore to eat lunch just eight minutes before the terrific explosion. Aboard the S.S. Henderson was a preliminary explosion, followed by a major one, and the vessel was virtually blown out of existence, according to witnesses.

Only two bodies of the crew of forty-one aboard were recovered. (You would have been notified if one were your husband). The concussion created a wave which rolled over the Bari wharves, sweeping workers into the harbor, and knocking down a warehouse and the roof of a cathedral 100 years old.

Engineer Davis was the only survivor. The captain and all officers were lost. The Henderson had put out from Newport News, Va. and was discharging the bombs when the explosion occurred. Cause was undetermined.

The blast set fire to three other merchant ships in the harbor but the flames were brought under control.

Mr. Davis flew home from Italy and arrived in N.Y. the first week in May, but sailed again a week later. He felt very badly as he lost many friends. Some of the men had gone on several trips together.

There is no possible chance of him (Mr. Flaker) being alive if he were on the ship. I am very sorry to have such bad news for you.

We have two small children and I am so very thankful that Mr. Davis was saved... I will give your letter to Mr. Davis when he returns...

With sincere sympathy, I remain

Mrs. Oscar T. Davis,
Latham Hotel,
New York City, N.Y.[26]

The mystery of why the S.S. Charles Henderson exploded has never been solved and it is unlikely that it ever will be. Mrs. Ann Flaker was shocked by two other developments. On April 10, 1945, a Burial certificate was filed for an unknown person whose name was scratched out and Wendell George Flaker added; his fingerprint(s) were identified by the Coast Guard. Seemingly, a portion of Seamen Flaker's hand(s) were recovered and identification of his fingerprint(s) was made. The remains of his body were buried in the military cemetery in Bari. However, the fingerprint didn't match that on his Merchant Marine document.

Even more bizarre, Mrs. Flaker received a telegram from Wendell Flaker dated April 13, 1945, (four days after the explosion). It stated,

VERY HAPPY TO HEAR FROM YOU DEAREST AM FIT AND WELL YOU ARE MORE THAN EVER IN MY THOUGHTS AT THIS TIME ARE YOU ALL RIGHT WORRIED ABOUT YOU.
WENDELL FLAKER.[27]

The only plausible explanation was that the telegram (entitled INTL+CD SANSORIGINE VIA RCA) had been collected and was delayed in reaching its destination.

More information concerning Bari and the S.S. Charles Henderson tragedy was supplied by Karl Hamberger of Ocklawaha, Florida.

I sailed as an A.B. on the S.S. *Thomas Nuttall* on a trip that took thirteen months. We left New York on March 17, 1945 for Charleston, South Carolina, to load ammunition (bombs). Though we didn't know it at the time, our destination was to be Italy.

Upon arrival we were held offshore in the Mediterranean near Taranto for the following reason. We learned that the S.S. *Charles Henderson* had departed Charleston, S.C., approximately one month before we did carrying a similar cargo of bombs. While unloading at Bari, she exploded at the dock killing thousands. Two Italian barges came alongside and we unloaded our cargo of bombs that were thought to be the cause of the S.S. *Charles Henderson* exploding at the dock.

These bombs were dumped out into the Mediterranean. I was told that these bombs were originally meant for mustard gas and had a lining inside to prevent the corrosive mustard gas from destroying the outer shell. However, instead of mustard gas, they were loaded with conventional explosive material. This made them highly sensitive to any shock or bump, similar to T.N.T. This information was given to me by an Army Security officer who sailed with us.

We then sailed to Bari, Italy and tied up at the same dock as the S.S. *Charles Henderson*. What was left of the *Charles Henderson* was only a portion of the bow and stern. Everything else was gone. I understand the midship house was thrown approximately one mile toward the city. The sea wall (made of large stone blocks) was pushed inland by the force of the explosion. *Total destruction!*

We started to unload the remainder of bombs when the war came to an end in Europe. We thought we were going home, (WRONG!) ...[28]

Further details of this cargo and the wanderings of the S.S. Nuttall *for the next eleven months are in Chapter 13 by Bernie Flatow. The S.S.* Nuttall *became another* Flying Dutchman, *doomed to wander the world with its perilous cargo.*

8

THE INDIAN OCEAN

*E*arly in the war, the German high command considered extending their sea-control eastward toward Japan. It was part of a grand plan to first capture Gibraltar and Suez. Turkey would eventually fall, leaving the Italian navy to control the Mediterranean. The plan was put on hold when Hitler turned his attention toward Russia. Meanwhile, Germany and Japan formed a defensive alliance in September of 1940. "... neither side trusted the other side with basic secrets, neither informed the other of major operations, and both fought for their individual purposes ... The great dream of a German-Japanese pincer on the Indian Ocean existed only in the minds of German planners."[1] Germany did send a complement of submarines and armed merchant ships called raiders into the Indian Ocean which successfully raised havoc and sank many Allied ships.

Between December 1941 and February 1942, the Japanese rapidly conquered Guam, Wake, British Malaysia,

Singapore, Thailand, Burma, and the Dutch East Indies (Indonesia). The Japanese now had to decide whether to attack Britain's Eastern fleet headquartered in Ceylon (Sri Lanka). Britain's defeat there would give the Japanese control of the Indian Ocean. This was strategically important because Japan would be able to protect its western flank, have access to the rich natural resources and oil from this area, and be able to concentrate on the American forces in the Pacific. The Japanese formulated a supporting plan called Operations Against Allied Lines of Communication. Point (2) stated:

> The Japanese expected to accomplish much through the use of German submarine blockade tactics, and plans were made to employ such tactics in the Pacific and Indian Oceans. Carrier and land based aircraft were to be employed whenever possible against lines of communication. They also planned to operate auxiliary cruisers in the Southern Pacific and East Indian Oceans at the outbreak of the war.[2]

Fortunately for the Allies, Japan never followed through because there weren't enough troops to support this westward advance.

At the first Washington Conference held by Roosevelt and Churchill in the latter part of December 1941, it was agreed that Germany was still the number one enemy. However, in defeating Germany first, it was still essential to deny Japan access to raw materials. According to the Memorandum by the United States and British Chiefs of Staff dated December 31, 1941 concerning the Maintenance of Communications, among the main sea routes to be secured were: "The routes in the Indian Ocean to the Red Sea and Persian Gulf, to India and Burma, to the East Indies, and to Australasia.[3]

Later in 1942, Roosevelt and Churchill divided up the Allied theatres of responsibility. The Indian Ocean and Middle East were to remain in British hands.

A major obstacle in the Allies' war plan was the Island of Madagascar, controlled by the Vichy French. Madagascar was centrally located near the British shipping lanes to the Middle

East and India. Of equal importance were the return shipping routes for the precious cargoes of oil. Both German and Japanese submarines operated in these waters with tremendous success. On May 5, 1942, British troops invaded the Island with little resistance. However, the Vichy Governor refused to surrender. Japanese submarines inflicted serious damage on Allied ships between May and July. It was not until November that the Vichy Governor surrendered. This was an important victory, especially in light of the Japanese victories and advance in the Far East.

~~~

The first story is from Stanley Willner of Palm Beach Gardens, Florida. He was aboard the M.S. Sawokla when it was torpedoed on November 29, 1942. His account and the aftermath of survival as a P.O.W. were told in his 1988 letter to the Veterans Administration seeking Compensation Pension. Parts of a speech given by Stanley at West Point to a meeting of fellow merchant mariners are also included to give more detail to his story. Stanley Willner was one of the plaintiffs in the case that won Veteran's benefits for the merchant mariners; Schumacher, Willner, et al., v. Aldridge, 665 F. Supp. 41 (D.D.C. 1987)

In 1938, I was appointed a Deck Cadet with the U.S. Maritime Commission by U.S. Senator Byrd (Virginia). After serving as Deck Cadet, I received my Mate's license and a commission in the U.S. Naval Reserve.

When the war was declared, I was on a ship in Portugal. Upon returning to the States, I went to the Navy Department in New York City to find out if I had been called to active duty. I was told by the Navy department to sail on the M.S. *Sawokla*, an Army transport ship operated by American Export Lines. I was thankful that we were one of the few ships not torpedoed before we were out of the Caribbean. The ship made it to our destination (Colombo, Ceylon). On the return trip, in November 1942, in the Indian Ocean, about 400 miles east of Madagascar, the *Sawokla*

The Sawokla *was built in Tampa, Florida in 1920 and sailed under the house flag of American Export Lines as the* Excellency. *Dennis A. Roland.*

was sunk by the German raider *Michel*, using superior guns and torpedo boats. I was the Officer on watch. The weather was overcast, it was dark and the seas choppy, when I spotted an object on the horizon. I pressed the buzzer to the Captain's cabin.

The next thing I knew I was in the water clinging to a piece of wreckage. It was pitch dark. I was picked out of the water by the Raider and told I had been in the water between five to eight hours. The Germans told us the *Sawokla* was ablaze and went completely under in about four to five minutes.

> The freighter went down in eight minutes. Although the ship was armed, there was no time for defensive action. The raider pulled thirty-five survivors out of the water within three hours. They found four of the gun crew the next day when the ship returned to take one more look around. The thirty-nine men were taken prisoner and held on the raider for the next eighty-one days before being put ashore in Singapore, February 17, 1943.[4]

The next day, the raider sent their scout plane out and launched the torpedo boats to pick up all wreckage. No trace was found of our ship. We were declared officially dead. Enclosed is a copy of the death certificate from the Navy Department. I was wounded in the penis, left testicle, right thigh, and loaded with shrapnel. I was in the hospital on the raider for over two months. I received good medical treatment and I was operated on numerous times. The Germans would treat POW's for any injuries they caused. Two other ships were sunk by the raider during the approximately ninety days we were aboard.

After ninety days on the raider, we were turned over to the Japanese in Singapore. On our trip from the ship to Changi jail, we passed Raffles Square and saw several nude, decomposed female bodies hanging from the rafters. We were told that was warning to other women not to refuse to sleep with the Japanese.

The first time we lined up in Changi, the British interpreter asked if we had any questions. I handed him a letter the German doctor had given me. The interpreter handed it to the Japanese sergeant, who tore it up and hit me with a rifle butt. Changi jail was a maximum security jail built for about 1,000 hardened criminals. The Japanese had almost 10,000 P.O.W.'s crammed inside the jail. Fortunately, we were put in outside open huts. Actually, the time we stayed in Changi jail was not too harsh. The British, Australian, Dutch and Americans who

ADDRESS COMMUNICATIONS TO THE
DIRECTOR OF NAVAL OFFICER PROCUREMENT
NEW YORK, N. Y.

TELEPHONE WHITEHALL 3-404

IN REPLY REFER TO:

QR2/KGC:B

BUREAU OF NAVAL PERSONNEL

NAVY DEPARTMENT

OFFICE OF NAVAL OFFICER PROCUREMENT

NEW YORK. N. Y.

33 PINE STREET

NEW YORK. N. Y.

March 5, 1943.

Mrs. Stanley Willner
391 Central Avenue
Jersey City, New Jersey

My dear Mrs. Willner:

We are sending you, by direction of the Navy Department, your husband's commission as an Ensign in the United States Naval Reserve.

We extend to you our very deep sympathy in your personal loss and beg leave to share your great pride in so splendid an officer.

Very sincerely,

KENNETH G. CASTLEMAN
Captain U.S.Navy Retired
Director.

This letter from the Navy Department announcing Stanley Willner's death was a bit premature. Stanley Willner.

surrendered in Singapore had all their gear, clothing, utensils, etc. In Changi the food was scarce, but there wasn't too much brutality.

Then the rude awakening came. I was put in an officers working party of 8,000 called 'H' force. 'H' force consisted mostly of British, Australian, Dutch and some Americans. The Americans consisted of a Texas field artillery unit that had surrendered in Singapore, survivors of the cruiser *Houston*, a few flyers that had been shot down over the Hump (Himalayan Mountain Range), and survivors from the *Sawokla*. We left Singapore in small covered box cars. POW's loaded like sardines, standing and really packed in. If someone passed out from the heat or other reasons he could not fall. After several days the railroad cars smelled like sewer barges. We were put off the railway in Thailand and had to walk at least fifty miles to the River Kwai.

Of the 8,000 POW's in 'H' force, less than 3,000 made it back to Singapore. Both the Germans and Japanese treated the captured merchant seaman as POW's — not as civilian trainees. We worked on the railroad for the next few years — even working on the infamous Bridge Over the River Kwai. The railroad was known as the Death Railway because over 100,000 POW's and native laborers died in about 150 miles of railroad.

It is very difficult to answer some of the questions easily. The majority of people cannot imagine what forced slave labor is like. Brutal incidents stick in your mind; they are so horrible, you begin to wonder if they really happened. When you have a nightmare — you know it is real. I credit a British doctor, Captain Ronnie Phillips, with saving my life. He looked after the very few Americans who slaved on the River Kwai railroad. I would have migraine headaches so badly that occasionally I would slip into the jungle and spend the night, joining the working party next morning at dawn.

We were subjected to three years of brutal treatment, starvation diets, working sunup to sundown, seven days a week — rain or shine. My body was covered from top to bottom with ring-worm, tape worms, ulcer sores, etc. I weighed about seventy-five pounds when I was released, down from my normal weight of 135. Some of the marines off the *Houston* originally weighed over 200 pounds. When they lost 100 pounds, they were bone. I didn't shave or have a haircut for three years. I also didn't have any shoes or clothes. Toward the end, we were like zombies — just skin and bone and sores and bruises.

On working parties to some camps, and loading barges on the river, I noticed a green plant that looked like hibiscus. I would grab a handful and eat them. I think they helped me greatly, but not much help for dysentery. The only medical treatment was boiled water, and very little of that, about a pint per day per POW.

The closest friend I had was Dennis Roland, the second mate on the *Sawokla*. We went through the entire POW years together. We were extremely close until he passed away about four years ago. We spoke to each other at least once a week. I guess he was one of the few people I was ever comfortable with.

We were in a jungle camp on the railroad when Roland took sick. He had appendicitis. An Australian doctor operated on him with just boiling water, a knife, and some kind of gut for sewing him up. On one of the Thai barges a Thai native had a duck. One day the Thai slipped when he was unloading the rice bags. I took the duck and smuggled it into camp. If I could find about six snails the duck would lay an egg. There was a British soldier who had one arm and one leg who used to heat the water in a fifty-five gallon drum for the Jap officer. We let him keep the duck near the Jap's hut, so everyone thought the duck belonged to the Jap officer. We gave him one egg a week and the other six to Roland. We even heated the shells and pulverized it on the rocks into powder, and made him drink it. The scheme worked for about six weeks and then we had to move out so we ate the duck.

Just before we moved camps, we were lined up one night after we had just finished work. It seemed the British soldier had made the water too hot for the Jap officer's bath. We had to stand by until the water started to boil and they threw the British soldier in. The screams are etched in my mind — they will never go away.

Roland always worked to get veterans' status for the merchant marine. It was an obsession with him till he passed away over four years ago. He was on the legal case and worked for years with Joan McAvoy. Roland made me promise that I would replace him in the legal suit if he passed on which I did.*

I was released in September 1945 and flown to the 142nd Army Hospital, outside of Calcutta. We stayed about a week or so. We were de-wormed and given numerous shots for dysentery, malaria, beri-beri, scurvy, etc. My Congressman and I have written the Army for transcripts of the treatment, but the Army cannot find them.

When the hospital was ready to discharge us to leave for home — the caste system really set in. The military were given new uniforms, medals, money, parties and preferred medical treatment upon arrival. The merchant seaman were left on their own.

When I finally got home I had nightmares every night, waking up in a sweat screaming. I also had diarrhea daily. I went to a marine hospital and the doctor who wrote the report said I was okay, just suffering from anxiety, gave me belladonna and discharged me. The doctor at the marine hospital left a lot to be desired. He showed no compassion and looked at me as if I were a freak. He could have informed me that he wasn't current on tropical diseases, but instead he said most was in my imagination. I wrote to the British Doctor Phillips, who sent me medicine for my stomach and a solution for the jungle rot on my chest. They were a great help.

The dental chart from the marine hospital said that my teeth were okay. My dentist worked on my teeth for over three years, most had rotted under the gums. It was a long, hard, and expensive process to save them.

During the forty-five odd years since my return, I have become a great 'Actor.' I can hide my pain and feelings and put

---

* *In Captain Arthur Moore's book* A Careless Word A Needless Sinking, *Dennis Roland's story is told on page 574. According to Moore, Dennis A. Roland passed away at the age of 76 in December 1984 at his home in Astoria, N.Y. He fought for years to get recognition from the U.S. Government for the U.S. Merchant Seamen who served in World War II ... He was one of the few survivors of the infamous Burma-Thai Railway. His account was written and sent to me a few weeks before he died.*[5]

on a good front, even though my nerves are shot. I always feel inferior. I've even had an artificial eye made for me at Bethesda Naval Hospital.

When I came home my blood pressure was extra low for years … I suffered from dizziness and would get queasy feelings in my stomach and pass out … My fingers are almost always swollen in the morning and evening.

Due to my physical and mental disabilities, I resorted to working in my family's small retail business. Worked night and day to try and forget my horrible experiences and brooding. I began to have the excruciating migraines (similar to the ones when I was a POW). The burning on my feet is still there. I still get diarrhea often … My nerves have gotten worse. About three years ago I had a pinched nerve in my back and a neurosurgeon removed a disc in my back. I was hit with a rifle butt numerous times by camp guards on that spot and other places.

The only remuneration I have received from the U.S. Government was for four weeks medical, when I was first brought home. I even joined an Australian/New Zealand POW suit against the Japanese for slave labor, about forty-five years ago. You cannot get one cent from them.

I went to a POW reunion at the Bridge Over the River Kwai about twenty-five years ago. There were ex-Allied POWs and about fifteen to twenty Jap guards. The morning before we were to cross the Bridge, we went to the Allied cemetery in Katchanburi on the river. Not a single blade of grass is out of place, the markers all clean and even. I recognized quite a few names and knew they had died in various camps. I was the only one who refused to walk over the Bridge with the Japanese.

Very truly yours,
Stanley Willner[6]

The Raider, Michel (Capt. Gumprich) was sunk on October 17, 1943 while approaching Tokyo Bay by the USS Tarpon (SS-175). Two hundred and sixty-three Germans, including the Captain, were lost.

Of the thirty-nine men that were taken prisoner, by some miracle, all the men lived through this hell and were repatriated to the U.S. after the war was over.[7]

Sawokla

In their wake they left Columbo-
Jute and linen down below-
They were sailing on for Cape Town-
Not expecting any show.

Then that fateful Sunday evening-
With the chief mate sick below-
The second mate heard one bell struck-
But still they did not know.

With the jarring crash the salvo hit-
And the second still below-
Haze and blaze and acrid fume-
Men running to and fro.

T'was the German raider *Michel*-
Whose torpedo struck below-
Whose 5.9s tore up her bridge-
And set her decks aglow.

There were many ships much like her-
Ask the merchantmen they know-
But, don't forget *Sawokla*-
Coral shrouded down below.

Ian A. Millar[8]

The Death Railway

Come along young merchant seaman-
Far from your ocean home-
Help us build this deathly railroad-
As through Burma we shall roam.

Help us lay the rails of tyranny-
Come along you have no choice-
For we'll work and starve, and beat you-
And we'll mute your freedom's voice.

Help drive the spike that holds the rails-
For every spike will cost a man-
When disease and fever take you-
Try escaping if you can.

Come along young merchant seaman-
When you're starving, sick, and weak-
Come serve *bushido*'s teachings-
We've a schedule to keep.

Forget your shipboard daydreams-
We hold no value on your life-
Except your slaving on this railway-
Forget your home and wife.

Forget your fallen shipmates-
And forget your carefree ways-
The emperor wants his railroad-
And you the price will pay.

You'll tell your friends who won't believe-
Of the barbaric things we've done-
And you'll find a firm reminder-
In the morning's rising sun.

Come along young merchant seaman-
You've shared with all the rest-
In the building of our railroad-
A railroad built with death.

Ian A. Millar[9]

~~~

This next story is a letter from Jesse C. Crawford to his dear friend Jack Marshall. Jack sent his letter to me on March 29th, 1997. Jesse passed over the bar about ten or twelve years ago according to the periodical Master, Mates, and Pilots. *A final thought from Jack Marshall was, "It is hard to think of all the shipmates I had from 1942/43 until 1966. I only keep in touch with three, so many have passed on."*

Dear Jack,

My Liberty ship [Jesse Crawford, as was proper, never identified his ship, but it was the S.S. *Robert Bacon*] stayed at the Mandeville Docks until March 12, taking on cargo of twenty-five General Sherman tanks, sheet metal, Dodge trucks, Ford parts, canned meat, news print marked PALESTINE IN TRANSIT, lubricating oil in drums marked SUEZ IN TRANSIT, two invasion barges, 3000 cases of Canadian Club whisky, 2000 cases of gin, and a few cases of NAAFI [Navy, Army and Air Force Institutes] stuff such as combs, razor blades, etc. for the British canteens. I went back around the U.S.O. several times, but Kitt told me you had caught a tanker and I figured you must have put right out to sea.

We moved down the river a few miles to the ammunition docks and took on 2000 tons of explosive; thirty-one box-car loads of TNT made in Chattanooga, several carloads of 40 millimeter ammunition, and some gelignite.

We left the Mississippi River March 19, and made up a convoy of about twenty-five tankers and twelve cargo ships and transports. The tankers broke away from us at the Florida Keys and went up the East Coast. Our orders were to make the anchorage at Key West, but the weather was pretty rough and our orders were changed when we were within sight of Key West. Seas broke over the boat deck, so we had to take in No. 3 and 5 boats and that night the mate broke us out to swing in the No. 6 boat which was about to be carried away. We went around the north side of Cuba and anchored overnight in Guantanamo Bay where we made convoy next morning for the Canal. We had one evening ashore in Cristobal and Colon where I earned the old bos'n's respect and friendship by drinking beer for beer with him.

We passed through the Panama Canal and out into the Pacific alone April 2 with orders to go to Durban. In the thirty-one days it took us to make South Africa I settled down to the routine of my four-to-eight watch as an ordinary seaman. Everybody from the captain on down had their heads shaved when we crossed the Line. The third mate and the Ensign didn't want their hair cut, but we cut it just the same. We had an easy passage around Cape Horn and across the South Atlantic. Our orders were changed; we were to make Cape Town. Two nights before we got there everybody on the bridge saw the wake of a torpedo that just missed our stern. The Old Man crowded on all the revolutions we could make and beat it into Cape Town like a scared rabbit.

I got ashore twice in Cape Town and really had a good time. Cape Town is a beautiful city built on the lower slopes of a mountain that rises four thousand feet from the sea. The people are friendly. Merchant seamen and Yanks, as they call all Americans, are especially welcome.

We sailed in a slow convoy along the South African coast to Durban where we lay out in the stream and waited for orders. We sailed in convoy to the south-east from Durban three days. The convoy broke up and we went south-east alone four more days. We turned to the north-east and then the north and went up through the Indian Ocean to the east of Madagascar. We hit the roughest water I have seen yet in the Indian Ocean. A sea broke every now and then on the flying bridge. I saw a good many gallons go down the stack. We stopped at Aden for orders and went right on up the Red Sea to Port Tewfik which is the modern part of Suez. We were three weeks discharging cargo. We painted the hull of the ship during this time. The deck gang had little else to do except stand gangway watches. I went over to Cairo and saw the Pyramids and the Sphinx and the Moham-medan mosques and the beautiful gardens on the Nile.

The common people in Egypt are a sorry lot. They don't believe in washing their clothes or themselves. They are lousy and full of fleas. I saw them hunting through the garbage cans like half starved hound dogs for scraps of food. There are many fine homes and mansions in Cairo where the rich people live, but the common people are lucky to have as much as a packing case or a shelter about like a dog house to sleep in. I would like to send all the American citizens that call themselves Communists and spend all their time cussing the "capitalists" and the government over to Egypt. They would appreciate the United States better as it is now.

I put in fifty-eight hours overtime in one week coming back down the Red Sea and the Gulf of Aden. We had to throw the dunnage (cargo packing materials) overboard and clean out the holds. When we hit the Indian Ocean we made only eighty-two miles the first twenty-four hours. We had to fill no. 5 hold half full of water as ballast to hold the propeller in the water. We put in at Mombasa for orders. Mombasa looked like a tropical paradise after the endless sand and rock of Arabia and Egypt. We took on a coxswain from the gun crew of another ship who had been left in the British hospital for forty-five days with a bad case of dysentery. The British told our ensign there were known to be five subs operating between Mombasa and Cape Town. [*According to Jurgen Rohwer, the following German submarines were in the area during July 1943: U-511, 198, 197, 181, 178, 177, and the following Japanese submarines: I-29, 27, and 10.*][8]

We left Mombasa July 11. We were torpedoed July 14 by the *U-178* (Capt. Dommes)[9]. The moon had set. It was the darkest part of the night. The 4-to-8 watch had not been called, so I figure it must have been about three o'clock in the morning.

There are differences in the published accounts of what time the Bacon *was hit and sunk. The next story, furnished by Edward O'Connell, who was also on board, agrees with Crawford's account in that he states the ship was hit at about 0235. Crawford continues:*

I was asleep in my bunk but woke up quickly enough when the torpedo hit. The alarm was ringing steadily. Somebody ran up the alleyway yelling, "This is it, boys! Go to your boats!" I turned on the light in my fo'c'sle and grabbed my life preserver. The light went out. I ran out to my boat, No. 1, screwed in the plug and cut the frapping line. About the same time the 3rd Assistant got there with an emergency light. The boat was half full of fuel oil and the reels that hold the long part of the falls were flat on the deck.

We abandoned the boat and ran back to the boat deck. There was smoke and fumes from the torpedo everywhere. No. 2 boat was full of timber and other wreckage. I got to No. 4 boat just as they were fixing to lower away. I was helping breast off the boat from the ship's side when I saw where the torpedo had hit. There was a hole in the hull along about No. 2 hold big enough to drive a wagon loaded with hay through it above the water level and no telling how big it was below the water level. Fourteen of us got into the boat before we released the sea painter (line securing the boat). The Deck Maintenance was in command. We pushed back around the stern of the ship. The propeller was stopped and half out of the water.

We got clear of the ship and waited for daylight with the sea anchor out. Our ship was hit by two more torpedoes before it sank. We saw the sub silhouetted against the sunrise as it cruised back and forth among the boats and the wreckage. We sighted one other boat with about ten men in it, a little float away raft with two men on it and a big raft with about eleven men on it. We knew we were somewhere in the Mozambique Channel, so we set sail and steered to the west. There was a fair wind and a following sea (behind the boat) and, as we found out later, a four knot current, all in our favor.

We sighted a ship and shot up two flares that same day about sunset. We sighted land a few minutes later. The ship, an English freighter (S.S. *English Prince*) on its first trip, sent off a radio message to shore giving the approximate position of our Liberty when it was sunk. The English were mighty nice to us. They took us to the Portuguese East African port of Beira. The Naval Intelligence questioned us all about the attack and we were put on C-type ships headed for Cape Town and New York.

At Cape Town I was put on an army transport that was built at Pascagoula, Mississippi. We made it to New York in nineteen days. We would have made it in sixteen days if we hadn't zig-zagged and gone so much out of our way.

I was the first survivor of my ship to reach New York. They advanced $300 toward my pay, but will not pay off completely until some of the officers get in. I was glad to hear that only two of the merchant crew of our ship are still missing. Some sailed into the coast. Some were picked up by different ships here there and yonder.

According to Browning, two men never reached the lifeboats, and a third died ashore from exposure.[10] *According to Moore, "... 3 crew members and 2 Navy gun crew were lost."*[11]

I sure like going to sea on a freighter with a good union crew and I hope to catch another one about the last week in September. I have to go to New Orleans to get my duplicate seaman's papers and Coast Guard pass, so I might as well ship out from there.

I don't guess this letter will catch you at home. Whenever you do get home, write and tell me about your sea-going and how you like tankers. I haven't seen any of the St. Petersburg boys since I left New Orleans and I sure like to swap yarns with some of them.

Your old pal,
J.C. Crawford[12]

<div style="text-align: center">~~~</div>

The next story is a companion piece to J.C. Crawford's letter because it tells of the miraculous survival of Cadet Edward S. O'Connell on one of the Robert Bacon's *rafts. But instead of being picked up the next day, they were adrift over thirteen days.*

Thirteen Days On A Raft

The first torpedo struck the ship on the port side at a point well forward of the deck house. It was about 0235 and the writer

[Cadet O'Connell] was sleeping. Just as soon as the writer heard the explosion he dressed and went to his post. The general alarm was ringing and the abandon ship was sounded almost immediately after the explosion. Boats No. 1 & 2 were damaged in the blast & unable to be launched. The writer then went to No. 3 boat and was about to board it when he noticed that there was only one man standing by the after fall; the writer then asked if he could lend a hand to O.S. John Beadles who was standing by the fall aft. Boat No. 5 was swamped in launching and was floating on her air tanks only. Cadet midshipman George D. McCall (U.S.N.R.) attempted to get in it to see if it could not be used. However he became fouled up in the embarkation net and the swells which were heavy must have tossed the boat against McCall and injured him so that he could not climb up the net again. All during the abandon ship process McCall could be heard shouting for help. After No. 3 boat was launched I attempted to get in it but this was impossible.

Seeing no other boats near the ship the writer ran back to No. 3 raft where A.B. James W. Colton & Joseph B. Whitehorse S 1/c had set a line fast on deck and were preparing to slide down to the raft which they had launched. Colton suggested that we heave on the painter and pull the raft up amidships & rescue McCall. We groped under the water for the painter and being excited & nervous we let the toggle come adrift and it was impossible for us to get to McCall.

We drifted to a point about four points off starboard quarter and saw second torpedo strike the vessel under the stack so that it must have been very near McCall. We then thought we heard the motor life boat but realized later it was the submarine which moved toward the forward end of the ship and fired the third torpedo from a point slightly abaft (toward the stern) the beam (widest part of the ship). The second one was fired at about 0255 and the third at about 0305. The submarine then came back and asked the name of the vessel and her nationality. He then said, "Good Night," and left us. At about daylight or a little before we could still see the ship. She seemed to be going down by the head but we did not see her take the final plunge.

That afternoon we met another raft with ten men on her. We took four of them on our raft. We drifted for seven days together then decided to split up. We rowed but the others claimed they were too weak. At 0530 on 27 July 1943 the *Steaua Romana*, a British tanker, picked us up and we arrived at Beira, at 1700 on 29 July 1943. We lived ashore at the Beira Hotel until 11 August when we boarded the M.V. *Kota Gede* of the Hall and Africa Line. The writer left the *Kota Gede* at about 0100 on Tuesday 19 October and went straight to his home.

Respectfully submitted
Cadet Edward S. O'Connell[13]

In a letter to this compiler, Ed added that he arrived home and thirty days later joined the Bernard N. Baker, *an American Export Liberty ship and in November set sail for Murmansk. His convoy was attacked by the German pocket-battleship* Scharnhorst *on December 26, 1943. Evasive action was taken, no merchantmen were lost and the* Scharnhorst *was sunk later that day by the HMS* Duke of York.[14]

A final note: the U-178 was scuttled in Bordeaux, France on August 25[20?] 1944.[15]

9

THE PACIFIC OCEAN

After the Japanese surrender, General Hideki Tojo gave General Douglas MacArthur three reasons that, in his opinion, caused the Japanese to lose the war: (1) the Allies' "leapfrogging" strategy which bypassed important centers of Japanese military power like Rabaul, Wewak and Mindanao; (2) the far-ranging activities of Fast Carrier Forces Pacific Fleet; and (3) the destruction of Japanese merchant shipping by United States submarines.[1]

General Tojo overlooked a fourth factor; logistics. In Military Science, logistics is the procurement, management, and transporting of supplies and personnel. As the war progressed in the Pacific, every soldier, pilot, and ship had a supply line of ammunition, gas, food and all other necessary supplies linked back to the United States — the U.S. Merchant Marine.

The war in the Pacific differed from the other theatres in several respects. Among the major problems were distances

176

between ports and fewer deep-water ports to unload the war materials. The distances were twice those in the Atlantic. The same problems faced the Japanese. It took "forty-eight days for a Japanese merchant ship to reach New Guinea or the Solomons, sixty days to reach Hawaii, forty days to reach Alaska."[2] With few ports available to Allied shipping, amphibious watercraft were used to ferry shipments to land, doubling the normal unloading time.

The great American counter offensive in the Pacific, involving incredible logistic support, would have been impossible without the use of a vast merchant fleet, a greater percentage of which was composed of Liberty ships. By 1944 hundreds of these ships were streaming across the Pacific, delivering millions of tons of food, ammunition, guns, and other military supplies. They took part in all the landings after Guadalcanal ... [3]

It was also a theatre of distinctly different military philosophies than those on the other side of the globe. In the Pacific, the Allies faced a ruthless enemy that would commit suicide rather than be captured or defeated. The Japanese (Kamikaze) pilots were prepared to die by crashing their planes into Allied ships. Occasionally, a German submarine captain might offer assistance and directions; Japanese submarine captains were brutally inhumane in their conduct toward captives. The Imperial Naval Order to the Commander of Submarines, issued right after Pearl Harbor, was blunt:

Do not stop with the sinking of enemy ships and cargoes; at the same time you will carry out the complete destruction of the crews of the enemy's ships; if possible seize part of the crew and endeavor to secure information about the enemy.[4]

The price the merchant marine paid for victory was high. "...Many Liberty ships and hundreds of merchant sailors were lost getting their cargoes across the vast ocean area."[5] "For the merchant marine, the Mindoro landings in the Philippines were the most expensive in terms of ships and men. More merchant

*mariners lost their lives at Mindoro, according to the War
Shipping Administration, than did members of the Armed Forces
taking part in the D-Day invasion.*"[6]

How important was the U.S. Merchant Marine in the
Pacific? General Douglas MacArthur had this to say:

> I wish to commend to you the valor of the merchant seamen
> participating with us in the liberation of the Philippines. With us they
> shared the heaviest enemy fire. On this island I have ordered them
> off the ships and into foxholes when their ships became untenable
> targets of attack. At our side they have suffered in bloodshed and in
> death. The high caliber of efficiency and the courage they displayed
> in their part of the invasion of the Philippines marked their conduct
> throughout the entire campaign in the southwest Pacific area. They
> have contributed tremendously to our success. I hold no branch in
> higher esteem than the Merchant Marine services.[7]

~~~

*Captain Milton H. Houpis (Ret.) was the second officer
aboard the M/V* Cape Fear. *Houpis had been previously on board
the MS* Staghound *which had been torpedoed and sunk by the
Italian submarine,* Barbarigo, *in March of 1943. Captain Houpis
was a 1942 graduate of the U.S. Merchant Marine Academy.*

The Battle of Tarawa

Tarawa was the capital of the Gilbert and Ellice Islands
(Tuvalu) colony. The island was L shaped and consisted of eight
square miles. It was the scene of a tremendous, hard-fought battle
with the loss of 3,000 dead or injured U.S. Marines.

The attack itself was to last only two days with U.S.
battleships pounding the island for approximately three days
beforehand with their nine 16-inch guns. A quick victory was
sought, but the marines approached the island from the weather
side and were not aware of the hidden coral reefs. The landing
crafts were not able to beach and instead got hung up on the coral
causing a heavy loss of life. Another hindrance were the bunkers

After the war, the Cape Fear *went through several owners and name changes. Shown here as the* Solmich *circa 1969, she was scrapped in Taiwan in July of 1971. Airfoto, Malacca.*

Milton H. Houpis as a cadet midshipman at Kings Point in 1942. Milton H. Houpis.

dug out of the coral reefs by the Japanese. They would come out and pepper gunfire every time the U.S. marines tried to land.

I anchored half a mile off the beach in the enclosed lagoon on the third day with 3,000 tons of ammunition and 250 Seabees (Navy Construction Battalions).

The Seabees were a great outfit that were equipped for the first time with new A-K 14 automatic rifles, much to the displeasure of the Marines who would have like to have used this weapon in their landings. The island was finally secured for our Seabees to land with their construction equipment to repair the airstrip for immediate landing of American aircraft.

During my seven days at anchor two Japanese bombers approached at 10,000 feet level and bombed the air strip under repair by the Seabees. There was no damage or loss of life. The "Bottom Line" was that the good Lord was kind and didn't let those Jap bombers drop any bombs onto our ship.

God bless our U.S. Marines, Seabees and our U.S. Merchant Marine that stood by all those nine days without panicking or wavering from duty and country.[8]

> If there had been boredom and seeming lack of purpose in these island runs, it all ended when the merchant ships joined convoys for the invasion of the Philippines at Leyte in October, 1944. In two weeks, the Libertys and other merchant ships delivered 30,000 troops and 500,000 tons of supplies to Leyte, fighting off continuous air attacks. They were credited with shooting down at least 107 enemy planes in ten weeks after D-Day. Much of this shooting was done by merchant seamen who took the places of Navy gunners killed or injured in air attacks.[9]

~~~

The following letter and diary were submitted by Glen Trimble of Kansas. His diary tells of the frightening tension and conditions that his ship's crew went through while waiting at Tacloban (Philippine Islands) to unload its hazardous cargo. At the same time he gives a comprehensive, detailed view of what it was like to be there — a good look at life aboard ship. His story is typical of thousands of merchant mariners in similar circumstances. The place names and specific details may vary, but the experiences were the same.

Dear Mr. Reminick:

Received your letter the latter part of July. Your project is really worthwhile and about 40 years past due. During this month we have lost two of our most active members (now three) and the amount of information that has been lost forever during the past few decades as these old sailors pass on is a treasure trove that will never be recovered.

We have been spending a lot of time getting a memorial to the WW II mariners built and dedicated and now it is just an ongoing project. I do believe a project like yours will also be a memorial. I have tried over the last six years to encourage members to write their experiences and over that period of time I have two . . .

My own time was all spent in the Pacific from the Solomon Islands, to New Guinea and the invasions of Leyte (P.I.) and Okinawa. I made five trips on a ship that carried only bombs. The most memorable of these trips was the invasion of Leyte when there wasn't a safe place to warehouse bombs so we were the warehouse for two months. We had over 350 alerts and 114 attacks on our section of the anchorage during this time. We had a near miss of forty feet off the bow, seventy feet off the stern (sprung the prop) and a Kamikaze crash on the #3 hatch kingpost but he exploded before hitting the deck and did not penetrate. The closest call at Okinawa was a Kamikaze about sixty feet out and bombs about 200 feet out, but that time of exposure was only two

This memorial to merchant marine veterans is located in Wichita, Kansas. Glen Trimble was intrumental in its creation. Glen Trimble.

weeks instead of two months!!! I kept a diary during these two invasions and with the Armed Guard officers reports plus Kings Point Academy cadets reports I was able to make a pretty good day by day story...[10]

Witness To The Birth Of The Kamikaze

This is the story of a boy growing up, learning that the world does not consist of people of like minds, like values or like beliefs.

I turned eighteen in the fall of 1942 and now not needing my parent's (mother's) consent, rushed to the Navy recruiting office to enlist. I was told the backlog for boot camps was so large new names were not being added. I insisted I'd been attending NYA radio school and already had some good training. I was told to contact the U.S. Maritime Office in Topeka, Kansas.

I didn't know anything about the Maritime Service, but went to Topeka and enlisted. Same old story, boot camps were full, but at least I was accepted and put on inactive status. My call came the last of April and I was sent to Sheepshead Bay, Brooklyn, New York. I was accepted into radio school, spent eight weeks at Huntington, L.I., and then was sent to Gallup's Island, Boston. This was not an easy six months, but I did get a FCC license in January 1944, with an additional two weeks of Navy convoy instructions and then, after a couple of weeks at home, reported for duty at San Francisco, California.

There were more new radio operators than ships registered at the assignment desk, so after a couple of weeks I was talking to the man making assignments every day, saying I'd take just anything to get to sea. I was soon awarded what seemed like the first prize — assignment as a first assistant on a C-1; an 18-knot ship just a year old. My jaw dropped a little when I reported aboard and found our cargo was all 1,000 pound bombs. We left S.F. at 1800, March 17th, 1944 and arrived at Espiritu Santo April 3 with an average speed of 13.55 knots. We left on April 7th with two escorts and a destination of the Solomon Islands.

The first trip was delivery to Guadalcanal and Bougainville where we were shelled for four days and nights while unloading. The Japanese had guns in caves in the mountains and about every thirty minutes one of them would lob a shell into the harbor. I never did see a ship hit, but have heard since that it happened, but rarely. The run was completed, back to S.F., reloaded, same cargo, and back to New Caledonia, Tulagi and Guadalcanal in the Solomons. Then back to S.F. for another load.

To this point it had been exciting but pretty routine and there was never any consideration of leaving this great ship, the S.S. *Cape Constance*. We loaded for my third trip and I guess I thought it would be another voyage to the tropics and all the new things a Kansas farm boy found in the South Pacific. Except for one stop in Honolulu and one in Noumea, New Caledonia, there had not been much "liberty" time, but lots of beach combing, shell gathering, fresh coconuts, etc.

We sailed to Milne Bay, New Guinea arriving in September, 1944. We left for Finschhafen on the 15th of September arriving on the 16th. We sat there for almost thirty days, not knowing why. I celebrated my twentieth birthday there, with three cans of warm beer. We received orders to proceed to Hollandia on the thirteenth of October and the rumors of a big convoy being formed was not hard to believe with all the ships anchored in the area. We flew the red "Baker" flag and no one anchored very close to us or any of the other "Baker" ships as this was the sign of high explosive cargos. Although it was against the rules and regulations, I started keeping a diary in a little 4"x7" lined book.

I wish I had done a better job as days would go by without a date and all times were local time which sometimes is hard to convert to Greenwich Mean Time (GMT). GMT is used on all official accounts and was the time we used on all our radio logs. I do have the USN Armed Guard (AG) reports that prove very valuable when it comes to daily dates, plus reports the cadets on board sent their Kings Point Cadet Corps supervisor.

Per the diary, we anchored at Hollandia on October 14th, and left at 0815 on the 18th in a convoy of thirty-five Maritime ships and thirty-four LST's. The Armed Guard report gives a total convoy of seventy-eight ships plus twelve escort vessels. We were #13 in the convoy! My diary date for arrival in Leyte is October 23rd, but the AG report says the 24th. I do not know if this is due to the difference between GMT and local time or not.

We went into Tacloban (Philippines) anchorage early in the AM into a heavy smoke screen. Major vessels were shelling inland areas and about 0820, twenty-three planes came over. Seven were shot down. One crashed into a LCI (landing craft) inbound and not much was left. That was our initiation with the enemy. One aircraft was shot down by a Liberty on our port side and the plane crashed between us. We did not observe any hits from the bombers, but did observe three or four U.S. Navy planes in the area at the time. Reports that one Liberty was crashed were circulated by the gun crew.

The reason we were kept in Tacloban so long was the fact that the weather was very stormy. There were typhoons and so much rain that the Army engineers could not keep their crushed coral base they were trying to lay down for runways and storage areas from continually sinking. There was no place to store our bombs so we were unloaded as needed.

The Liberty reported being crashed was the SS *Augustus Thomas*. She was beached, but there were no deaths and only a few injuries. The next day, (the 25th per the AG reports,) we were under alert conditions almost continuously from 0430 to 2000 with a total of four attacking planes shot down around the area. The airstrip construction area was bombed at least twice. One engine crew member on deck at about 1800 received shrapnel in the stomach and chest, evidently from a shell that hit at #3 hatch. [*The* Augustus Thomas, *was "further damaged in an air attack on November 17, and eventually towed to Hollandia a total loss... then towed to Suisun Bay, California and finally scrapped in 1957.*[11]]

During invasions, all fire control signals for the Navy gunnery officer came through the radio room. We had an amplifier with two long cords running from the radio room up to the bridge deck where the gunnery officer is stationed. The signals are simple: Flash Red Control Yellow indicates enemy in the area, but use caution as our own planes are in the area also. Flash Red Control Green indicates enemy in the area, fire at will when appropriate. About 1830 we received the Control Green signal as four planes were approaching the area. I relayed the information to the gunnery officer. A very short time later, the signal was changed to Control Yellow (the four planes consisted of three enemy and one of our Navy planes in pursuit.) I could not get the gunnery officer to answer; we had lost contact. Without thinking, I left the radio room for the ladder to the upper deck just outside the radio room door. I just reached the top of the ladder when I felt a sting in my right arm and at the same time looked up to see the Navy plane losing altitude with black smoke showing. I had received shrapnel pieces to the lower right arm and hand as I was going up the ladder. The wound was minor, but I dressed and reported to the Purser-Medic aboard ship. (In April, 1946, I received the Mariner's Medal.)

October 25th was a very busy day. During the early morning hours the sky to the south was very bright and you could feel the vibrations in the air. We believed it to be a high level of shelling by the battleships and cruisers down the coast, south of Dulag. Official reports state that at noon of the 24th, Admiral Kincaid advised all Navy and merchant ships to prepare for night engagement. The ships anchored off Red Beach, to my knowledge, never received any such information. It turns out the firing we witnessed was Admiral Oldendorf's force intercepting the southern part of the Japanese fleet enroute to the beaches of Leyte. This action is known as the battle of Surigao Strait.[*]

Due to heroic actions of the baby carriers, pilots and especially destroyer attacking battleships, Japanese Admiral Takeo Kurita turned back just when he had about cleared all obstacles between his fleet and the beaches at Leyte. The largest battleship ever built, the *Yamato*, was the flag ship of his fleet, and was within fifty miles or less of being within range to shell the Tacloban anchorage with its 18.1-inch guns. I'll always regard October 25th as my very lucky day!

---

[*] *The Last Big-Gun Naval Battle, the Battle of Surigao Strait,* an eyewitness account by Howard Sauer aboard USS *Maryland*, is available through The Glencannon Press.

The 26th was almost a continual alert from 0600 until 2200. At 0615 one plane came in low. We were hit on one of the signal lights and one of the gun tubs from the fire of ships close to us. You could certainly hear the ricochet of 20mm shells glancing off the king posts and such. A plane was downed. Five more times attacking planes were in our area. During the afternoon, the SS *Benjamin Ide Wheeler*, was dived on. We now have had 27 actual attacks in our immediate area since arrival. [*The* Wheeler, *sank in shallow water after attack by Kamikaze suicide aircraft. Refloated and used as a depot ship. Received further battle and storm damage in Leyte Gulf. Scrapped in the USA in 1948.*[12]]

The 27th started with an alert at 0545 with a large group of fifteen to twenty attackers enroute. Only one got through to our area. A group of P-38 planes landed on the "so-called" airstrip today. Another three Jap planes were downed this PM with the P-38's getting two of them. One crashed the stern of a ship. About 2200 the air strip was bombed, no report of damage. The gun crew was on alert till 0345. We have been under continuous smoke screen (dawn to dusk, except on stormy days) since arrival. Everything smells like kerosene and I have a dull headache all the time. [*MS* Cape Romano, *was hit. The plane struck the port side of the bridge. Two crew members and two Navy men were wounded in the first attack.*[13]]

On the 28th we moved in close to Tacloban. In fact, we'll be the first ship in line when the planes come in over the hills. About 0700 one plane came over, but did not drop any bombs. Another attack at 1633 and we were the first ship to open fire. A Jap plane dropped his bombs in open water and left the area. During the evening the first typhoon came into the area with winds of about 60 knots. Small craft were washed up on the beach. I noticed something new the last couple of days — bodies coming to the surface; going out with the tide in the evening and coming back on the morning tide.

The 29th (Sunday) started with the first alert at 0100 and another at 0615 with one plane shot down. There were a couple more alerts and at 1900 a watch with a rifle was posted in the bow.

Snipers in the hills were firing at intervals. The winds are still blowing at 60 knots.

No planes got through on the 30th even though we had five alerts. The alerts keep your blood pressure up even without actual attacks going on!

October 31st has been relatively quiet; only three alerts with three planes getting into the area. It appears that a fuel storage tank was hit over by the runway area. The last alert started at 2350.

The alert continued on November 1st and a lone plane came over us about 0200 and ended up strafing a spot light just to the west of us in a CB area. He got the light! An LST anchored close by was strafed and a bomb was dropped. I understand that three crew members were wounded by shrapnel. There were a total of five alerts today.

We had seven alerts on the 2nd, with one plane dropping four bombs close by about 0340. There was some strafing by one plane at 0510, but he got away. Only the port side 20mm guns were fired.

November 3rd brought another seven alerts and action in this area is getting very heavy. Four planes were shot down today with one crashing into a Liberty ship anchored about 600 yards off our stern. The ship had troops aboard. About midnight a single plane came in very low and dropped a large bomb about 50 yards or so off our stern. The boys on the aft gun made a direct hit on him, but he was evidently so close the shell didn't explode. The plane went down over toward Samar. This totals six today and now we'll have a Jap flag to paint on the stack. [*SS* Matthew P. Deady, *complement numbered thirty-seven crew members, twenty-seven Naval Armed Guard, and 680 U.S. troops. Two Navy gunners in #2 tub, and twenty-six troops were killed. About 200 troops had been discharged before the attack.[14]*]

It doesn't let up; about 0520 a lone plane came in from behind the mountains and made directly for us. Our gun crew set him on fire and he crashed us. By a miracle, the booms were left rigged last night, so he tried to hit us and he hit the #3 kingpost boom and exploded. The main part of the plane went over the bridge to the aft section of the ship and over the side, burning all the way. The AG officer has shrapnel in his back and one of the gunners was bruised on his back, but it was a real miracle no one else was hurt except for minor flash burns as most of the gunners had rain gear on. The #3 kingpost was bent almost double back to the bridge, shrapnel had penetrated through the stack, the railing around the starboard side of the hurricane deck was wiped out and we lost all the radio aerials. Part of the cockpit landed on one of the gun tubs and the whole ship appeared to be in flames, but the crew soon had the hoses going and the fires were put out.

I'll always remember when the explosion happened; everything seemed like a red fog for a long time. I thought to myself, "Well, it didn't hurt, did it?" Guess I thought we had blew and it was o.k. as long as it didn't hurt!!! The Navy radio man was on a cot just outside the radio room door and when the guns started firing he just rolled into the radio room. After it was over, we discovered a shell casing from the plane had gone through the awning and through the cot. I still have that empty casing, bent with the primer intact.

A total of thirty some alerts today and nineteen actual raids in our area. We received a report on the first plane that dropped the bomb off our stern. It was a German seaplane and the pilot was not on board, so he evidently escaped. One of the gunners from the aft gun now can't hear from one ear due to the bomb and gun explosions. We now will have two flags on the stack if we ever get out of here.

November 6th brought us an early visit by a Jap plane that dropped a flare, evidently for taking pictures. He was shot down by a P-61 night fighter. Only one shot down today. This point is getting so hot all the small craft have been moved away and the CB camp has also been moved. Hope we get out of here soon and get some real unloading done.

November 7th started quiet until about 0530 when a plane came over with its lights on! He circled around and dropped a bomb about 40 feet off the port bow. Shrapnel flew over the bow and bridge, but no one hit. The lights fooled the gun crew!!! Only three alerts today.

November 8th brings rain and high winds. Barometer is really dropping. Only two alerts today and at 1800 watches were cautioned to keep sharp lookout for drifting ships. Winds are really getting worse.

November 9th brings better weather conditions. On the positive side, only two alerts today.

On November 10th, alerts started right at midnight and almost continue till 1000. At noon we weighed anchor and moved into the pier at Tacloban. All secure by 1330. One evening alert lasted for one hour. Only one plane dropped bombs even close today. I just got ashore and ran into Archie Brown, classmate from Gallup's Island. He is on a Liberty just off the dock area. The navy bosun did a great job on the two flags on our stack. Looks great!!!

November 11th brought only three alerts with booms being dropped about 1815. All clear by 1930. Cargo being unloaded.

November 12th — I can't believe it. Someone is evidently complaining about our cargo being at the dock! Got underway at noon and moved to Red Beach area just off the airstrip. From one hot spot to another! We arrived at anchorage just as another raid started. One of the largest we have had and still only 30% of the cargo is off.

Three planes were shot down, two by AA (antiaircraft) fire and one by one of our planes. One dived into what I believe was a LCI. At 1800 a plane dived into a Liberty anchored aft of us. Lots of fire and it really looks bad. I can hear the screams clear over here. Almost continual alerts till 2030. (Later have learned the Liberty was not the *Marcus Daily* that we thought, but the SS *Jeremiah M. Daily*. She carried troops and it was worse than we even imagined. The bridge was wiped out, including the radio room. [*The entire bridge section was destroyed as were the quarters on the starboard side of the bridge and boat decks. The starboard lifeboats were also destroyed. The fire from the range oil spread throughout the midship house and caused extensive loss of life among the troops on deck in #3 tween deck ... Four crew members including the Master, were killed. Two Navy gunners and about 100 troops were also killed. Ten Navy gunners and about 150 Army troops were also injured. After emergency repairs, the ship departed from Leyte and arrived in San Francisco on January 3.*[15]]

The deck is littered with shrapnel from all the AA fire during the afternoon. Have learned that the Dulag Beach area was hard hit. Four ships hit: *Alexander Majors, Leonidas Merritt, Thomas Nelson, Morrison R. Waite.* A very bad day at Dulag which is about eight miles down the coast from Tacloban.

November 13 — a quiet day; only three alerts.

November 14 brought its first alert at 0025. One plane shot down at 0600 and crashed close. Another shot down about 0720 that tried to crash us but missed about fifty feet. The plane burned out in the water. Another plane shot down by a P-38 and crashed on the beach. Tokyo Rose is bragging about the work of their suicide squadrons! This is very hard to accept that we are observing someone just committing suicide.

November 15 brought three alerts and the 16th brought only two, but a pretty good storm going on today. Clearing up this evening.

November 17 brought a very active day. At 0715 a large flight came over. One was shot down by a P-38. I was on deck watching with the glasses and glanced down at the water just as twenty-five or thirty small bombs were hitting parallel to our port

The Alexander Majors *discharging over the side into barges and landing craft earlier in the war. Imperial War Museum.*

This photo, taken in 1956, shows the Thomas Nelson *after having her hull modified and her engine replaced with twin diesels giving her a speed of over 15 knots. United States Lines.*

side about 200 or so feet out. I didn't know you could get under cover so fast. You have to be crazy to be on deck during a raid when it isn't necessary!! Some big bombs dropped over by the destroyer anchorage. Two planes set afire and one dived into a Liberty filled with barrels of gas. Five boats rushed out and put out the fire before the hatch covers melted through. The Liberty ship was the SS *Gilbert Stuart*. Several reported killed. [*Five crew members were killed and 8 seriously wounded. One Navy gunner was killed and many injured from strafing and the explosion of the plane. Five of an Army work party aboard were killed and many others injured.[16]*]

The other plane hit the stern of a Navy Liberty and glanced off into the water without any serious damage that we know of. Another went down in flames into the water. Late this evening another plane was shot down over by the air strip. We know of five shot down today and two ships hit. They are starting to discharge us into barges in between raids. This may take forever!

November 18th took all doubts from my mind that we were seeing deliberate suicide action going on. At 0700 I went out on deck and happened to glance up toward a cloud bank over in the east. There were three alerts, but three zeros came out of that cloud and went for three of the C-1 ships anchored in a straight line off our port side. Two seemed to be lucky and only had glancing hits with no big damage. The third one made a direct hit on the bridge and his bomb went off at impact. Early reports indicate eighteen casualties. The planes never tried to drop bombs and not a shot had been fired. The C-1 hit was the SS *Alcoa Pioneer*. [*Five Navy men were killed and 9 injured. Five of the ship's crew were also injured but all survived.*[17]] It is hard to see how the casualties were that light.

November 19 brought three alerts, but no raids. Storm blowing almost typhoon intensity.

November 20 had some alerts, but hard rain almost all day. Very little cargo being moved.

November 21 brought several alerts, but weather still bad.

November 22 brought almost continuous alerts.

November 23 brought first alert at 0730 with fifteen high altitude bombers bombing both the airstrip and our harbor area. No bomb damage observed. One zero and one two-motored bomber shot down. One plane came in very low and dived into a Liberty with his bomb still attached. She burned all night and all day. Finally they beached her for salvage. Almost a full moon again and back to the smoke screen. Haven't discharged anything the past two days. It was reported that there were troops

The Alcoa Pioneer *under charter, after the war. Built by the Bethlehem Steel Co. of San Francisco, she was placed in the Reserve Fleet in 1963 and scrapped in Valencia, Spain in July of 1970.*

aboard the Liberty. [*The ship was the SS* Gus W. Darnell. *No one was killed but six crew members and five Navy men were injured and required hospitalization. This ship was named in honor of Gus W. Darnell, master of the SS* Tillie Lykes *which was torpedoed and sunk with all hands on June 18, 1942.*[18]]

November 24 and we started discharging bombs once more, but early AM more bombers flew over than any time since we first arrived. Counted sixteen overhead almost all out of reach of AA fire, only a few guns were getting that high. Two were shot down. The first bombs dropped about 200 yards from us and worked in toward the air strip. Two ships were straddled, but no one was hit. One bomb hit two P-38's on the ground. One fighter was shot down by a P-38. About 1115 a lone flyer came in and as he went behind the mountains he was trailing smoke. Later reports say it was one of our P-47's. A P-38 got a fighter just off our starboard beam. He crashed across the bay in Samar. A lone Jap flew the entire length of the bay just above the water without being hit. He dropped his bomb, but no damage. Raid #5 started about 1915 and lasted almost 4 hours. Few bombs were dropped from high altitude, but no hits and no planes shot down during this entire raid. (Leyte radio reported 35 bombers and 7 fighters were shot down before they got into our area.) AA fire and shrapnel are more hazardous at times then the Japs are!!!

November 25 had nine alerts today, but no attacks until 2250. Search lights picked out two high altitude bombers too high for AA. They dropped their bombs and started a large fire between Tacloban and the air strip. A lone bomber was picked out at 2315, but was still too high for AA. The moon is almost full and the Japs are making the most of it.

November 26 had eight alerts today starting at 0030 when a lone Jap strafed a search light off our port bow, but was shot down and burned just south of the air strip. At 0045 another one started strafing the airfield; he was set on fire and stayed up several minutes making a great target for the boys on the 20mm. He finally exploded across the bay on Samar. No more Japs till 1130 when two came over, but were too high for the AA. At 1137 another one made an attack on the lower end of the bay, but we couldn't determine if he got away or not. At 2010, 2040, and at 2130 they flew over, but were too high for AA. Their bombs did no damage that we could see.

November 27th started on a quiet note with no planes until 1145. They were down at Dulag beachhead about 8 miles south of us. The heaviest AA yet started; so heavy you could feel the vibrations of the ship. We could see the flak in the air, but due to a light rain falling, we couldn't see the planes. We have since learned that the Japs tried to land troops there by air. We have no reports as to the number that tried to land, the number of planes or the number killed. The reports are two of our ships were hit with 19 killed on one; no report on the other. Several small Navy craft came by with parachutes from Dulag.

Only one plane came up here and he dropped a bomb in the floating dry dock, no report on damage. About 2100 tonight a Jap scored a lucky hit on the air field with one bomb and burned several planes. Several more passed over, but were too high for the AA fire and caused no damage. One was even spotted by search lights. They expect an airborne attempt to take the air field here any time.

November 28th with seven alerts.

November 29th started with four early raids, at 0145, 0200, 0215 and 0230. They were too high for AA and caused no damage. Several more alerts, but no more planes.

November 30th had several alerts, but no planes. The Captain got tired of sitting here with all the unloading crew leaving each time an alert sounded. He ordered out barges to be tied alongside and our own crew would do the unloading. When a barge is loaded we call for a tug or whatever can take the load to Red Beach.

I want to note that our Thanksgiving Day dinner consisted of stew (Army), beets, dehydrated potatoes and apple pie! We won't have that for Christmas if we don't get back to New Guinea for some supplies.

Notice some ships have been loading troops for the next operation and all foodstuffs have been stripped from the ships here. We now have a supply of nothing but Australian chile with mutton. That supply should last a while even though that is what we have three times a day.

December 6th brought the first actual planes over us for almost a week! We have had three to seven alerts each day, but have not observed anyone getting to this area. This changed about 0315 when several planes came over and again about twenty minutes later. Bombs were dropped between us and the air strip, but there was no apparent damage. They were too high for effective AA. At 1900 an aerial torpedo attack was made on the shipping here in the bay. One plane came clear across the bay, passing about 500 yards off our port bow. He wasn't shot down. Several explosions were observed on Samar, but couldn't tell if they were bombs or planes shot down. AA fire was extremely heavy.

A few minutes after, this plane came in over the beach very low and with his lights on. He got almost to the air strip before the AA gunners decided he was a Jap. He was set afire and crashed on the strip. Several explosions were heard. Two more raids, but no damage observed.

December 7th brought several alerts starting at 0158 with high altitude bombers too high for AA fire, but no damage observed. It is reported that the plane that crashed on the strip last night destroyed five planes. The pilot tried to jump, but was too late and he just made a dirty spot where he hit.

The Japs evidently had a bad day today. However, almost every one of our planes that came back to the strip made from one to three victory rolls!

December 8th and confirmation that the Japs did have a bad day. Our 77th Div. landed behind the lines at Ormoc on the west coast. We hear the Japs lost fifty-seven planes in the air alone. We had hard rain most of the day, but the good news is that we are finally unloaded!!!

December 9th and we moved to an empty ship anchorage — hope the Japs know that these are empty ships!! Only one alert all day.

December 10th brought five alerts and some excitement. About 0320 a severe explosion shook the ship enough to wake everyone. It was an oil storage tank blowing up with damage to others. Reports indicate possible sabotage from troops that were dropped by parachute. An attack was made on shipping south of Dulag about 1710. It is reported one plane downed and one ship [SS *William Ladd*] hit. Another fuel dump exploded at Dulag about 1830. No reports yet.

December 11th brought only four alerts and only three on December 12th. We must be getting ready to leave as the AG gave the LST 472 three cases of smoke bombs.

December 13th had five alerts, but no planes. Additional reports on the oil tank explosion indicates a TNT dump blown up which set the tanks off. Reports indicate heavy casualties among a company of Negro troops stationed nearby.

December 14th brought several alerts, but no planes till 1845 when a Jap slipped in over the air field and dropped four bombs. Only a few shots were fired at him. No reports on damage. Early this evening a large convoy of about 150 ships left. We expect to hear of a new landing soon. They included 32 destroyers, 4 cruisers and 24 PT boats.

December 15th — the day we have been looking for! Left anchorage at 1345 and bound for New Guinea and, we hope, mail. Haven't had mail since October 13th. The records indicate we had over 300 air alerts and 114 actual attacks on our section of the anchorage since arrival. I guess two near misses and one Kamikaze crash isn't too bad especially since we got rid of all the cargo!

December 22nd and arrived at Hollandia, New Guinea. Received mail, lots of mail, took on food supplies and refueled from a tanker on the 24th. Left Hollandia and arrived Finschhafen on the 26th, but received orders to proceed to Port Moresby. Arrived Port M. on the 27th and started taking on Army personnel on the 28th and left at 1125 for the States. During the trip up the Liberty SS *John Burke* was dived on by a Kamikaze and its load of explosives just disintegrated with not a trace remaining; the SS *Lewis L. Dyche* was also dived on and vaporized. A ship that we spent lots of time with in the New Guinea area was the SS *Juan De Fuca*. She was hit by a Kamikaze and then when arriving in Mindoro was bombed so badly she was beached for cargo salvage. The SS *Simeone Reed* was bombed and beached in the same raid as was the SS *John Clayton*. The SS *William Sharon* was dived on and her entire superstructure was set afire. [*Many of the ships leaving this area to go to the island of Mindoro in late December and early January met with disastrous results.*]

Within a few days of leaving Port Moresby the engine crew discovered the prop shaft bearing was overheating. It was believed the bomb we took off the stern at 2355 on November 3rd had sprung the prop. We now go for a while and then stop and the bearing housing is wrapped with burlap and watered down.

We arrived in Pearl Harbor for emergency repairs on January 28th. A whole month of stop and go from New Guinea to PH. Within a week we were enroute to San Francisco.

I was next assigned as CRO (Chief Radio Officer) on a new Victory, the SS *Grinnell Victory,* still in the Richmond (California) yards. We loaded the same cargo and made the Okinawa invasion. Although the amount of Kamikazes increased we were in and out of Hugushi Beach in two weeks. I do not know how many alerts and how many actual attacks, but our time was short. The closest bombs were 300 feet away and the closest Kamikaze crashed off our side about 60 feet away. After Leyte, we were getting more used to this type of action.

I came back to SF in July and was assigned to the SS *Joplin Victory* for the Japanese homeland invasion. We loaded our usual cargo and left on August 12th. When Japan surrendered on the 15th we knew we would receive instructions to go to Pearl or return to SF. No such luck; we went into Ulithi in the Caroline Islands and no one wanted bombs anymore. We sat there from the last of August till the last of November, where we were routed up to Saipan and we unloaded into barges. The rumors were the loads were taken out to deep water and put overboard.[19]

~~~

The following story was submitted by Paul A. Tumminia of Staten Island, New York.

The Sea Saga of the *Juan De Fuca*

In May 1944 we headed back to New York and Rhode Island to pick up a crew and cargo. From there we proceeded to make up a small convoy off Guantanamo Bay, sail through the Panama Canal and on to Pearl Harbor. We unloaded and returned to Long Beach, California. We took on cargo in San Francisco and sailed alone to Brisbane and Sydney, Australia. We dropped off some cargo at Lae, New Guinea and proceeded to Hollandia where we joined a convoy going to Leyte Island in the Philippines.

After a few weeks we formed into another convoy and we sailed for what was called "MacArthur's Gamble," Mindoro. Halfway there our convoy was attacked by a group of Kamikazes. One of the planes crashed dived into our number #2 hold and killed three soldiers. The explosion also blew one of our Navy signalmen over the ship's side. We made San Jose Harbor (Mindoro, Philippines) with the three other merchant ships. The next day we were reunited with the Navy man that was blown over the side. An LST picked him up during the attack.

On Christmas Eve the Japs decided they wanted to take the island back so we upped anchor and moved out to sea, but our planes and PT boats turned them back. From the time we arrived in the [San Jose] harbor we were under constant strafing and bombing attacks at night. By New Year's Eve many of the other merchant ships had been damaged and sunk. We lifted anchor again and sailed close to the island to prevent us being a target for the planes. At three o'clock on New Year's morning we were torpedoed and run aground after we took on too much water. We finally abandoned ship at approximately 5:00 A.M. by taking to the lifeboats. We landed on the island of Ambulong. Two days later the Navy picked us all up and took us to the mainland of Mindoro. There the commander told us about his problem; that he needed the cargo of pilings that we were carrying and without them he couldn't dock his boats. He asked us in the deck and engine room departments to volunteer and stay to unload the cargo. Eighteen of the crew went home and the rest of us went back to the small island to make up camp and proceed to go to the ship and take off the pilings. This was done by mere arm power, rowing back and forth, and it took a couple of weeks.

After completing the job in three weeks, ten of us decided to go home. From the airfield at San Jose, we hitched a ride on a plane going east. After reaching the Admiralty Islands we were given priority by the War Shipping Administration and proceeded as passengers to Pearl Harbor. There our priority ended and we were put up at a hotel for eight days until we boarded a passenger ship and sailed for San Francisco ten days later.[20]

In the congratulatory letter that Emory Land, WSA Administrator, sent to Paul, his name was spelled incorrectly as Paola A. Turmania. The WSA also sent the commendation to the wrong address. A second mailing was sent to the company headquarters of Paul's employer, but, not surprisingly, no one in the company recognized the name. Finally, in February 1996, after fifty years, Paul received his commendation. He had requested information from the Maritime Administration and a clerk discovered the yellowed commendation sitting in Paul's file based on the serial number from Paul's correspondence.

~~~

The following story and poem were contributed by Walter L. Welch. They are from his father Alvin Lee Welch's diary. Alvin passed away in 1994. The diary and poem describe Alvin's first visit to Tacloban in the Philippines aboard the SS Henry White.

Sunday, November 12, 1944 — Our Baptism of Fire.
On our way into Leyte Island, our first sign of the Japs was a Zero, evidently hit by shore batteries, heading for Davy Jones' Locker. Some of our boys reported seeing the plane hit, burst into flames, and go down. Later (about 5:30 or 6:00 a.m.),

the body of the Jap pilot was seen floating alongside. One man mistook him for a turtle in the gray dawn. All this I learned from the preceding watch.

At 7:30 a.m., G.Q. sounded and I had just reached my battle station when the fellows topside sent up a cheer. "They sure got that Zero fast." From my station in the wheelhouse, I couldn't see anything, but that made two planes down already. Then just as the fellows thought that a P-38 was going to get it from another Zero a second P-38 scored the 3rd victory we could confirm.

All was quiet until 2 p.m. when the alarm was sent in. We were anchored, so I was in my sack. Five Zeros were in the sky, filled with flak. There were also a lot of our fighters up there. One Zero was in a dive with a P-40 on its tail. The Zero never pulled out of that dive. Then another was making a strafing and bombing run on a Liberty. His only bomb scored a direct hit on the Liberty just as he burst into flames from ack-ack (antiaircraft) and fighter fire. He crashed into the bridge of another Liberty. Suddenly, three planes were diving between us and another ship on our port beam. They were, in order from one to three, a Zero, P-38, and a P-40. The P-38 fired at the Zero and then headed for the clouds. The Zero made for us, with the P-40 on its tail, firing. Our 20mm's opened up and he pulled away from us. As the P-40 fired its last burst and followed the P-38, the Zero leveled off with a thin stream of smoke coming from its cowling. He dropped two bombs at a ship on our port quarter, but missed. Then he cut across our stern and our big gun fired once and blew the left wing off and half of the port fuselage. He tried to manoeuvre into a ship off our stern, but fell short 75 or 100 yards. Two ships confirmed our victory.

At 6 p.m. another raid about three miles away started sending up an awful barrage. I was looking right at an L.S.T. when it took a direct bomb hit and burst into flames. It burned till about 8 p.m. About sixty seconds after the LST was hit, the Zero got hit, crashed into the water and burst into flames. It burned for perhaps twenty minutes. Score seven Zeros.

At 12 p.m., no other raids have occurred. One thing I have to say for these Japs is that they are excellent pilots, with plenty of guts. One can't help but to admire them after what I saw today. Finis for tonight, 11/12/44

Monday, November 13, 1944, 8 P.M. at Dulag, Leyte, P.I.

Today we moved our anchorage. We are about 300 yards from one of the Liberties that got hit. (SS *Jeremiah M. Daily*) A Zero dived into her. Up forward she is quite a mess. The plane hit the forepart of the house and entered the vicinity of the Chief Engineer's room. We had an alert about 5 a.m., one at 2:30 p.m. and one at 7 p.m. Each one lasted at least an hour. There was no apparent damage. Our guns fired on a plane at 2:30 p.m. raid. It was reported to be an observation plane.

Starting this morning the deck crew have to remain inside the wheel house. Yesterday we were allowed on the wing, but no more. He says that your battle station is in the wheelhouse. Stay at your station. Hope Tojo doesn't come over any more tonight.

9:00 P.M. Tuesday, November 14, 1944

All last night we had raids. Another Jap Zero tried to get us at dawn, but our guns scared him away. A shore battery got him as he was leaving. No damage done to our forces. The radio said forty Jap planes started our way. Twelve were chased back and twenty-four were shot down. We saw the remaining four in our area. Tojo seems as if he will start to come over at 5 a.m. regularly. For the last three days he seemed to make it at just about that time. One good thing about his early morning visits is that we're up long enough to work up a good appetite for breakfast. If tonight is anything like last night, no sleep for us. I'm really tired.

9 P.M. Saturday, November 18, 1944

Tojo has been keeping us pretty busy lately. There goes G.Q.

11 p.m. As I started to say, (at 9 o'clock) Tojo keeps us pretty busy. Saw three Zero's go down.

8 P.M. Sunday November 19, 1944

Just came in from 42nd alert. The Japs have averaged

being over six times a day since we have been here. We get up every time they're over. Gets monotonous after a while.

They layed about 70 or 100 eggs (bombs) this last raid. They were after the bomber field.

6 P.M. Monday November 20, 1944

We left the States 6 months ago, to the hour. Long time at sea. It has been raining all day, so we have had three raids today. There didn't appear to be any action anywhere, tho. I believe they have just been sending up a plane or two on nuisance raids. A storm was reported due tomorrow, so we moved anchorage. I hope it isn't very bad.

It appears that we will get the $125 bonus for Sunday (12th) air raid. The steward had "The Voice," (union paper) and it states, "any ship in immediate danger of damage due to enemy action will receive the $125 bonus." We were certainly in "immediate danger of damage due to enemy action." That Zero was certainly headed for us!!! Thank God the 20mm's opened up in time to turn him; and also for a straight shooting 5-inch gun crew. The last raid was the 46th.

Saturday, November 25, 1944

I haven't written for almost a week now. The Japs are still keeping us busy. Friday morning while we were on the alert, a Zero dropped out of the clouds almost dead astern from us. Our 20's opened up on him immediately, but our 5-inch didn't get a chance to fire. I think our 20's nicked him. Our 3-inch missed him twice and he dropped a bomb at a ship off our port bow about five hundred yards. He almost hit the ship. He evidently got away, but he was sure catching hell. About ten minutes later I went into the wheelhouse to sleep, and came in and said that they had got one Zero. He came down in five or six pieces.

To date, we have had nearly seventy alerts in not quite two weeks.

Thursday, November 30th, 1944

In the past five days, a lot has happened. The Japs tried to retake Leyte. Paratroopers were dropped about six miles from here. About twenty miles away there was a naval battle going on between our ships and the Jap task force. I don't believe they made the beach.

We have had almost 130 air raids so far. The Jap's have averaged at least 1 raid every four hours. They are from fifteen minutes to four and a half hours long. They come over at all times of the day and night, but very few of them go back home. The planes that our crew have seen go down in our area at Dulag total thirty-eight or forty. That is besides the seven we saw downed at Tacloban. We can only see about 8 or 9 miles here.

Monday

Chips and I took the Captain and 2nd Eng. to Tacloban in the boat. As we got near one of the strips, a P-38 came over in a V roll.

Wednesday

There was a big fire on the water about half a mile from us. It seemed that there had been a lot of H.O. [high octane] gas pumped out of a barge because it had water in it. A "buffalo" [LVT or amphibious tracked vehicle] went through it, and it caught fire. Three men were killed.

Wednesday, December 6, 1944

The Japs are still pestering us. Tonight we saw them for the first time in a week in our area. Last night they had a pretty heavy bombing attack at Tacloban. Tonight they were at Tacloban and here at Dulag. Four of them were shot down here. I saw two. One was over the strip, (about twelve mi. from here) coming in our direction, with the shore batteries giving him hell. Then the Liberties' 20's opened up. We weren't firing. He burst into flames and started climbing. They ordered our big guns to keep on him, and if he came for us, to blow him to pieces. But he crashed on the beach.

Another was diving on the strip when they hit him. He blew up when he got hit. All the planes were coming in low tonight. A couple of ships were hit by our tracers. There was also a naval battle going (Ormoc offensive). Don't know much about that.

Thursday, December 7, 1944

All has been pretty quiet today. Only three alerts. No firing that we could see. I learned today, that the Japs had landed 300 paratroopers about six miles from here in that attack last night. Our boys killed most of them. One of the planes we saw go down was a big Jap transport. There were about twenty Jap paratroopers alive and our aircorps pulled them out and eliminated them. The Flips [Filipinos] sure give the Japs a rough go when they catch 'em. They helped out with the paratroopers, too.

We have some Infantry boys on board helping to discharge us. They are back from the front for a twenty-four hr. rest.

The 24th and the 32nd are fighting and winning, but they are taking a helluva beating to do so. The 18th landed the other day and are giving them a hand.

The Japs here said that they "Don't intend to lose the Philippines," and they are putting up a sure enough battle.

We have only one field at Tacloban for our bombers to use. On one strip here at Dulag, our B-25's can land, if they are forced to, but it isn't long enough to take off on. It is a fighter field. We have one strip and are fighting to get the other (Buri) back. More tomorrow.

Monday, December 11, 1944

There was nothing much new, until last night, since the seventh. Yesterday there was a fire on the beach, and it was a pretty big one too. I don't know what started it, but it burned as if it were a gasoline dump.

Then, about 6 p.m. we had another raid. The SS *Ladd* (*William Ladd*) was hit and sunk. A damaged Jap Zero dived into her. About 9 p.m. she was observed burning from stem to stern. Then there was a big explosion, which appeared to be in her engine room. She sank stern first. Two planes were brought down, one of which hit the *Ladd*. [*She was anchored eleven miles south of Dulag with about 500 barrels of gasoline and 150 tons of ammunition still to be unloaded. No one was killed but six crew members were injured and hospitalized at Leyte. The vessel was completely gutted from No. 2 hold aft.[21]*

This morning while I was in the lifeboat, I saw a P-38 go into an Immelmann (a turn in flight where a plane does half a loop and then rolls over to complete the turn), come out of it on top in a v-roll, and then another. Two less Zeros. Boy, I sure hope we go home when we discharge this load. We have been on the hook here at Leyte almost a month. In fact, tomorrow makes a month.

December 22, 1944, Friday

Well, after 40 days at Leyte Island, in the Philippines, we are leaving. It is pretty swell to be under way again. Now all we have to do is get through the straits and past Mindanao. For the past ten days there hasn't been much enemy air action where we were. Last week we moved our anchorage from Dulag to Tacloban, about five or ten miles from the docks. The night after we got there we had a raid. We only saw one plane, flying low, and he got hit and was probably downed. There was plenty of firing going on too.

I guess Curly, the baker, is in for a lot of trouble now. He is charged with desertion. He has been on the beach since Wednesday, and today, just before we sailed, the skipper took all of Curly's gear ashore.

When we were coming back from Tac., a Corsair came in for a landing and cracked up. Couldn't see anything for the dust. Kept the other planes from landing for half to three quarters of an hour. Sure hope the pilot wasn't hurt.

Unless something happens before we're clear of Mindanao, I shall not write any more of Leyte. For now, it's Finished.[22]

Alvin Welch wrote this poem, dated and copied on January 15, 1945. It is untitled, so I have taken the liberty to title it for Alvin.

The *Henry White*, A Liberty

On her maiden voyage, headed out to sea,
Sailed the *Henry White*, a Liberty.
She left the States, 20th day of May,
And sailed the sea for many a day.
The days and nights were filled with wonder,
With wind and sun and rain and thunder.
We sailed into port, no docks to see,
In a place called Moresby, in old N.G.
We then proceed, after a few days
to a point farther north, called Humbolt Bay.
Then up to Biak Island and
The Shuttling of the *White* began.
We sailed up and down the coast of Guinea,
The months spent there were a few too many.
So, the Army said to us one day,
"Philippines for you, Isle of Leyte."
Off we sailed on another run,
To an island held by the rising sun.
Seven months is really a long, long time,
More so when you have the same old grind.
But as yet the crew is all still sane,
And our guns have brought down one Jap plane.
But I often wonder, and I'm not alone,
Why the hell don't they send us home!!!![23]

~~~

The following story submitted by Richard Hanly of Vancouver, Washington, involved that most unpleasant of places: jail. Dick passed away in 1998.

WARNING
STEALING U.S. GOV'T PROPERTY IS
PUNISHABLE BY $10,000 FINE AND 10
YEARS IMPRISONMENT

You've all seen this sign aboard ships —

September 22, 1946: The Liberty ship S.S. *James C. Birney*, was along side the dock in Naha, Okinawa. We were loading used Army equipment — trucks, etc., for Manila.

A bullet pock-marked Shinto Arch was standing half a mile from the ship. (It still stands today near the Col. Sanders and the Seaman's Club.) As we were due to leave the following day, five of us decided to go get our photographs taken under the arch.

After the photos were taken, we headed back to the ship and saw three 6x6's loaded with gunny sacks. The drivers were sitting around eating their lunches. We asked them what was in the sacks, and they said, "Combat Boots." We asked if we could have some. They replied, "Help yourself, we're taking them to give to the 'Gooks.'"

We climbed up and started rummaging through the sacks to find a pair. One guy had found a pair that fit him, when a Lieutenant pulled up in a jeep. "What are you men doing up there?" When we told him, he ordered us down. The one with the pair jumped down, still holding the boots. The Lieutenant took the boots and ordered us to precede him to Provost Marshal's office. We just laughed and started back to our ship. Then he pulled out his .45 and aimed it at us and ordered us to march! MARCH WE DID!! Across the Bailey Bridge and up the hill we walked, with him behind, his .45 trained on us.

When we got to the Marshal's office, we were ordered into a cage. It was really a cage! Bars on the overhead, sides and bottom.

After a while, the Provost Marshal came in and told us he was going to "Throw the book" at us. He wasn't going to have Okinawa turned into another "Manila." [*A reference to the large amount of thievery that took place in the Philippines.*] By then, it wasn't funny anymore. When night came, we were given blankets to roll up and lay between the bars so we could sleep. Who could?!

The next morning our Captain Ericson showed up and told the Marshal a typhoon was headed this way and he had orders to leave, but he needed his five A.B.'s. After some discussion, we were allowed to leave — with the stipulation we would be handed over to the Military upon our arrival in Manila.

After almost foundering in the storm, we arrived in Manila. The Old Man had a message waiting for us. He was to turn us over to the Military immediately! He told us not to go ashore (we were at anchor.) After four or five messages, which he didn't reply to, they quit.

The Military at that time didn't look too kindly on merchant seamen.[24]

10

STORMS AND HEAVY WEATHER

*E*lmer Vick, of Columbiana, Ohio, tried to enlist in the Marines and the Navy, but was rejected because of a genetic dental defect. Later, he was accepted on waiver by the merchant marine. He graduated from Hoffman Island, New York, in November 1942. He was assigned to an old freighter, S.S. Lena Luckenbach, as an oiler.

S.S. *Lena Luckenbach*

In March 1943, sailing in a convoy to England, there were many sub alerts and sinkings. Our ship was badly damaged by a collision with another convoy freighter (SS *James Fenimore Cooper*) on April 20, 1943. It occurred early in the morning while in heavy seas in the North Atlantic. The other ship rammed us and her bow tore a huge hole on our port side, forward of the bridge. The other ship was not seriously damaged and rejoined the convoy. We were taking on a lot of water, listing and sinking.

The Lena Luckenbach *was built in Hioga, Japan and eventually became part of Mulberry A, an artificial harbor created by sunken ships for the D-Day landings at Normandy. Steamship Historical Society of America.*

When the engine room started to flood the skipper ordered us to abandon ship and we took to the lifeboats. Some hours later, a lone American diesel ship bound for England happened by, rescued us and took us to Liverpool. We were waiting for passage home when word came that our ship had not sunk completely. It was towed to Scotland, beached, patched temporarily, towed to dry dock in Glasgow, repaired and overhauled. The crew stayed in a hotel for the five month time, then sailed home. I sailed her one more trip after that. I've been told that the ship was deliberately sunk as part of a breakwater during the invasion of Normandy.[1] [*The ship was sunk on August 4, 1944 as a unit of Gooseberry I breakwater, part of the artificial harbor known as Mulberry A, which was located off Vierville, France.*[2]]

~~~

This letter was written by Jack F. Marshal to his mother and it describes the horrific conditions that he and his ship, the SS Cedar Mills *encountered during a typhoon while enroute from Australia to India. Jack received a Citation for Meritorious Service for his brave actions that helped save the crew aboard a French Destroyer.*

February 9, 1944

Dear Mother:

This is the only kind of paper I can find on the ship and it is better than most of the stationary we could get in most of the countries we have made port in.

As I haven't been able to tell you all or any of the news of this trip, I will try and tell most of it now as this letter won't be censored.

We left San Francisco the morning of October 14 (1943) on our way to Melbourne, Australia. It started off like all trips, four hours on and eight off, until we got to the equator on the 21st of October. We then spent half a day celebrating by cutting one another's hair off. When it was all over, even the ones that had been across before were without hair also. There were only a few that had crossed the equator before. Then "Father Neptune" gave the order for all to line up and get a shampoo. No! They didn't use a well known brand. It was something entirely new, prepared by the bos'n, it was made of graphite grease, lamp black, and fish oil and said to be a cure-all. But "Alabama Joe" the steward came out on the bad end as usual, for some of the boys used towels to get the mess off their heads. We missed out clear and clean on Halloween night, because we crossed the International Date Line early that morning and that put us over to November the first.

Our cargo was high test gas, 12 P-51 fighter planes and two army men to look after the planes. As our route was to take us around New Zealand, we were getting on down south where it was getting cooler each day. We had the coldest weather down here we have had to date. We had to go down to latitude 49 degrees South, but it was never colder than 42 degrees above.

About five days out of Melbourne the engine broke down. All hands were called out, except for the engine crew, to make a sea anchor on the bow. We were cross-ways to some swells that were making us roll so that while we were on the bow working you could almost spit on the boys on the other side of the bow. We had it only half finished when they found they could fix the engine in another hour so the "Old Man" called it off.

We got into Melbourne, Australia, the 10th of November. I got ashore once there, but didn't have time to go to the zoo; sure wish I had. The people here are very friendly.

We left there and went up the coast to Adelaide and Port Pirie where I mailed you a letter. Then we went to Fremantle to go in convoy to India; we were there on Thanksgiving Day. We left Fremantle late Thanksgiving afternoon with a large Dutch cargo ship and a French destroyer, the *La Triumphant*.* She had made quite a name for herself at the beginning of the war by knocking off German ships. She was of the class they were building in '36 and '37 that would do 47 knots.

We were to refuel her after four or five days out and make ten knots at the same time which was all right to talk about, but just didn't work out. We had just gotten started when she came in against us and flattened the hose, that was the end of refueling for that day. The next morning we got all the fire hose on the ship put together, got a two inch wire cable, made her fast to us and started refueling again, this time with better luck. We were standing still for about sixteen hours in the South Indian Ocean which isn't a nice feeling in war time. The Dutch ship signalled they were going on alone for they had a load of T.N.T. and didn't want to stop. We sure couldn't blame them for that. Before we left Fremantle an officer told the "Old Man" that we would have to tow the destroyer before we got in.

Everything was quiet after the refueling for a day or so then on the 2nd of December we hit a hurricane that by morning had almost capsized us two or three times and had taken three of our life rafts and had the Destroyer sending out one S.O.S. after another.

About six o'clock in the morning of the third of December, we were just getting out of the storm when our radio man picked up their S.O.S. They said later they had been sending since ten P.M. the night before they were using a different beat from us. After receiving their message, we sent "coming," got their bearing with our radio direction finder and were on our way back in the storm.

The destroyer was sighted about one o'clock and she was in a hell of a fix. She had better than a 40 degree list in her and

---

* Actually *Le Triomphant,* she was launched April 4, 1934 and rated at a maximum speed of 37 knots.

each wave looked like it would turn her over. The night before, one of her engines had gone out and she got crosswise to the waves and she would roll over so far that water went down the stack and put out the fires in the boiler. She was then at the mercy of the sea. I was told by one of her sailors that she rolled over so far that half of the wheel house was under water at times.

When the trouble started their chief mate [*he probably means the executive officer as French destroyers don't carry chief mates*], a doctor and two sailors started forward from aft and all four were washed over board, but the sailors were then washed back aboard and made it back to the mess room. The mate and doctor were never seen again and were the only men lost.

They said the captain would give the order to abandon ship and then stop them. This was said to have happened three times. The captain had tossed his cap and life belt overboard and said he would go down with his ship. They would most all have been lost, if not all, if they had abandoned ship, for the waves were too big for man, raft or lifeboat to live in. There were some water tight compartments that held her up, for all the quarters, mess room and engine rooms, were filled with water. All the crew were having to stand on the starboard side of the deck and hold on to the rail. They had nothing to eat and only wine to drink. But you have heard about a Frenchman and his wine, you just can't kill him so long as he has it.

There was nothing we could do that day for the sea was too rough, but by the next day we put two motor life boats in the water and took all her crew except 100 off, which meant we would have to put 125 men on the old *Cedar Mills*. We were standing by within a mile or two for at this time they were still expecting her to sink.

Our "Old Man" and chief mate decided the next morning that a lifeboat still couldn't live in those waves that were plenty high and breaking so it was put off until noon and by then it had quieted some and there were some men on the destroyer that had been burned the first night and they could not get to their medicine. They decided to put three boats in the water and go get the sick first and as many more as we could before night.

The chief mate took one boat and the bos'n the other with four men in each boat. They are both top seamen, I'm glad to say. I was able to get a seat in the chief mate's boat by the same way you get a pullman today, by being ahead of the next fellow. I had asked him a day ahead. About 12 noon the motor on our boat was started up and run for a while as it was water cooled from the sea and they didn't want to get it too hot. We were to start it again as they were letting us down. First a wave would hit the bottom of our boat and then you would look over the side and the water would be 25 feet from you, so they had to lower us away motor or no motor. We let the boat go from the falls, got our oars and for the next few minutes it was a life or death thing to get away from the ship. We were on the lee side and the wind was blowing the ship faster than we could row.

We came up even with the main deck more than once and banged against the side. By some good work of the "Old Man," quartermaster, and engine room they were able to get the ship off us. One good thing about it, we were too busy to get scared.

After finding our motor wouldn't start, we would just row enough to keep her bow to the waves. If you didn't do this, you would capsize in a matter of minutes. It was later found that there was water in the gas tank. How it got there, no one knows.

By now, the bos'n and his boat were in the water, their motor was running and they were coming to tie us to them. We had a 30 foot line in our boat for that job. After making fast to them, we were on our way to the destroyer which was about 1/4 of a mile away. You may think this is a tale, but at the end of that 30 foot line part of the time we couldn't see the other boat. It was just like a roller coaster, we would be riding down the side of one wave and they would be going up the side of another. Then as we went up, they would be going down the other side and we couldn't see them.

As it was impossible to get close to the destroyer without turning over, the men from the destroyer would have to jump in the water, the ship would drift away from them in a few minutes and then we would go in and pull them out of the water. You will have to admit it takes nerve to jump in that rough sea and hope someone will pull you out. Two or three of the men's legs were burned so badly they couldn't walk, others couldn't swim. But they all had good life belts.

We got about 25 men aboard that afternoon and our boat back aboard, which was also some job. It was about dark by now so the other men abandoned their boat, but by luck we found it the next morning. By morning it had quieted down a little more. I wanted to go again in the boat, but so did "Red" Farmer. He talked me into standing his wheel watch so he could go. Before it was over I was glad that he went, that darn motor stopped again and they had to row about half a mile and I was pretty sore from rowing so hard the day before.

The second day they were able to get close enough to put water and food aboard the destroyer. The Frenchmen gave the boatswain and crew a gallon of wine. The boatswain was carrying 25 men a trip, in a 20 man boat, besides his own crew of four men. By late afternoon, we had the destroyer made fast with a large cable and were on our way once again. Yet we could only make six knots for the destroyer still had a bad list. The British were radioed about where to carry her, but they radioed back that they would send a cruiser after her, which met us about a week later.

The "Old Man" and crew have gotten some nice "Thank You" messages from the British. When leaving the *La Triumphant*," we made one circle around them, they gave us a big cheer like you will never hear at a football game. Our "Old Man" gave them a V on the whistle. We were then on our way to Karachi, India, the way we like to run: alone.

On December 17th, we pulled into Karachi to discharge the planes. The next day I went ashore with the A.B. on my watch. We got a hack to see the town. It is said to be the cleanest town in India, but it was the damnedest place I have ever been in. The smell would almost make you sick. There was a dead horse on the street. Instead of dragging him off they let the buzzards pick him on the street.

There are no bug houses so they let the crazy go free. We saw one grown man walking down the main street without any clothes on. There were beggars everywhere. While we were stopped once, a woman came up with a little child on her hip. The child would put its hands together and bow to you, like you were some God or something and the mother wanted us to give her money. This was all she would say, "Baby no Papa, another coming, no papa," and would then pat her stomach. That will give you an idea what India is like.

We left Karachi Sunday noon, and it sure was a pleasure to get out of there. We went into the Persian Gulf to an oil dock below Baghdad. We were there Christmas Day. I didn't go ashore as there was nothing to see there. Anyway, we were on the Iran side of the river.

We left there the 26th of December with a load of gas for Port Elizabeth, South Africa, which is a very nice town. Then on down to Cape Town, from there to Trinidad, then we came back to New York.[3]

~~~

Norris Wainwright, Ship's Carpenter, gave me permission to publish his remarkable story that first appeared in the April 12, 1945 issue of the Ossining Citizen Registrar. *Norris was working for an antiques store where he ran the repairing and refinishing shop in White River, Vermont, when it was announced that the merchant marine had been granted veterans status. He visited the V.A. and was granted a 100% disability with all benefits and a full pension back to 1988. At the age of seventy-six he quit work and moved to Pennsylvania where he married a retired school teacher. Norris's first wife died in 1976.*

(Copyright. Reprinted by permission of Gannett Suburban Newspapers)

Crew Goes All Out For
"Guy With Guts"
Norris Wainwright, Merchant Marine

. . . It was more than a month ago when [Norris Wainwright's] wife first received word that her husband had been injured. How badly, she was not told, and it wasn't until she went to New York to bring him home that she learned the full extent of his injuries and the story of the stormy seas that brought about the accident.

Working with his fellow crew members, Wainwright was hastening to secure his ship [SS *Benjamin Holt*] for heavy weather when a hatch fell on him, cutting off part of his left arm, and three fingers of his right hand.

"This very element that caused the sailor's misfortune made his rescue doubly difficult," according to the official Merchant Marine release on the story. "Since his ship had only limited medical facilities, it was imperative that he be transferred to one of the escorts as soon as possible. His shipmates bound the stumps as best they could and signalled the Convoy Commodore their problem. The Commodore in turn requested assistance from the Escort Commander. Due to the nature of the sea, the job was strictly a voluntary one. When directed by the Escort Commander to go in and render any assistance possible, this Coast Guard manned Destroyer Escort maneuvered alongside and, by virtue of its remarkable maneuverability and the skill of its Commanding Officer, managed to maintain station alongside the merchantman for almost an hour. It was a superb job of ship handling and seamanship, both on the part of its young Commanding Officer and its crew.

The heavy seas constantly threatened to crush the light escort against the merchantman. No less skillful was the manner in which

Taken aboard the Moses Cleveland *in 1944, this photo shows Norris Wainwright, left, before he signed on the* Benjamin Holt *as carpenter. Norris Wainwright.*

the merchant captain and crew carried their part of the job. The ship was held on course by masterful steering and constant vigilance on the part of the captain.

The first two shot lines passed from the escort were broken by the force of the seas. There remained only one more line. If this were lost Wainwright's chances would have taken a sudden slump. By virtue of a superhuman effort on the part of the merchant seaman, this last line was taken aboard with amazing speed. Almost before you could realize it, the hawser had been made fast and the wire basket was sent across. As soon as the seas permitted the ships to assume a favorable position, the basket was sent back with its human burden.

The rest of the story is one of pure guts and nothing else, Wainwright was hustled aft to the sickbay by many eager hands. He actually tried to walk back but that wouldn't do. When the doctor examined the bloody remnants of what had been his arms and hands, he calmly gave all the details as he remembered them. Bleeding was checked, he was treated for shock and made comfortable in a bunk close by the sickbay. For the next three days he was still in shock and suffered from seasickness; but despite all his trials his spirits were high.

At the end of this time, the medico (physician) felt the weather to be calm enough to go to work. He intended cleaning up the wounds and making them ready for further repair work in a hospital ashore. The ship was really no fit location for surgery and of course it was hardly steady enough to do any fine cutting or suturing. This did not deter Wainwright. He persuaded the doctor to go ahead and cut, come hell or high water. This the doctor did, using a local anaesthesia. Wainwright lay calmly and chatted with a pharmacists mate while the medico was sawing bones and sewing him up. He was truly a marvelous patient.

Admiring courage as they do the crew could not help going out for a guy with the guts this merchant seaman showed. They flocked to his bunk day and night, and his slightest wish was a command as far as they were concerned. They want the folks from his home town to know that he is "really a right guy and can take it, but plenty."

The entire crew and armed guard of the *Holt* signed a letter to Vice Admiral Emory S. Land, War Shipping Administrator, to say that thanks to the quick action and superior seamanship of Capt. Lill of the *Holt*, a man's life was saved.

Norris was aboard the DE five weeks, then spent 3 weeks in Staten Island Marine Hospital where he underwent surgery so he could be fitted with an artificial arm. He then returned HOME to stay.[4]

~~~

The final story of this chapter was submitted by Matthew Loughran of Deer Park, New York. Matty survived the war but was almost done in by a vicious storm on May 11, 1945.

I enlisted in the U.S.M.S. on July 10, 1944 at the age of seventeen, after being rejected by the Navy. I took basic training at Sheepshead Bay and shipped on September 12, 1944 on the *Fred W. Weller*, a Standard Oil of New Jersey tanker.

After trips on the *Esso Camden*, and *Esso Raleigh*, I shipped on the *Esso Pittsburgh* as a P.O. Mess on April 17, 1945. We made a run to Curacao, N.W.I., under Captain John Petterson. We loaded 114,031 barrels of Admiralty Fuel Oil and returned in convoy to New York, arriving May 5th. Fortunately, we were home for VE Day and I had a chance to return home which at that time was in Middle Village, New York and celebrate the occasion.

I returned to the ship and sailed on May 9th 1945 at 0530 in a convoy of 45 ships and 6 escort vessels. Two days from New York, we met very rough weather (force 5 to 6) and rough following seas. About 1830 on May 11, 1945, I was sitting in the mess listening to V disc records.* I heard a loud thud and the ship lifted slightly. A crack was discovered in the way of the #5 port wing tank. This did not interfere with our proceeding. At 2150 of the same date I heard another loud thump, the vessel lifted and we discovered cracked plates on the starboard side in the # 4 and #5 wing tanks.

---

* V disks or "Victory Disks" were 12-inch, 78 rpm records containing popular music. They were produced during World War II.

At this time we were sent to our lifeboat stations. I remember the lights were on, and we looked down at the condition of the sea, and I knew the boats could not be lowered. Our ship was rolling and tossing so badly it would have been impossible to launch the boats. We were recalled from abandon ship. I returned to mess and talked about our condition. I remember clearly that standing at the lifeboat and looking at the sea. I was scared shitless! I learned after that we nearly collided with a vessel aft of us (*Macuba*) which was carrying high octane gas.

By 2345 we were cleared of the Convoy (HX-355). The HMCS *Quesnel* K-133 was ordered to stand by and assist us if needed. At 0300 and 0350 on May 12th additional cracking occurred and at 1450 further cracks developed. Believing that the ship could split in half, all crew were ordered aft which was considered safer by Captain Petterson. The ship was steered from the after station.

Because of the condition of the ship, it was decided to reduce the crew. I can remember drawing lots to see who would go. I was a lucky one along with my buddy, Russ Porter (A.B.). At 2000, May 12th, #5 lifeboat was lowered and the 16mm crew and one Armed Guard were moved to the *Quesnel*.

I remember how well we were treated by the Canadian crew. The food was great (creamed cauliflower) which I really enjoy. I think we also received a shot of rum. We slept on cushions in the after part of the ship. We arrived in Halifax on May 14th. The *Pittsburgh* arrived the same date under tow of the *Foundation Franklin*. The cargo was slowly taken off to avoid strain. The divers examined the damage and reported that only the deck plates and keel held her together.

We left Halifax June 3rd and arrived Point Breeze, Philadelphia on June 7, 1945. At the pay off the next day, very few signed aboard for the next trip.

In researching the *Pittsburgh*, I learned that in February 1945 at Ulithi, she fueled the USS *Chipola* (AO63). The fueling took twenty-two hours to discharge and fenders were used. This may have weakened the *Pittsburgh*.[5]

11

LIFE AT SEA
AND
IN PORT

L *ife at sea is an escape from the mundane. Although shipboard life has its monotonous periods, no other occupation affords a person the wealth of beauty, energy and rage that the sea provides. And in World War II, the constant tension of an enemy lurking beneath or above the sea added another element. And yet, these mariners kept going back. Once the salt of the sea gets into a seaman's blood, it courses through his veins forever!*

A major interest aboard ship was food. Emory Land, WSA Administrator, wrote, "Seamen need food — good food. To assure an adequate supply of the best available, the WSA saw to it that ship suppliers had large quantities of scarce stocks of essential foods so that there would be enough on hand at all times to supply ships."[1] For the most part, merchant seaman ate well although at times food did become scarce especially when ships stores were given to troops or when ships ran out of food on extremely long voyages. Captain L. Roy Murray in an interview remarked that once he had to take supplies to Russia via the Pacific. The ship had been at sea for fifty days and off the west coast of Australia they ran out of the their regular fare. So, for the next two to three weeks the ship's crew had only Spam, dried beans, dried eggs and powdered milk.[2]

Aboard ship, recreation consisted of boxing on some ships, exercising with equipment, running on make-shift tracks, throwing balls around, and playing card games, cribbage, chess, checkers, or reading. Shore leave presented other forms of entertainment. The United Seaman's Service, organized by the WSA was comparable to the USO.

> At its peak, USS operated 126 facilities — rest homes, clubs, hotels, recreation centers — on six continents with a total personnel of 2,000. In 1944, about 170,000 American merchant seaman paid more than 2,600,000 visits to these establishments and, from 1942 to May 1, 1945, approximately 1,503,595 overnight accommodations had been provided for seamen.[3]

This chapter will present a few stories which deal with the lighter side of a mariner's life. They are humorous and at the time, were a godsend to keeping one's sanity in a world turned upside down.

~~~

Between November 1943 and March 1944, I served as Purser on the SS *Maria Mitchell*. In early 1944, after completing our mission of delivering military supplies and material for Russia at the Persian Gulf port of Khorramshahr, our ship joined a small convoy at Masriah Island in the Arabian Sea consisting of ten loaded tankers, one troop ship with only its crew and our empty Liberty ship heading for the Red Sea.

The 23rd of February 1944 would prove to be a momentous day that would remain long in my memory. After the evening meal on the 22nd, the ship's baker baked the week's supply of bread and set all the loaves on the galley's serving counter to cool off.

At 0330 of the 23rd, the convoy was attacked by submarines and two tankers were hit. At 0430 another attack and one tanker was hit. At this time GQ was sounded because a torpedo was headed for our midships. With the sounding of GQ at 0430, my mind went blank and I remembered NOTHING until I was aware that I was in my assigned 20mm gun tub. I then discovered that under my left arm was my attache case with all the ship's papers and money, and under my right arm was a loaf of fresh bread.

The drive for survival expresses itself in many ways!

Capt. Winfield H. Adam, (Ret.) USCG[4]

The Maria Mitchell *survived the war and was scrapped in Bilbao, Spain in July 1971.*[5]

~~~

In the Fall of 1944 the S.S. *Makua*, a Transmarine ship, had been lying at anchor in Ulithi for thirty-five days and would remain for an additional two weeks. We had only corned beef hash, dehydrated potatoes, powdered milk, powdered eggs and flour — complete with weevils. We were unable to get additional provisions because of the upcoming invasion of Leyte in the Philippines. Admiral Halsey's fleet was due in early December.

The day before Thanksgiving, we were told we could come over to a concrete barge and pick up Thanksgiving provisions. The Chief Mate, myself, one other A.B. and two Armed Guards took another motor lifeboat about three-fourths of a mile to where the barge was anchored. One A.B. remained in the boat. The four of us went aboard where a Chief Petty officer, with a list, directed us to take two frozen turkeys and then he walked on. I grabbed four, ran to the side and dropped them into the boat, where the man below tucked them under a tarp.

Every time we were given something, we doubled it as soon as the officer's back was turned. Whether he knew what we were doing or not, I still don't know. How they expected fifty men to eat the provisions allotted us is a mystery!

Besides the above, we were able to purloin candy, a couple of hams, canned vegetables and fruit. The boat was loaded when we returned to a "HERO'S WELCOME."

THANKSGIVING DAY WAS A FEAST TO REMEMBER!!

Dick Hanly[6]

~~~

This story was submitted by Joe S. Harris of Ocala, Florida. Joe was a cook and baker in the merchant marine. He sailed all over the world and seemingly had a great and fun-loving time as noted in his experiences. The ships he served on were attacked, bombed, torpedoed and Joe came through it all unscathed. He attributes it to reading the Bible every day while at sea, which he still practices today.

I was seventeen when I graduated from high school in Jonesville, Virginia in 1943. I told daddy and mommy I was going to Kingsport, Tennessee to look for a job and would write them in a few days to let them know where I was staying. But instead of going to Kingsport, I went to Pennington Gap, Virginia and bought a train ticket to California. I knew if I told them I wanted to go to California they would not let me go. I sent them a postal card from Texas, saying, "Somewhere in Texas on the way to California." I went to see my uncle and aunt in Glendale and stayed three months with them, and I worked for Pacific Airmotive in Burbank in the day and in a theater at night.

Then after three months I wanted to serve my country, so I chose the merchant marine. I joined in Los Angeles, September 28th 1943. I took my basic training on Catalina Island at Avalon,

California. Then began my journey that would take me to different parts of the world. Myself and three others were in Cook and Bakers School in New York and we worked part time in a restaurant near by. We roomed on the fifth floor of a rooming house and the man who owned the house kept telling us we were making too much noise and bothering the other tenants. But it wasn't us, it was the roomers next door and we told the owner, but he kept nagging us. So, one night we bought a lot of caramel popcorn and put it on each stair step from the 5th floor down to first floor and ground it in good with our feet. It stuck good on the short nap carpet, and of course he never did know it was us who did it or we would have been kicked out.

I made eleven voyages to different parts of the World, and was always doing something dangerous, or playing a prank on someone. I helped a Frenchman in Le Havre, France stow-away on ship. He was caught three days out of port, but he never told the captain or anyone that I put him on board. And would you believe the captain assigned the Frenchman to me in the galley. So I put him to work peeling potatoes, carrots, and onions. He seemed to like the chores I gave him and he got to eat all he wanted to. When we were one day from the port of New York, the Captain had him locked up so he would not jump ship. I felt sorry for him, as he didn't understand enough English to know why we were locking him up. Next day when we docked, he was taken to Ellis Island to be deported back to France.

Another time I purchased white shirts, sheets, and pillow cases in New York and sold them to the Arabs in Oran, North Africa. When we got shore leave I would always take a buddy with me as the Arabs were not to be trusted. In the streets the Arabs would say, "Joe got any sheets or soap?" They called all Americans "Joe." They would pay a high price for them as certain tribes of them would bury their dead in white, and that is why they were easy to sell. Also, I would buy Octagon soap for 5 cents a bar and sell it for a $1.00 a bar to the Arabs.

Once, a shipmate and myself were at Mindanao, Philippines on shore leave. We came upon a large group of natives that were making their bets for a cock fight about to take place. I slipped to one side of the ring and my shipmate to the other side. We cut the roosters loose and at the same time ran as fast as we could with about half the people after us. If they had caught us they would have killed us as they did not have all their betting done and were not ready to start.

The foreign lands and peoples that I visited were so much different than I expected. In talking to them they thought all Americans were rich. I was quick to tell them that we had the poor and under privileged just as they did.

As I observed the Navy gunners on the ships I was on, I had great respect for them as I knew they had good training and were ready to put it to use. I saw them demonstrate it many times and I even got to help them. After the war was over I was thankful I came through it. And now after a fifty year interval, I am glad I was able to serve my country and I am proud to be an American.[7]

~~~

The following two stories were submitted by Fred Allen of Springfield, Oregon.

The International Hotel

Our arrival in Murmansk was interesting. Several ships were sunk in the harbor and the town had been obliterated by bombing from the German held air fields in Norway. As soon as we tied up, three representatives of the Russian government came aboard. We were to refer to them as the "Unholy Three." They seemed to be led by a rather attractive woman, predictably named "Olga." She and a tall man named Simon did all the talking. The third member was a shorter, brutish looking individual who never spoke at all.

We were given some introductory information, much of it Russian propaganda. However, we were told that entertainment had been arranged for us at "The International Club." It was made quite clear that our wanderings ashore would be between the ship and this hotel.

I am fully aware of the great losses these people had and their determined resistance to the Germans, and, when I comment that the "International Club" was an old warehouse that had miraculously not blown down, I realize it was certainly all that was within their means. So, in the evening after the evening meal, those of us who were inclined, would wander through the debris and rubble to the "Club."

There the ever present and vocal Olga would welcome us. There would be a short propaganda speech, then a movie would be shown on a projector that somehow survived the bombing. I began to realize the movies were American showing strife and suffering in the United States — no Andy Hardy, Fred Astaire or Ginger Rogers bits.

After the movie there would be limited amounts of vodka. This was a greenish hued liquor of amazing potency. The Russians took pride in being able to bolt about three fingers without moving a muscle. This is work for heroes.

The humor showed up in the form of our radio operator. He was a young fellow from Brooklyn. All these kids from Brooklyn learned how to jitterbug at an early age. This is really and advanced art form and requires skill, coordination and a certain amount of inventiveness.

Just after the movie, a truck would back up to the front door and about a dozen Russian girls would hop out. They had somehow learned of this dance craze, probably from the movies, or who really knows.

Our radio operator was named Flatow, and it wasn't surprising that he acquired a nickname of "Flat Top," after a comic character in Dick Tracy. "Flatop," would hold dancing school. The Russian girls would crowd around him trying to be next.

The "Old Man" would come ashore wearing four full stripes and head up to the Club. The girls would ignore him and give complete attention to Flatop. There he would be out on the floor, with the typical bored look, executing perfectly, the intricate steps. The "Old Man" would just simmer.

The Russian girls at the "Club" would be in the charge of a large severe-looking, raw-boned, square-jawed Russian female

Sergeant. There was no foolishness whatsoever. At about 10 P.M. this lady baritone would bellow out something in Russian and the girls would scramble to get back in the truck. We never knew where they came from or where they went.[8]

Bernie Flatow is a member of AMMV [American Merchant Marine Veterans] — North Atlantic Chapter. I met Bernie at the October 1997 meeting and Fred Allen's story arrived two weeks later. I related it to Bernie who commented, "It was all true!"

July 1943. We came into Table Bay, Cape Town, and dropped the hook. We were on our way home from Suez, where we had dropped a load of goodies, mostly ammunition, for our 8th Army.

The problem was that we were anchored way out in the bay and it was necessary to get a bum boat to get back to the ship. The Chief Steward and I had come off the ship in the afternoon with the agent.

It was now late in the evening and we were weary after exploring the local soft drink industry and Seaman's Missions. Getting a bum boat was out of the question, so we accepted the fact we would have to seek accommodations ashore. The prestige hotel in Cape Town is the Assembly. We were told that there were no rooms left, but he gave us the address of another hostelry.

I suspected at the time that the hotel had a general rule of not renting to merchant seamen, and one cannot really fault this house policy. A taxi deposited us at the entrance to an establishment called the Avalon. Not four star, but not bad either.

On registering, I noted the Registration Book had recent entries of early American political leaders. There was Mr. and Mrs. Hamilton, Mr. and Mrs. Madison, just to mention a few. I strongly suspected these were not the true names of the guests and decided to break with tradition. I registered as Felix Mendelsohn.

You know how it is, sometimes late at night you think you are so clever. After a brief argument as to how many letter "s" were in Mendelsohn, we were requested to retire for the evening.

This we did and then came down for breakfast in the morning. The steward and I had the shock of our lives. There were Mr. and Mrs. Hamilton, Mr. and Mrs. Madison, etc., dining. But the gentleman part of each duo were remarkably like our shipmates. The ladies were what you might call non-descript.

The steward and I warmly greeted them by their names we had seen in the registry the night before. They seemed uncomfortable with our cheery greetings.[9]

~~~

The next story concerns recreation aboard ship. The story was sent by Thomas Quinn of McKeesport, Pennsylvania, and relates the exciting build-up for a boxing match.

My merchant marine service encompassed twenty trips (troops, equipment transportation,) crossing the Atlantic, three voyages into the Mediterranean and a trip to Calcutta, India and around the world. Our ship shuttled eight trips from Southampton, England to both Omaha and Utah beachheads which our ship drew enemy fire and eight personnel were wounded, but no casualties. We kept right on doing our duty. But the most interesting and memorable voyage was the eight-month trip around the world.

Aboard this relatively new C-2 vessel was an excellent merchant marine crew and very friendly Armed Guard buddies. We got to know almost all by name and their back-home environments, stories, pictures and past love-affairs.

The Armed Guard crew was under the command of a twenty-four-year-old ensign, fresh out of Officer's Training School. He was a strapping muscular man, about six feet, three inches on a 190 lb. frame. He was very athletic with a great high school or college background of sports in a small Minnesota town. After a few months aboard the ship, the Ensign became very friendly and spent much of his time with the crews. He was constantly jogging around a crew-made track around the outer perimeter of the ship, weight lifting, shadow boxing, doing push-ups and training. He was a well-defined, good-looking, impressive person.

In the merchant marine crew there was a sort of quiet professional boxer (age twenty-six) with three professional fights which he won, all by knock-outs. He fought in the 150-160 lb. class under the name of "Kid Chicago." He was a bookworm, always reading and a library regular. He was absolutely uninterested in the training facilities; however, he was built with arms of steel — very huge and muscular. When we crossed the equator, "Kid Chicago," was reluctant to go through the paddle wheel rite, but eventually did, and this seemed to loosen him up to becoming more friendly.

After several weeks passed and the good relationships of the mostly young officers and seamen developed further, the crews built a boxing ring on the after deck which led to some boxing matches. None of the matches were serious, but when you were off watch duty, it was something to do.

Some of the guys were good at weight lifting and general calisthenics which now "Kid Chicago," would sometimes take a small part in. He would take part in the general exercising and using the large punching bag.

However, "Kid Chicago," constantly refused to step in the ring. As time went by, he was requested and later harassed about fighting the well-trained ensign. The ensign was willing to go for a three-round friendly match, but "Kid Chicago," always refused saying, "I can't fight a friendly match."

As time went by, there came a day when a make-believe promoter arranged for a three-round Sunday match at 1:00 PM, weather permitting. Our ship was on its way to Cape Town without a naval escort and it was sure hot in the Southern Hemisphere. The promoter decided to change the match time to 9:00 AM. All of this information was heard over the ship's loudspeaker system. Most every sailor was on deck for the ship's main event.

The bell rang, the ensign danced around the ring jabbing lefts and dropping back. After doing this maneuvering for about a minute or two, "Kid Chicago," followed the ensign on the drop back and threw two punches. The Ensign was down and knocked-out. The audience went silent.

The cruise continued and we docked in New York, but conditions on board ship were never the same. We were all friendly, but there wasn't the same old camaraderie. However, there were no hard feelings among the crew.[10]

~~~

The following story was submitted by Peter Salvo of Pennsylvania. The story was submitted by him to the Liberty Ship Archives of the S.S. John W. Brown *Museum.*

It was in the summer of 1943 and we were leaving Santos, Brazil aboard the Liberty ship S.S. *Joseph Wheeler.* We accompanied another Liberty ship and we were without an escort. A few miles out to sea, a German sub was waiting for us. The other ship was hit, but we escaped back to port.

Word spread fast that an American ship was sunk. The natives of Santos, seeing us return, thought we were the survivors and they gave us a large party. We had a ball, eating their food, drinking their liquor and entertaining their daughters!

But the next day the real survivors came ashore and we had a lot of explaining to do to the natives of Santos as we were running toward our ship.

On the next voyage, the S.S. *Joseph Wheeler* was one of seventeen Allied ships sunk at Bari, Italy. There was a heavy loss of life when a German plane dropped tin foil over the harbor, knocking out the radar system and allowing their bombers a field day. We referred to this event as the "Pearl Harbor of Europe."[11]

~~~

The following story was sent by George H. Marks, Sr. of Connecticut.

I shipped out on this Army transport enroute to San Juan, Puerto Rico on August 31, 1942. This was formerly a Staten Island Ferry traveling between St. George, Staten Island and South Ferry, Manhattan, New York. There was a twelve man crew plus officers. I shipped as an A.B. (Able Bodied Seaman). This was a twelve day trip with one stop at Guantanimo Bay, Cuba. We ran out of water several days out and we all bathed nude on deck during any rain storm. I often wonder what a German submarine officer was thinking when and if he saw this double ender going south along the coast. I'm sure he could not find it in his silhouette book on Allied ships. We did make it and for four months we sailed to all the islands from Jamaica to Trinidad carrying native troops. Because of illness I had to leave and never heard of the ship's fate.[12]

12

D-Day

A *s the German war machine began to collapse, the question became not if continental Europe would be invaded but where. The obvious place was Calais, at the narrowest point in the English Channel. Other landing sites were debated and a decision was made to invade from Normandy. The invasion plan was code-named "Operation Overlord."*

Although much of its infantry was destroyed in Russia, the remaining German army was still a formidable force. The Normandy beaches were well-protected and their defense the responsibility of none other than Field Marshal Erwin Rommel. Fortunately for the Allies, the German high command considered the landings at Normandy a diversion, designed to draw their attention away from Calais.

The invasion force was the greatest assembled in the history of man. Supreme Allied Commander General Dwight D. Eisenhower, after intensive deliberation of strategic considerations and weather reconnaisance, selected a two day period, June 5-6, 1944 for the invasion. The weather turned stormy, but a small clearing trend was forecast and General Eisenhower said, "Go," on June 6th which became known as D-Day. * "Over 1,300 warships, 1,600 merchant ships, and 4,000 landing ships were available for the liberation campaign together with 13,000 aircraft (including 5,000 fighters, and 4,000 bombers) and 3,500 gliders."[1]*

During the first days more than 150,000 men and nearly 7,000 vehicles were put ashore. By the end of the month there were almost a million men, over half a million tons of supplies, and more than 100,000 vehicles of various kinds.

There were two major obstacles to overcome: first, enormous amounts of equipment and supplies had to be brought ashore at Normandy, and second, there were no ports to disembark the men and materials. To keep the supply lines open, two artificial harbors (code-named Mulberries) were constructed. The need to protect these harbors from rough waters was vital. Hence breakwaters (Gooseberries) were created by sinking ships and huge floating caissons (Phoenixes) that were towed from England. These artificially-protected harbors were large enough to accommodate seven Liberty ships. Floating roads and rail track were also constructed in these artificial harbors.

... 32 American merchant ships were to be sunk off the beachhead to form a breakwater. They were manned by more than 1,000 merchant seaman and officers who volunteered for the hazardous duty. These ships, many of which had previously suffered severe battle damage, were charged with explosives for quick scuttling. They sailed from England through mined waters, filed into position off the Normandy beach under severe shelling from German shore batteries, and were sunk by the crews to form the artificial harbor. Behind this breakwater, prefabricated units were towed in to handle the subsequent debarkation of men and equipment, to make invasion of Fortress Europe possible.

---

* All debarkation days are known as D-Day, just as all hours of attack are known as H-Hour. This particular debarkation day became so famous it has become "the" D-Day.

Ten oceangoing Tugs operated by the WSA and manned by merchant crews assisted in the famous Mulberry operation by towing the harbor units into position. Seven of these tugs had towed pre-built sections from the United States to England en route to their assignment. From D-day until the last tug departed the Channel area, they towed 182 units including 75 "phoenixes," . . . plus 27 disabled ships from the landing area back to the safety of British harbors. This project stands as one of the most remarkable water-borne engineering accomplishments of all time.

All merchant seaman and officers in the operation were commended and the ten masters of the tugs decorated by Admiral Sir Bertram H. Ramsey, Allied Naval Commander in Chief...

Later, the English Channel was nicknamed by the merchant crews "Liberty Lane," because of the number of these cargo ships ferrying back and forth in a shuttle run supplying the Anglo-American armies in France.[2]

How important was the United States Merchant Marine to the D-Day invasion? Supreme Commander General Dwight D. Eisenhower said:

Every man in the Allied command is quick to express his admiration for the loyalty, courage, and fortitude of the officers and men of the Merchant Marine. We count upon their efficiency and their utter devotion to duty as we do our own; they have never failed us yet and in all the struggles yet to come we know that they will never be deterred by any danger, hardship, or privation.

When final victory is ours there is no organization that will share its credit more deservedly than the Merchant Marine.[3]

~~~

This story was submitted by Lester E. Ellison. He wrote: "Very little has been written about the important part played by merchant mariners on U.S. Army Tugs, during the Normandy Invasion. I was at Omaha Beach from 0600 on June 7, 1944 to August 28, 1944 on U.S. Army Tugs ST-761 and ST-247."[4]

My sea career started October 12, 1942 when I reported to the United States Merchant Marine Academy. My first trip to sea was on the MS *West Grama*, built in 1919 in Los Angeles. This freighter was deliberately sunk on June 8, 1944 as part of Gooseberry 1, breakwater in Mulberry "A," an artificial harbor at Omaha Beach … It was sad to see the first ship I sailed on being sunk. The captain on the MS *West Grama* had very little use for cadets, his orders were to give them all the dangerous assignments. If they got killed, there would be very little lost. This trip ended April 17, 1943. Under this captain I learned what work was and how to do it.

After sailing on various Liberty ships, I went to work for the Army Transportation Corp. as the mate on a U.S. Army Tug, and I was soon on my way to Europe. This was February 1944. The next few months were spent training. Little did I know that we would be at Omaha Beach at 0600 on D+1 to build and operate an artificial harbor. We were issued an AGO Card by the U.S. Army which read as follows:

> This is to certify that Lester E. Ellison whose signature, photograph and fingerprints appear hereon, is a civilian, employed as First Officer with the Armed Forces of the United States; that, as such, he is an noncombatant and is entitled to the law and usages of war.

Launched in 1918 in Los Angeles, the West Grama *was operated by Grace Line, Inc. for the War Shipping Administration. Mariners Museum, Newport News, Virginia.*

Meanwhile, as we were pushing a barge loaded with ammunition to the beach that had not been cleared of mines, and the bullets and shells were all around us, I had the feeling that we were more than noncombatants.[5]

Tugs and the Normandy Invasion

The Normandy Invasion was a massive Allied effort and the beginning of a turning point in the war. Among the Allied naval forces preparing to confront the Germans were six battleships, twenty-three cruisers, 105 destroyers, 1,076 other warships like minesweepers and anti-submarine vessels, 2,500 landing craft and 2,700 merchant ships. There were 158 tugs involved in Operation Mulberry.

The Mulberries, the two artificial harbors established immediately after the initial landings, were absolutely essential for the success of the Normandy Invasion. For, as we found out in World War II, the most difficult thing in the amphibious operation is not to establish the initial beachhead (that can almost always be done if sufficient force is employed) but to sustain and reinforce the ground troops. Massive as was the assault on the Normandy beaches, it had to be followed immediately by even greater increments of men, armor, vehicles and supplies to make it succeed. There was no possibility of getting all this ashore over wave-lashed beaches where spring tides rose twenty-one feet. One or more ports were essential to maintain an even flow of men and material. But all the French (ports), notably the nearest ones at Cherbourg and Le Havre, were so strongly held by the enemy that the capture of one would employ forces badly needed elsewhere for at least six weeks.

The Task Force commander, Captain A. Dayton Clark, participated in the planning, the training and the execution, of Operation Mulberry. The need of secrecy was so paramount that very few men among the detailed planners knew what the entire operation was about. The Phoenixes — enormous concrete caissons as big as a five-story apartment house; the Whales — pontoon-supported ramps capable of handling heavy armor; and the Gooseberries — vessels to be sunk as an outer line of protection — had to be built or procured at a dozen different ports of the United Kingdom. Men had to be specially trained to operate them, tugs procured to tow them, combatant ships found to escort them, salvage and towboat experts engaged who were capable of solving these new and unprecedented problems . . .

For training, the crew on the U.S. Army Tug *ST 761* practiced moving the Phoenix units and block ships that would be sunk to create Mulberry "A," an artificial port that the Americans undertook (with Mulberry "B," by the British) to permit the landing for the invasion of Europe. These Phoenix units had never been moved through the English Channel. We trained under various conditions, taking off from the Isle of Wight, off the coast of England into the Channel. There was a tremendous tide and the current there is very swift. Each tug was assigned to a different work area. In our group, four tugs were required to hold one block ship in position while it was being sunk. They (the block ships) had dynamite charges in them, which just blew their bottoms and sides out. The tugs had to hold them in position while they sank in fifteen or twenty feet of water.

Besides sinking concrete Phoenix units designed to make the harbor, old and newer ships consigned to this purpose were sent to the bottom. Among them was the MS *West Grama.*

Participating in the Normandy invasion was particularly hazardous duty. First, there was the matter of the explosive designed to scuttle the ships. Then there were the Germans firing away at anything that moved in the harbor or on the beach. The danger of being struck by a floating mine was ever-present. And then there were activities that, because of the size and complexity of the invasion, couldn't go by "standard operating procedure."

We were assigned to move a barge loaded with ammunition onto a beach that had not been cleared of mines. It was just one of those things you're told to do, and you do it. Usually, the beach would have been swept for mines first. But they needed the ammunition on the beach.

Luckily, we carried out our assignment without mishap. But now I think back to how deadly the Normandy Invasion proved to be. It didn't get dark until around 11 o'clock at night. Then we would tie up alongside a block ship and try to get some

ST-type tugs were medium-sized tugs designed for harbor work. Their diesel engine developed 400 horsepower. Marine Engineering.

sleep. The first thing we'd have to do in the morning was to remove the bodies that had washed up between the tug and the block ships. We saw many bodies of dead soldiers.

The American Mulberry "A," was assembled off Omaha Beach on D-plus-8-day (14 June 1944), twenty-four hours ahead of the expected time. That in itself was a marvelous achievement, and it functioned so smoothly that on 14-18 June inclusive an average of 8,500 tons of cargo poured ashore over it daily. Then, on 20 June, there blew up the strongest summer gale known in the English Channel for forty years. At the end of two days bashing by wind and waves, and vessels that dragged anchors and pounded against it, Mulberry "A," looked like a complete wreck. But the officers and men responsible for it managed by extraordinary energy, resourcefulness and a complete disregard for the common necessities of food, shelter and sleep, to repair Mulberry "A," so that on 23 June the tonnage landed rose to 10,000 tons and on the 26th to 14,500. The other U.S. installation off Utah Beach, which had some natural protection from the Cherbourg Peninsula, came through the storm almost intact and the British Mulberry "B," behind Calvados Reef survived.

During most of the storm, we did rescue work evacuating soldiers off the Phoenixes who were their gun crews. After the storm subsided on June 22, we were among the tugs helping to restore Mulberry "A," as much as possible. Merchant ships were used to plug holes in the breakwater. Then we were among the tugs operating the harbor.

I should add that at this time we were under command of the U.S. Navy. Even at this date it is hard to explain to anyone that you were a merchant mariner, sailing with the U.S. Army Transport, under the command of the U.S. Navy. We arrived at Omaha Beach at 0600 on June 7th 1944 and were there until August 28, 1944. For the work we did at Omaha Beach, we received two letters of Commendation.

One, from the commander of Task Force 128 (Captain A.D. Clark, U.S. Navy). It reads, in part:

> To the officers and men of your craft, I wish to convey my heart (felt) commendation for the assignment well done off the U.S. Assault Beaches in the Baie de la Seine during the Allied invasion of France in June 1944. Your craft served with the U.S. Naval Forces under my command and rendered loyal and efficient service which contributed to the successful accomplishment of the mission. It was a pleasure to have such an able and willing team in my organization.

We also received a letter dated 10 August 1944, marked SECRET, from the Harbor Master of U.S. Naval Advance Base 11 (Lieut E. B. Olsen, USN). It reads:

> ST-761 - Operations of.
>
> 1. Since its arrival at this Base, D plus One at 0500 hours, subject tug has participated in many varied activities which contribute to the success of the operation. Of these activities the formation of an artificial harbor was the most important, during which time subject tug assisted in the siting of over fifty (50) Phoenix units, weighing from three to six thousand tons each, and twenty-three (23) block ships. The formation of this artificial harbor made it possible for the successful landing of many important troops, vehicles, and supplies. Besides assisting in the siting of the above, subject tug has also assisted in many salvage operations and general harbor tug work.

2. During the period from 6 June 1944 through 10 August 1944, subject tug has not missed one day or night of operations for any reason and has been ready for any assignment at any time.

3. In adequately performing the above duties, it has sometimes been necessary to expend the subject tug and its gear, because of the nature of its duties, at times in the open channel, in all conditions of wind and weather, day or night, subject tug received a most serious pounding, which accounts for the present condition of tug, and its gear.

4. To the Officers and men of U.S. Army Tug *ST 761*, we express our sincerest gratitude for a difficult operation very well done, under the most trying conditions of wind, weather, and enemy action.

I am proud as a Merchant Mariner to have participated in the Normandy Invasion some 50 years ago.[6]

~~~

Richard Powers of Jupiter, Florida, wrote the following story which was published on June 6, 1994, 50 years after D-Day.

D-Day 1944

On the first day of March 1944, in Baltimore, Maryland, the WSA (War Shipping Administration) told me to report to the S.S. *Vitruvius,* a ship docked in Baltimore. The WSA informed me it was to be delivered to England, and afterwards, I was to return to the States on the *Queen Mary.* This sounded great, and I couldn't wait to get aboard and get that ship delivered.

After getting aboard and looking around I couldn't help but notice this was a different ship from anything I had been on before. It was made of concrete!! From stem to stern it was solid concrete. I thought, will this thing float? And if so, will it get us across the Atlantic? In the ship's hold, workers were loading thousands of tons of lumber. This made me feel somewhat better!

We left Baltimore the second of March and met our convoy of ships just outside of Charleston, S.C.. There were fifteen very old ships, the oldest being the S.S. *Olambala* built in 1901, and many World War I ships. Our convoy left for England March 10th, and our average speed was three knots. It took thirty-six days to arrive in Liverpool, England. Once in Liverpool, we started unloading the lumber and I asked about the trip back on the *Queen Mary*, but no one could give me a straight answer. News spread that there was a concrete ship in port and lots of Englishmen came to see the ship. Some with walking canes tapped on the sides to make sure it was concrete.

After all the cargo was unloaded we just sat there with nothing happening until one day a group of army engineers came aboard with cases of dynamite and started putting it in the hold of the ship. The next thing I knew it's the 1st day of June and we are headed out for sea with a ship full of dynamite!! About two days out, the captain called "All Hands On Deck," pulled out an envelope with a letter from General Eisenhower telling us this was the big one and we will be part of the D-Day invasion. We rendezvoused at Portsmouth, England with thirty-two ships to be used as blockships to make a breakwater so other ships could dock and let off supplies to our troops.

We were in France on D-Day and what a sight to see! Troopships, battleships, every kind of ship you could think of were there, and plenty of action going on by the Germans, our troops, and Navy ships, as well as aircraft. We were supposed to be in place and sunk on D-Day, but due to German fire, didn't

The John Smeaton, *above, was a sister ship to the* Vitruvius. *Built in Tampa, Florida of concrete over reinforced steel, the ships were propelled by a 1,300 horsepower triple expansion steam reciprocating engine. Their top speed was seven knots. Bob Childs collection.*

make it until D+4. Before the engineers sunk our ship, a troop ship picked us up. Looking back at our ship we saw a big puff of smoke and our ship sank quickly to the bottom in the shallow water, with about half the ship still showing.

The troop ship took us to Bournemouth, England, where the British gave us a good meal of cabbage, boiled potatoes, and hard rolls. We really lapped it up as our ship had all but run out of food. From Bournemouth everyone was put on board the *Queen Mary* to return to the States, but I decided to stay longer. I volunteered to stay as a replacement for anyone who got sick or hurt and had to be replaced. In July I was told to report to Belfast, Ireland as a replacement on a Liberty ship. I returned to the States that August. I missed my chance to come home on the *Queen Mary*![7]

~~~

Peter J. Dilullo of McKeesport, Pennsylvania submitted the following story describing his experience aboard one of the Tug boats used in the D-Day activities.

I worked on Tug *ST-247* all through the Normandy invasion. There is very little written on the part we played, but we were there!

About twelve men went aboard the *247* in Liverpool. We sailed her down to the Isle of Wight (south of Southampton) and joined the convoy to Utah beachhead. We worked there about a week and went up to Omaha beachhead. We helped line up ships and then sunk them to build a harbor. In the process, we hit some underwater obstruction and began taking on water. We ran her aground where it took the Army welders about three days to repair the bottom. All this work was soon destroyed by a large storm (*The American Mulberry Harbor at Omaha Beach was destroyed in the "Great Storm" with over thirty knot gale winds from June 19-23, 1944, seriously damaging the flow of equipment and supplies to the front lines.*), but we did the job until Cherbourg was taken. We were then ordered to run a supply dump for our ships.

It was interesting being a merchant mariner (civilian) and then working for the Army. A friend of mine was hit by shell fire on a Liberty ship that took part in the invasion. He survived and so did I. As a young man it was fun just being there![8]

~~~

Walter W. Luikart, who contributed an earlier story to this anthology, kept a diary of his D-Day shuttling experiences aboard the S.S. Nicholas Herkimer.

This ship was the most interesting of the nine I was on. I signed on as an Ordinary Seaman and we left New York on May 26th in a dense fog and joined a convoy of sixty-nine ships and eight escorts. On May 28 we were joined by thirty-three more which included converted carriers. I kept a diary of this voyage every day and herein is the condensed version:

6/7/44 — mines sighted. Gas masks issued to Merchant Crew. Moving from anchorage to anchorage and dock to dock because of broken crane.

6/23/44 — received word or rumor that we were to remain in this area for indefinite time for operational duty. In Glasgow we resupplied the ship. We have sailed from N.Y. to Glasgow to Milford Haven to Southampton. From there we made eight shuttles to Utah Beach, three more to Normandy Beach, one run to Rouen, from Rouen to Cherbourg, one run from Southampton to Le Havre, one from Southampton to Cherbourg, one more from Southhampton to Le Havre, and Southampton to New York.

6/25/44 — we had an air attack today and all the ships at the anchorage opened up to get this one lone plane. They all must have missed and it looked like the Fourth of July, all put together. These are some of the interesting things that occurred on these shuttles:

1st Shuttle 7/11-7/15/44 - In Glasgow we took on 550 troops for the run to Southampton. We removed the torpedo nets and rigged for smoke and attached the balloon (The

Barrage Balloon was an antiaircraft device that was attached to a steel cable. It was flown to deter German pilots from sweeping in low over the ships. The cable could very easily rip through the wing of a diving plane.) The balloon was lost the first day. We also had a general alarm because flying bombs from the shore batteries were dropping in our area. There were sixteen Libertys and three escorts in this crossing. We anchored at the beachhead and could hear heavy firing because we were close to the front lines and we could see the flashes from gun fire. We unloaded and returned to Southampton.

2nd Shuttle 7/19-7/26/44 - The second trip we had an artillery battalion, and again we attached a balloon for the trip. This trip was rough with choppy seas and heavy winds and rain that kept the troops in the hole most of the time. What a mess as there seemed to be not enough barges to unload the ships.

3rd Shuttle 7/31-8/9/44 - On the third trip we carried 510 Free French officers and men. It was not uncommon for the winches to malfunction and on this trip we snapped a cable and it took us five days to unload cargo.

4th Shuttle 8/13-8/19/44 - We carried troops and vehicles on this trip. The weather was rough and we lost our balloon and it took us four days to discharge the cargo.

5th-7th Shuttles 8/21-9/16/44 - routine trips.

8th Shuttle 9/21-9/28/44 - Was a routine trip except for heavy fog and weather. We moved very slowly because of it, and we had trouble with the jumbo boom. The unloading took five days. The ships supplies were getting very low.

9th Shuttle 10/5-10/25/44 - We made very slow progress because of gale force winds on Oct. 6. We had damage to cargo because of shifting and badly secured cargo. I think the *Charles Morgan* got bombed today and abandoned. (*The* Morgan *was bombed and sunk on June 10, 1944 off Utah Beach.... an Able Seaman and seven U.S. Army men were killed.*[9] *The ship that Walter was referring to was the SS* Elinor Wylie *which was mined on Oct. 6, off the southern coast of France, towed to Toulon to discharge and then towed to Oran, Algeria by a U.S. Navy Tug for repairs. There were no casualties.*[10]) We departed for Omaha Beachhead where we remained at anchor for eight days because of a blackout which prevented us from working at night. During this stay we were also ordered to dock, but then had to return to the anchorage because we were the wrong ship.

10th Shuttle 10/29-11/19/44 - We carried 150 troops and had bad weather.

11th Shuttle 11/21-11/30/44 - We departed for France, but after ten miles out we were called back for some unknown reason. Some of the crew had been picked up by the SUP [Shore Patrol] in Southampton and five of them were brought to headquarters. If it wasn't for the chief mate they would have been jailed. He demanded to see the commander of the outfit. He successfully told the guy off about how the Navy and Army were crapping on the merchant marine and that they weren't going to do that to the guys on his ship and they let them go. I can attest to the plight of the merchant marine because if we wanted to send something home we had about ten miles of red-tape whereas servicemen had no trouble at all. It was as if we were the enemy.

The trip got more interesting as we went up the Seine River to Rouen, France. The country was beautiful, but kind of beat up. When we went ashore we were challenged a number of times because of the curfew in effect. One of the AB's could speak French and he got acquainted with some of the people. Their stories were fascinating, especially about the Germans taking seventy-five hostages for every German that was killed.

We picked up troops here and went to Cherbourg on 11/29 and unloaded them and picked up some Polish, French, Czechs and Germans. I think they were refugees and we took them to Southampton. Last night we lost our anchor and drifted about four miles. No one knew it was gone until we heaved the anchor line up. When I was ashore I picked up a lot of 20mm shells and we saw a lot of land mines that were disarmed, but we were warned against wandering off too far.

In Cherbourg I had an artist come ashore and for a couple of bucks he drew a picture of my girl friend. I still have it on display in my home. It was a good likeness.

There was a prisoner of war working our ship and I was able to get a brass submarine. I think the brass work was beautiful. I also got a second brass sub which I keep in my den and some day may donate to the Soldiers and Sailors Hall in Pittsburgh.

13th Shuttle 12/3-12/12/44 - We went to Le Havre on the 4th and we were met with a heck of a storm. We left the anchorage at 0130 and because of the severe weather we turned back. We left again at 0400 and we turned back a second time. At 0730 we were turned back a third time. We remained there for the night and left on the 6th. I can remember standing watch on the bridge and looking down at the ongoing destruction on the deck where trucks, Jeeps, trailers and even a bulldozer were smashing all over the deck. I thought I was watching a movie, it was very exciting. We arrived in Le Havre on Dec. 6.

14th Shuttle 12/17-12/21/44 - This trip was to Cherbourg.

15th Shuttle 12/25/44 - This trip was the last one and we went to LeHarve. There were many ships tied up there and we were tied up alongside another Liberty. We found out that they had clothing aboard. When we left the States we had only light clothing because of the time and not knowing that we would be gone so long. So, we pilfered the #4 hold and came up with some nice sweaters that were, of course, G.I. issue. We got some booze and had the third mate go aboard the other ship and keep the watch officer and crew busy. We lowered a line from our ship down the hole and winched up a couple of boxes of goods. It was very welcomed. Our skipper found out what was happening and from then on he called us the *Herkimer* Pirates.

On Dec. 30 we received orders to proceed to Bristol Channel. This was welcome news because it looked like we may be on our way home. From there we went to Swansea where we had some much needed liberty or shore time.

On Jan. 10 we joined the balance of the convoy and proceeded to New York arriving on Jan. 26, 1945. This ended my voyage on my third ship.[11]

The Nicholas Herkimer *was scrapped in Green Cove Springs, Florida in September 1967.*[12]

~~~

The final entry in this chapter is a letter written by the Deputy Administrator of the WSA, Captain Edward Macauley, USN, Retired.

An Open Letter to the American Seaman

The men of the Merchant Marine were among the first to see the issues of this war plainly. You were the first Americans to volunteer and your brothers of the sea were the first Americans to die in this fight for freedom. The landings on the shores of France are the fruits of their sacrifice.

In the name of those dead comrades I call on every seaman ashore to return to the sea to finish the task which they began. Our nation and the Allied cause need you. Many seamen have been drafted and many, many replacements are required to keep our ships sailing.

In the precise timing of the great invasion machine, the Merchant Marine is an integral and essential gear. On the Channel beachheads and beyond, our heroic fighting men of the Armed Forces are counting on the fighting Merchant Marine. I know you will not fail them. The food, equipment, ammunition and supplies which are the very blood of the invasion will be delivered. Stock piles, long building for this day, as they are used up will be built again. Across the Atlantic, across the Channel, the bridge of supplies which you held so long and against such odds will continue to hold secure. You will deliver the goods. God speed you.

Capt. Edward Macauley, U.S.N. (Retired)[13]

13

THE LAST TRIP

*J*ust as the first voyage for most mariners remains etched in
their memories, so does the last. But that last trip carries
with it something extra — a bit more nostalgia — at the
knowledge that life at sea is coming to an end.

The first story was contributed by Bill Erin of Boulder
City, Nevada.

My last trip during World War II began on July 20, 1944,
when I signed on the S.S. *Abbot L. Mills* in New York. As soon
as the crew was aboard, we took off for Norfolk to load the ship
and join a convoy which we later learned was headed for North
Africa.

Some nosing around by crew members revealed that we
were loading high explosives in the forward holds. This spread
quickly through the crew and left many in panic. Some tried to
get off the ship, but this had been anticipated and SP's (Shore

Patrol) were stationed at the gangplank. You needed a pass to get off and the captain wasn't issuing any.

A few even feigned illness and claimed they needed medical attention. They got it in the from of a Navy doctor who came aboard to examine them and refused to let them off the ship. As soon we were loaded we anchored away from the dock.

I was on the 12-4 watch with the first mate who turned out to have been promoted much too quickly for his ability and who made the trip memorable with his blunders. The first of these occurred two or three days out from Norfolk when the convoy was hit by one of those unbelievably strong North Atlantic storms. We were the lead ship of the next to last column on the port side of the convoy. By midnight when our watch took over, the Liberty was being thrown as much as twenty degrees on the compass by some of the waves that hit her. The waves that got under her shook her like a dog shaking a rag doll.

I had the first shift on the wheel on our watch the night the storm was at its worst and as far as I could determine, we caught a glimpse now and then of the ship to our starboard. By the end of our watch, however, the convoy to our starboard was no longer in sight. As dawn came, the mate had us off on our own somewhere leading the ships behind us in our line and the column to our left. We had our own little squadron.

It wasn't too long before a destroyer escort appeared and led the two columns back to the main convoy. The captain wasn't the only one who was furious. The commodore moved our ship back to the rear of our line.

The next blunder came when we entered the Strait of Gibraltar. The Strait is so narrow that the convoy had to thin out and pass through in a double line. We could see the Germans on the Spanish coast with huge telescopes noting the ships and their deck cargoes. The trick was to get through as fast as possible and form up the convoy again on the other side before the German bombers hit us.

Our two columns were the first to enter and, as it was our fo'c'sle's watch, the captain put me on the wheel because I had negotiated the Strait before. With the ships two abreast, the rocks to our starboard were close and very visible.

We were the last ship in line, but the next two columns snugged up right behind us. When we were about half-way through, the commodore, in the lead ship, cleared the Strait and struck the flags signaling a starboard turn in line. In other words, when we reached the position he was at, we were to turn right as he was now doing. When the First Mate saw the flags struck he ordered me, "Hard right."

Having been there before, and seeing the rocks not more than a couple of ship lengths to our starboard, I did something not in the book. I questioned the order. "Hard right, sir? Are you sure?"

"Hard right!" he yelled angrily. I saw the captain on the starboard bridge wing so I said a silent prayer and brought the wheel over enough to start the bow bobbing its way right. Almost immediately the captain stormed into the wheelhouse.

"What the hell's going on? Bring her back — hard left!" I was turning back almost before he gave the order and we didn't go into the rocks.

Now we entered the Mediterranean and made our right turn in order. The ships ahead slowed down to let the rest of the convoy get through the Strait and form up before we could get hit. The first mate, however, was delinquent in ordering the engine room to cut speed and we came right up the stern of the ship ahead. Now I was happy to obey a hard left order, but that wheeled us over toward the starboard side of the ship in the next column so we also had to pull out of line.

The mate panicked and signaled the engine room to stop. So we quickly lost headway which caused the ship behind us to pull out causing the ship next to it to also pull out of line. By this time there were about six big, clumsy freighters floundering around at all angles and more coming through the Strait.

At this point, the signalman on the commodore's ship started blinking furiously at us. Our Navy signalman was out on the port bridge wing and started writing on a pad. The mate opened the wheelhouse door and shouted at him, "Well, what's he saying?"

"He says, sir," the signalman said, "For Christ's sake get in line or get out of the convoy!"

Fortunately, the Germans were apparently too busy in Northern Europe fending off our invasion there that they didn't have anything left to throw at us and this time we were not attacked.

We went to a port in North Africa called Mers el Kebir and anchored out. This was puzzling. What was going on? Who was going to get the ammo and other supplies we had aboard? We were not allowed off the ship for any liberty because our operation was supposed to be highly secret. However, here we were in the midst of this huge convoy of ships. How could we be secret?

Somehow the rumor spread through the ship: We were headed for the Southern France invasion. I'll never figure out how anyone got that information, but it proved to be true. The problem was we sat in that hell-hole of a harbor in a blazing African sun for a solid month before we finally weighed anchor and headed for Toulon.

Because we had left the States in such a hurry to make our convoy, we had not fully re-supplied the ship. We ran out of fresh water and had to shower in sea water with that awful salt-water soap that never made any suds. We ran out of meat and got some Army rations aboard. The flour became infested with weevils, but we ate and it joked that is was the only protein we were getting.

The steel decks were so hot by mid-day that it was difficult to walk on them with shoes on. It was even too hot to do the traditional chipping (paint scraping) over the side with which captains traditionally kept crews busy. We couldn't go ashore, but the captain let us put a lifeboat in the water with a single sail and we did get some recreation and swimming that way. Sleeping was difficult not only because of the heat, but the Navy patrolling among the ships with small boats discharging small depth charges at regular intervals. This was meant to keep saboteurs from swimming out underwater with explosives and attaching them to the hulls of the ships. It had to be done, but the constant banging and clanging at night was not conducive to peaceful slumber.

We became so bored that one day we decided to try out the survival suits that hung in every fo'c'sle. On the wall was a large poster with instructions on how to use these. You were supposed to be able to get into one in thirty seconds before plunging into the North Atlantic. It was supposed to protect you against the freezing temperatures. It was a rubberized, insulated coverall that zipped up tight to the neck and was supposed to be waterproof. After the war I read in *Reader's Digest* a story about a merchant mariner who had been torpedoed in the North Atlantic and got into one of these suits before going overboard. He got on a raft with four other sailors. When a DE (Destroyer Escort) picked them up the next morning, the other four were dead but he was still alive. However, he had to have both arms and legs amputated. I wonder if it was worth it.

We had an ordinary (seamen) aboard who was a fat, jolly little guy and who had become the butt of most jokes. So we decided to put him in the suit and heave him overboard. However, he came up feet first and all the air inside the suit went to his feet so he couldn't turn over. There he was, floating in the ocean with his two feet kicking wildly above the water. Fortunately, we had two men standing by in the lifeboat and they were able to fish him out before he drowned.

Finally, the Southern France invasion got under way and so did we. We sailed into Toulon Harbor on day two and apparently the invasion force had driven the Germans out of Toulon, but the "green beans," as the FFI (Free French Interior) called them, still had artillery in the cliffs above the harbor. They were lobbing shells into the harbor with great regularity and a ship or two had already been hit. So they sent us down to Marseilles where the Germans had been pushed back a little farther and we unloaded there.

The problem was the Germans had mined all the bollards (metal or wooden posts to which mooring lines are secured) so we couldn't tie up at a dock and unload. We had to rig the booms ourselves, without any stevedores around, and unload the ammo one sling at a time into Army ducks (amphibious trucks) that came along side. They took off right to the front where I guess the material was badly needed. The first night, I was up the forward mast helping to rig the boom when we had an air raid. They were high level bombers, but they had us zeroed in pretty good. One landed in the water close enough to us to rattle the ship and send spray over us. We were lucky it didn't spring any plates. All the lights went off and everybody rushed to man the guns. I was loader in a forward 20mm gun tub just off the mast house above which I was working. So I scrambled down the mast as fast as I could and, instead of going down the ladder to the deck, decided I could jump over to the gun tub from the mast hose. Why this crazy idea came into my head I will never know, but you did crazy things at times under fire.

In the dark of the blackout, I missed my footing when I landed and came down on my butt on top of a cleat. This caused a pilonidal cyst which was quite painful for the rest of the trip and which, after I got back to the States, got me discharged. This came about because even though the cyst was drained, it was a recurring problem and there were no doctors aboard ship. So I was washed out.

At Marseilles once we started unloading, it had been so long since we were off the ship that the captain gave us a day off, one watch at a time. Somehow, he found that the ducks we were loading would go through Marseilles and we could ride along, getting off in the city. So, one at a time, we rode a sling down to the duck and sat alongside the driver for one of the wildest rides of my life.

They gunned it along narrow, winding roads at high speed with a sub-machine gun at their sides and orders to stop for nothing. When I asked why the gun and why the orders, the driver answered, "The fucking FFI. We gave them the guns and the know-how to hijack German trucks and now that the Germans are out of here it's business as usual against us."

We were heroes in Marseilles. Any American was greeted effusively and, being a maritime city, unlike our own country, they understood the value of merchant seamen. I remember wandering into a little wine shop to see if I could get a bottle of good French red. The shopkeeper was a little old man, but when he saw who I was he grabbed and hugged me. Then he took me down into the basement where, behind some barrels, he had hidden some good bottles "from the Green Beans."

I got along because I had taken four years of French literature in college. I could read and write it even though I spoke, with great difficulty, what was probably a broken pidgin French. This, combined with the Marseilles dialect, made verbal communication almost impossible. So I carried a pad and pen with me and wrote my way through Marseilles.

After we had the forward holds empty, the Seabees had cleared the bollards and we were able to dock to unload the rest of the ship. This gave us time to get acquainted with a squad of FFI who took up residence on our dock and stole some of the winter clothing we had in number four hold. Giving one of them a Ping Bar (the wartime version of a Mars bar) was equivalent to making a friend for life. I passed out all my rations of candy and cigarettes since I didn't smoke. They awarded me a 1917 German Luger they had taken off a prisoner and I have it to this day as a souvenir. By now it's probably valuable, but I wouldn't sell it under any circumstances.

I remember when I gave one of them a candy bar. He carefully shaved off a sliver of the ersatz chocolate, savored it with as much joy as I have ever seen a candy bar administer, and carefully wrapped up the rest to take home to his family. When we ate, they would line up outside the cook's window and, as our plates came back, Cookie would scrape off what we were wasting into their mess kits. When we caught on to this we began to leave a lot of food. It made us realize what the people in Europe had been through and how lucky we were to be Americans.

By the time we were unloaded, the German Air Force had become such a minor threat that we scooted back across the Mediterranean to Mers El Kebir all alone. They made us wait for a convoy back to the States since there were still a few random subs on the prowl.

It was winter by now and the North Atlantic was its usual mean, cold and rugged self. Spray froze on everything, including the men. You were constantly dealing with ice. It was underfoot, on the lines, on you. If the bow watch didn't keep moving, his relief often had to chop him loose with a fire axe.

We made it back home without an incident. However, for me, the war was over![1]

The Abbot L. Mills *was damaged by a mine off Dubrovnik, Yugoslavia; towed to port and was considered a total loss. She was sold in July of 1948, towed to Venice and repaired in 1949. She went through several name changes and owners, finally being scrapped in Spezia, Italy in December 1971.[2]*

~~~

Peter Dykovitz, who contributed an earlier story, was in Antwerp, Belgium with a damaged ship when the war ended.

Spring 1945

I was a third assistant [engineer] on a Liberty carrying war supplies to Europe. We had four locomotives and tenders as deck cargo. After an uneventful trip across the ocean the convoy anchored somewhere in the English Channel. Sometime in the early hours of the morning there was a thud and the ship listed to starboard nearly throwing me out of my bunk. I put on some clothes and ran out on deck. Someone said that we had hit another ship. It was pitch black with a strong wind. We all went inside and heard that the convoy had received orders to move ahead.

The next morning when I was on watch the telegraph rang: Half Speed and then Stop and Finished With Engines. The third mate came down into the engine room and said the bow had been damaged. The captain requested the log book and said there was going to be a hearing with the captains of the two vessels on shore in the afternoon. The rest of the convoy had sailed out of sight.

The War Shipping Administration blamed the other vessel as that captain gave the order to move first. That vessel should have gone slow ahead as soon as the anchor was raised. The wind swung the ship broadside and it hit us in the area of their no. 3 hatch.

We sailed for Antwerp early the next morning. When we arrived the next day the War Shipping Administration personnel came aboard to check the damage. I had gone on the dock and saw where the bow had been pushed in about fifteen feet at the top and about three feet above the water line three feet back. The captain said that when the ship was empty there wouldn't be any danger and he could sail it home. WSA thought otherwise.

As the cargo was being unloaded, men from the shipyard started to cut away the damaged bow with torches. Then another bow was removed from a Liberty that had been damaged and beached. The bow was lowered into place, welded and then painted.

The repair work was still going on after the cargo was unloaded. Then, suddenly, the war came to an end and nobody did any work for two days in celebration. The Army ran a fleet of trucks into the city and then the trolley cars came back into service. The USO shows were most enjoyable.

We sailed from the city and formed a convoy somewhere in the English Channel. The convoy had fifteen ships and one destroyer; and we sailed with all our lights on. It seemed strange at first after sailing for so many years blacked out. The destroyers were there in case a diehard Nazi commander was out there, but it was a quiet trip in a straight line.

The majority of the crew were not signing on for another trip, including me. We were sailing for New York and we were all happy to know that. Two days out of New York the ship was diverted to Norfolk. Talk about an unhappy crew! We were paid off in that port and when my relief came aboard I took the night train to New York and another train home.[3]

~~~

The following story was submitted by Bernard C. Flatow who obtained the final rank of Ensign, U.S. Maritime Service. He was the Chief Radio Officer aboard the SS Thomas Nuttall *where this story took place.*

This story began the last week of March 1945. I was the chief radio officer aboard the SS *Thomas Nuttall*, a Liberty ship. The *Nuttall* was in a convoy heading east across the Atlantic when two days before we reached Gibralter the convoy commodore informed us by blinker that we were to fall out of the convoy and proceed alone on a pre-determined alternate course to Augusta, Sicily. No explanation was given us to the reason for our leaving the convoy. The *Thomas Nuttall* was fully loaded with 10,000 tons of ammunition and our original destination was Bari, Italy.

We proceeded alone and anchored in the roadstead at Augusta. The NCSO (Naval Control Ship Operations) boarded our ship and informed the captain that there was a problem with some of the ammunition in our cargo and that we were to proceed to Taranto, Italy, anchor in the roadstead, and some of our cargo would be offloaded.

We still did not have any idea as to the reason of the offloading, but upon arrival at Taranto we were informed that we were carrying 100-pound fragmentation bombs. In the conversion process the munitions manufacturer had failed to remove the chemical lining on the inside of the bombs and just added the explosive powder. It seems that there was a chemical reaction between the lining of the bomb casing and the explosive and that they were very unstable and could explode at any time. Some of the bombs had already exploded on other ships and to the authorities' knowledge there were only four ships left carrying this type of bomb and the *Nuttall* was one of them.

It took thirty days to remove the defective bombs. They were removed from the hold two at a time on a cushioned lift and placed on mattresses on the deck of a mine layer which was tied up alongside the *Nuttall*. As soon as the mine layer was fully loaded it would depart and dump the bombs somewhere in the Mediterranean Sea, and then return for more bombs to be disposed of.

After thirty days we were ordered to proceed to Bari, Italy where unloading commenced. We were in Bari only a few days when the war ended in Europe and a decision was made to reload the ship and bring the 10,000 tons of ammunition to the Pacific by way of the Suez Canal, Red Sea, Indian Ocean, Ceylon, Darwin, Australia, Port Morsby, New Guinea, Manus, The Admiralty Islands, the Caroline Islands, Guam and finally to Saipan in the Marianas Islands. During this time we travelled alone with no escort.

At Saipan we anchored in the roadstead far from any ships. It seems that word had preceded us that there was a possibility that some of the defective bombs might still be on board.

Needless to say the ship was never unloaded and we never reached Okinawa which was our final destination. The war with Japan ended on August 15, 1945.

We remained at anchor in Saipan for more than six months and finally we set sail for the United States on January 19, 1946, across the Pacific via Hawaii, the Panama Canal, the Gulf of Mexico and finally to Galveston, Texas where we were again anchored in the roadstead far from the port. It was another two weeks and we finally received orders to proceed to the San Jacinto Ammunition Depot outside Houston, Texas where the ammo was finally unloaded.

The *Nuttall* did not dock from the time we left Bari in early May 1945 until we arrived in Houston in April of 1946. Word was that the count of the defective bombs was not accurate and that there were more bombs of this type on board than were listed on the manifest. We will never know the true story.[4]

The Thomas Nuttall *joined the Reserve Fleet and was finally scrapped in August 1972 in Kearny, New Jersey.*[5]

~~~

The Unsung Heroes

You can read about the heroes -
Army, Navy, Air Force too -
But what about the merchantmen?
They fought the battles too.

How quickly we've forgotten -
How courageous deeds were done -
When they sailed amid the wolf packs -
On the North Atlantic run.

We've forgotten frozen fingers -
And the Stukas of the north -
We've forgotten all the merchantmen -
Whose tradition set their course.

We've forgotten shark filled waters -
And the tanker's scorching pyre -
They battled hard to save their ships -
In the face of hostile fire.

There's not many who remember -
All the horror that they saw -
Or why among their unworn ribbons -
They hold the combat bar.

They're not ones for wearing medals -
At parades they're seldom seen -
A shame for our forgetting -
The backbone of our team.

Ian A. Millar[6]

EPILOGUE:
I REMEMBER

*T*he final scene is of those Merchant Marine Veterans who served in World War II. Their part in American history is slowly becoming known. Many thanks are due these magnificent heroes for contributing to this anthology. Their history — our history — has been preserved for future generations to read. They have become our teachers and through them we can all learn about America's maritime history.

~~~

Glen Trimble:

I remember how clear the air was, yet how beautiful sunsets could be. I remember how even the stars would leave shimmering trails of light across smooth water and the moon would leave a trail that seemed as wide as a road; incredibly luminous was the prop's wake as it churned up the phosphorus of

261

the sea on a dark calm night. All nights were not calm, especially storms coming out of the Gulf of Tehuantepec and making up elsewhere in the South Pacific.

I remember waves coming over the bridge, of the prop out of the water on the crest of a giant wave and how the ship would shudder when the prop bit into the sea; of measuring with our homemade plumb bob hanging on a nail; of rolls of more than fifty degrees.

I remember seeing three waterspouts at the same time in the area between Guadalcanal and Florida Island.

I remember seeing the Southern Cross for the first time; the first South Pacific island, part of Espiritu Santo, the first real jungles of Guadalcanal.

I remember the first excitement at Empress Augustus Bay of four days and nights of unloading a cargo of bombs and having a shell falling into the sea every thirty minutes or so, fired by Jap guns up in the mountain caves.

I remember picking up a Jap skull in the jungles of Finschhafen, New Guinea, to use as a paper weight, but when knocking it on a log to remove the ants, the brain pan broke and that was more than I could take and that plan was abandoned.

I remember the invasions of Leyte and Okinawa and how at times it seemed the guns were never going to stop.

I remember the screams of those burned when the Kamikaze crashed the Liberty anchored aft of us. I remember how long the red fog seemed to last when the Kamikaze crashed us and I thought our cargo of bombs had probably exploded.

I remember the typhoon winds at Leyte and some wild storms at Okinawa.

I remember Okinawa didn't seem so bad even with more Kamikaze raids — the closest crash to us was about 60 feet and we were only there two weeks, not two months, to discharge our bombs.

I remember also that you can't always be right. I sat on the concrete retaining wall outside the Royal Hawaiian Hotel and looked at Waikiki Beach. I couldn't imagine why all the fuss about a beach only about ten feet wide at the most and decided it would really amount to nothing!!!![1]

~~~

And Melvern Schroeder:

A world turned upside down taken to the tenth power. That's what it seemed to this naive youth from the wheat fields of Kansas. Why I happened to choose the merchant marine, about which I knew little, remains hazy. There were mixed reasons, precipitating factors. Among them, certainly, lurked the imminence of a draft board summons that would deny not only my freedom but also my freedom of choice. Adding frustration to uncertainty was the clouded future of a fading romance. I felt imprisoned by an undefined, restlessness. Hence the seductive attraction of escaping it all by going to sea. A classic solution familiar in the literature of fact and fiction.

I entered the U.S. Maritime Service in March 1944, trained at Catalina Island, and commenced my service with a trip each to the Hawaiian and the Marshall Islands. My focsle mate and fellow fireman-watertender on these trips was Casey. He is one of only two shipmates with whom I remain in touch. The other one is Al, focsle mate and fellow oiler with whom I sailed the Atlantic. I would not see these two special brothers again for thirty-five years. Welded by the experience of ship and sea — the sea, great, sweet mother of us all — men forge a bond, deep and primal. All of us who sailed back then intuitively belong to an exclusive fraternity. When we trade stories of those days, however skewed by an untrustworthy memory, we recognize our brotherhood in the knowing eye and slanted smile. Unconsciously, we're engaging in a ritual, the meaning of which rests in the metaphor those stories represent. Like shards of broken glass, they stick with us as badges of our own identity. In all their variety, they tell but one truth: what it was like. Thus have these tales from the briny become a feature at the monthly breakfasts attended by a number of old salts here in Wichita, Kansas.

My stories lack the drama that others can tell. The closest that I came to an unfriendly torpedo was the sound of exploding depth charges heard from the bowels of a ship. The only wound

I can claim is the still persistent fungus infection I caught while wading in the coral reef at the Marshall Islands. Should I care to boast, I can tell of the time at these islands that I flew on a submarine patrol in a PBY, surely against all regulations. Or the time at Pearl Harbor where I, against all statistical odds, ran into a friend from home. Once, midway through the Suez Canal and peaceful at anchor, my ship was rammed by the British troop carrier, *Corfu*. We saw her coming, knew she must hit, and helplessly watched. While several missionaries on their way to India dropped to their knees, I ran for my camera. More chilling, on another occasion, was my near date with Davy Jones's Locker. I foolishly swam near the gateway of a breakwater as the tide was falling and drifted out to sea. The details are mercifully blocked from my memory to the extent that I cannot even recall the port at which it happened. Was it at Iraklion, Crete or Colombo, Ceylon?

The subject of favorite ports always inspires debate. Mine was New York. In addition to her unlimited attractions, New York reminds me also of the two most unforgettable people that I would get to know. One was Jack, the chief electrician with whom I sailed as a second electrician. A consummate rascal, his lust for the edges of life had often exceeded the normal limits of the law. But, good-natured, with wit and charm to match, he must just as often have softened the jailor's heart. Under his chaperonage one night, I saw the fabled haunts of New York's 52nd Street and its celebrated Jack Dempsey's as few could ever have.

Dan, by contrast, personified breeding and cultivation. I first met him at the old Seamen's Institute where he was a featured entertainer. We became friends and through him I was introduced to New York's world of stage and opera. His apartment became my home away from home. From this kind man, now long deceased, I learned a great lesson about the dignity and oneness of all human beings. For, as I was not, Dan was gay.

"On every side the sky, on every side the sea." So wrote Virgil in the *Aeneid*. In Mansfield, it is "the lonely sea and the sky." I, too, found the sea a very special place. Here, removed from the distractions of land and shore, she provided the hospitality through which I discovered Will Durant and his writings on philosophy. Discovery led to heightened interest which, in time, became ungovernable. "Philosophy," said Plato, "is the highest music." How well I understand. Like the sea itself, my debt to her is immeasurable.

"There is a season and a time to every purpose," says the Good Book. Now, in the September of my life, I feel an urgency in the questions that memory evokes. More and more I wonder: what do the pages of time write about men who sailed with me on the *Fremont Older*, the *Alexander V. Fraser*, the S.S. *Titan,* and the *Roswell Victory*? Together, we breathed the air and walked the streets — yes, also flirted with the girls — of London, Venice, Trieste, and Bari, of Kavalla and Thessalonika, of Oran, Alexandria, Calcutta and Santos and more. I wonder, how is it with you? Sometimes I wonder desperately, for time is running out. And, not to forget, I wonder also about you, my brave little Yugoslavian lass. Are you still running from war? Pretty London nurse, rose-cheeked maiden in Nottingham, what cards has life dealt you? Julie, how could you always know the arrival of my ship in New York? Tell me soon, tell me soon.[2]

~~~

Peter Salvo, known as the Street Captain because of his union support and political involvement for the merchant marine, became a seaman in 1942. He shipped out of New York making eight trips during the war. Peter has written hundreds of letters to help inform American presidents, government officials and newspaper editors of the plight of the merchant marine veteran's status and current problems. Peter has never stopped writing. He participated in a medical experiment after the war which was an outgrowth of the atomic bomb explosion.

In 1950, while waiting to ship out of Baltimore, Maryland, I became a victim of a medical research project. My port agent received a telephone call from the Governor of

Maryland asking him for a volunteer desperately needed for an important government project. The agent and myself were friends, but he pointed at me as said, "You are a volunteer." I should have bitten his finger!

He accompanied me to what I called the House of Frankenstein. We met with government officials and high ranking officers who introduced me to some men in white coats as their subject. Being that I lost my identity I should have turned and ran; instead we sat down and discussed the project.

The officer spoke first, pointing out the Cocoanut Grove fire in Boston, Mass. in 1942 when 500 people died from lack of blood plasma. Furthermore, he conveyed the possibility of a similar incident happening in our cities upon an atomic bombing. The project was to develop a plasma substitute.

I was confined at the Baltimore Marine Hospital for ten days, my only roommates were live animal hearts preserved in jars, who were not very conversable. My only visitor was the port agent. Calling him some of Harry Truman's pet names and showing him my blue complextion, he said, "Don't worry. These are nice people."

My answer, "In jars, too!"

I was the only white guy sporting a blue complexion. Before the governor would call our port agent again, I caught the first ship leaving Baltimore.[3]

~~~

George Canaday is the Director of the United States Merchant Marine Museum in Anderson, Indiana. While G.I.s were getting their way paid through college, George, working in a filling station and his wife working two jobs, was able to graduate from college and become an accountant. Over the years, he owned a bowling alley, a bar, a go-kart track, an insurance agency, etc. In 1995, George founded the U.S. Merchant Marine Museum "to honor those seamen who went to war when we were needed, but were forgotten when they were no longer needed."[4] The following is from the brochure the Museum publishes.

May 22nd is National Maritime Day. Few people know that it is a day set aside to honor our Merchant Marine. Even fewer people know that Anderson, Indiana has a museum devoted entirely to the merchant seamen of WW II.

The museum was the creation of George R. Canaday who, with his older brother, Joe R. Canaday, served in the Merchant Marine during WW II. Unique is the fact that they served on

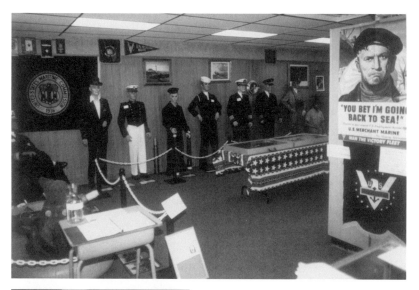

A few of the displays to be found at George Canaday's Merchant Marine Museum in Anderson, Indiana. George Canaday.

many of the same ships together, when both were enlisted men and again when they were officers. Most of their service was in the North Atlantic to England and France, although they saw service in the Mediterranean, Africa, Italy and Sicily.

The museum contains uniforms, medals, pins, seaman papers, insignia, ships models, ship instruments and a reference book library.[5]

~~~

Joseph Chomsky, Vice President of the AMMV Edwin J. O'Hara Chapter, wrote a poignant remembrance on the 50th Anniversary of World War II VE (Victory Europe) Day. The theme of that day was "A Grateful Nation Remembers."

What I remember is that, on graduating high school, I joined the merchant marine as a Cadet Midshipman, MMR/ USNR and after three months of basic school I went to sea, crossing the North Atlantic in convoy on a Liberty ship bound for Europe.

What I remember is that I was proud, as a merchant mariner during the war, to serve America and the Free World in that noble attempt to stop Hitler's Nazi juggernaut that was determined to destroy our way of life, take away our freedoms, and make the survivors serfs to a foreign power.

What I remember is that we served in every theatre we were sent to. While others sailed to Murmansk, the Persian Gulf, the Pacific or Indian Oceans, I went to Scotland, England, North Africa, Italy and France.

I remember that we not only delivered the goods our troops and allies needed but we took part in every invasion, landing and military operation that was on or near deep water.

I remember that not all of our shipmates survived; that more than 6,000 American merchant seamen died at sea when their ships were destroyed and that thousands more died afterward of injuries received when their ships were attacked. Thousands more, the "lucky ones," disabled, lived out their lives with no government support but with the injuries sustained when their shipmates died.

I also remember that during the war the Navy rarely sent search and rescue missions for survivors of sinkings of our merchant ships, even when these sinkings took place close to our shores. I have since learned that the Navy even tried to discourage the "Hooligan Navy," private yachtsmen and fishermen, from going out in search of survivors of the many sinkings along our coasts.

I remember that the surviving next of kin of killed or wounded merchant seamen who asked for financial help were told "no programs exist;" I remember that all such payments made to those who persisted stopped in 1947.

What I also remember is that when the fighting ended our government asked us (ordered many of us) in 1945 to continue sailing in support of our occupation troops to deliver the food, fuel and materials needed by everyone in the war-ravaged areas to help them re-establish their economies, to feed the hungry and shelter the homeless. While the men who were drafted into the armed forces were going home, we stayed on.

I remember that in August 1946 I received a "Certificate of Substantially Continuous Service," that said I had done my duty in the merchant marine in World War II, was no longer subject to the Selective Service System and could now go home and get on with my life: but with no job opportunities ashore, I kept sailing.

I remember that when I finally got home and tried to continue my education I was told by many colleges that they were only accepting applications from recent high school graduates and "veterans who will be attending under the G.I. Bill;" MERCHANT SEAMEN NEED NOT APPLY!

I remember that the various "veterans" organizations (the American Legion, the V.F.W., etc.) invited my brother, my cousins, my friends and neighbors who had been in the armed forces to join their clubs; I wasn't invited or wanted!

I remember, in August 1948, being reclassified 1A by my draft board and told I must continue sailing or be subject to induction into the army or go to jail.

I remember being bumped out of my job as a civilian employee in the Brooklyn Navy Yard in 1954 by a "veteran" who was drafted in September 1945 and only served a few months before being discharged; the U.S. Civil Service Commission and the U. S. Navy said he was a "veteran" and I wasn't.

I remember, when job hunting, being told by prospective employers that they wouldn't consider hiring me as long as they had job applicants who were "veterans"!

I remember being told, in the mid 50's, close to home at the Lake Success headquarters of Sperry Gyroscope, that they wouldn't hire me, no matter how good my qualifications, because "It was the policy of Sperry Gyroscope to not hire anyone who was ever in the merchant marine."

I remember the hard times, trying to raise a family on substandard wages because the only jobs open to a merchant marine veteran were the jobs no one else wanted; the jobs with low pay and lousy working conditions.

I remember every Veterans Day, every Memorial Day, every holiday when flags were flown and people marched in commemoration of the greatness that was America, that my stomach tied up in knots because they said my contribution in the war was without value; not worth remembering!

I remember that after the hostilities ended the government demanded that all persons remaining in the merchant marine be "politically correct;" the Coast Guard issued Identification cards to all approved seamen and waterfront workers. Those who were refused I.D.'s were denied the right to work in the maritime trades. Anyone who had been an active union member involved in the peace time years prior to World War II in any of the strikes for improved wages and working conditions was barred from the waterfront.

I remember that when the Supreme Court finally ruled that the foregoing practice was unconstitutional and must be stopped, that it opened a sixty day window to the injured parties to claim damages.

I remember that, after the war, any ex-G.I. who asked the Coast Guard for seamen's papers was automatically issued them, a much simpler system than had been applied to non-G.I.'s.

I remember that with jobs becoming more scarce as shipping needs declined and jobs ashore were still being denied to merchant marine veterans of wartime service, many of these ex-G.I.s with an extensive array of post-war benefits took jobs that were being denied to the men who had sailed and survived in the hazardous wartime merchant marine.

I remember that the Government had awarded these same wartime mariners the right to wear the Merchant Marine Defense Ribbon (medal added later) for service in the merchant marine between September 9, 1939 and December 7, 1941, (additional campaign ribbons were added later.) These were the years when, with Europe completely dominated by Hitler, it was so important to help the British Empire and the Soviet Union resist Nazi aggression, to "hold the line," till American troops could help.

That war should be safely behind us now but I still feel recurring resentment every time I see or hear the slogan: "A Grateful Nation Remembers."[6]

Welcome Home Our Many Heroes

Lest we forget
   Sometimes when the bands are playing
And the uniforms march by
   You will find a seaman watching
With a wistful-looking eye
   And you know just what he's thinking
As he hears the cheering crowd
   As the soldiers and the sailors
Swing along, erect and proud.
   He is thinking that his country
Saves its honor once again
   For the uniforms, forgetting
All the seas' forgotten men.
   He is thinking of the armies
And the food and fighting tanks
   That for every safe arrival
To the seamen owe their thanks
   He is thinking of those buddies

Who have paid the final score,
    Not in khaki or in the Navy
But the working clothes they wore.
    And we'd like to tell him something
That we think he may not know
    A reminder he can stow away
Wherever he may go.
    All your countrymen are proud of you
And though there's no brass band
    Not a bugle or a banner
When the merchant seamen land,
    We know just the job you're doing
In your worn-out work clothes
    On the sea where death is lurking
And a fellow's courage shows
    So be sure to keep your chin up
When the uniforms parade
    What a man wears doesn't matter
It's the stuff of which he's made.

                    Author Unknown[7]

ABOUT THE AUTHOR

Gerald Reminick lives on Long Island, New York. He is a Professor of Library Services at the Western Campus Library, Suffolk County Community College, Brentwood, New York. He was educated in the New York area, receiving his Bachelor of Science degree from Adelphi University in 1967, a Master of Arts from SUNY [State University of New York] at StonyBrook in 1975 and a Master of Science in Library and Information Science at Long Island University in 1979.

Formerly an avid sailor, he gave that up to research and write about maritime history. His published works include several books on library research and poetry. He is an associate member of the North Atlantic and Kings Point chapters of the American Merchant Marine Veterans.

A member of the Y.M.C.A. masters' swim team, Jerry is now working on a book about the German attack on Bari, Italy on December 2, 1943. This incident was known as "The Little Pearl Harbor."

He and his wife, Gail have two children, Danielle and Bradley.

273

Endnotes

Introduction

[1] Emory S. Land, *The United States Merchant Marine At War: Report of the War Shipping Administration to the President* (Washington, D.C.: 15 January, 1946), 3.

[2] "Sell Wartime Ships," *Business Week*, 17 July 1937, 42.

[3] U. S. Department of Commerce Maritime Administration, *The United States Merchant Marine: A Brief History* (Washington, D.C., 1972), 3.

[4] Felice Swados, "Seamen and the Law," *The New Republic*, 9 March 1938, 124.

[5] Felix Riesenberg, "Communists at Sea," *Nation*, 23 October 1937, 432.

[6] "Committee Reports Seamen Lack Discipline," *Scholastic*, 5 February 1938, 15 S.

[7] Swados, "Seamen and the Law," 125.

[8] Joseph P. Kennedy, "New Blood in American Shipping," *Vital Speeches of the Day*, 15 June 1937, 534.

[9] Thomas M. Woodward, "America's Maritime Power," *Forum and Century*, May 1939, 286.

[10] Felix Riesenberg, Jr., *Sea War: The Story Of The U.S. Merchant Marine In World War II* (New York: Rinehart & Company, Inc., 1956), 47.

[11] Ibid., 152.

[12] Ibid., 153.

[13] U.S. Department of Commerce Maritime Administration, *The United States Merchant Marine*, 3.

[14] Dan Horodysky and Toni Horodyski, "Merchant Marine Casualties of WW II," *United States Merchant Marine*, 20 July 1999, <http://www.usmm.org/>

[15] Land, *The United States Merchant Marine At War*, 31.

Foreword

[1] T. J. Whalen, *"Report of Casualty (Form DD-1300) for James Louis Randall,* 20 May 1994, Collection of Mary R. Parmalee.

[2] Matthew S. Loughran, "A True Veteran," *Newsday*, 16 March 1996.

[3] Ian A. Millar, "Forgotten Men," *In Praise of Merchantmen*, 1982.

[4] Ibid., "Dedication Page," Ibid.

Chapter 1, Pre-War

[1] "Lynn R. Fullington," *Anderson Daily Bulletin*, 2 August 1943.

[2] Donald MacIntyre, *The Naval War Against Hitler* (New York: Charles Scribner's Sons, Inc., 1971), 261.

[3] L. Roy Murray, Jr., "Rescue At Sea: The Odyssey of the S.S. *Nishmaha* and the Rescue of the Survivors of the Torpedoed British Cruiser HMS *Dunedin* Before the United States Entry Into World War II, 1995."

Chapter 2, Determination

[1] Trina Burton, "The Merchant Marine Memories of Dick Burton: Worthy To Serve, Lexington, Kentucky, 1996," Collection of Dick Burton.

Chapter 3, Enlistment and Training

[1] Emory S. Land, *The United States Merchant Marine At War: Report of the War Shipping Administration to the President* (Washington D.C., 15 January 1946), 54.

[2] Ibid., 55.

[3] Jack K. Bauer, *A Maritime History of the United States : The Role of America's Seas and Waterways* (Columbia, S.C.: University of South Carolina Pr., 1988), 310.

[4] Glen Trimble, Letter to Gerald Reminick, 15 September 1996, Collection of Gerald Reminick.

[5] U.S. Maritime Service, *This is Sheepshead Bay : The Picture Story of the U.S. Maritime Service Training Station, Sheepshead Bay, N.Y.* [n.d.], 2.

[6] William Kellett, Letter to Gerald Reminick, 23 August 1996, Collection of Gerald Reminick.

[7] Ibid., *Diary to Dear Mom*, 15 February - 31 March, 1945, Collection of William Kellett.

[8] Walter W. Luikart, "How I Got Into The Merchant Marine, December 1996." Collection of Walter W. Luikart.

[9] Ian A. Millar, "Merchantmen All," *In Praise of Merchantmen*, 1982.

Chapter 4, First Voyage

[1] Alfred A. New, "Maiden Voyage of the *Jonathan Trumbull*, 15 December 1987." Collection of Alfred A. New.

Chapter 5, The Atlantic Ocean

[1] *An Encyclopedia Of World History*, 1968 ed., s.v. "Naval Warfare And Blockade, 1939-1944."

[2] Terry Hughes and John Costello, *The Battle of the Atlantic* (New York: The Dial Press/James Wade, 1977), 42.

[3] Samuel Eliot Morison, *History Of United States Naval Operations In World War II. Vol. I. The Battle of the Atlantic* (Boston: Little, Brown and Company, 1966), 200.

[4] John Gorley Bunker, *Liberty Ships: The Ugly Ducklings Of World War II* (Salem, N.H.: Ayer Company Publishers, Inc., 1990), 83.

[5] Merton Barrus, Letter to Mr. And Mrs. Vail, 18 October 1942, Collection of Oysterponds Historical Society, Orient, New York.

[6] Robert M. Browning, Jr. *U.S. Merchant War Casualties Of World War II* (Annapolis, MD.: Naval Institute Pr., 1996), 129.

[7] Jurgen Rohwer, *Axis Submarine Success 1939-1945* (Annapolis, MD.: U.S. Naval Institute Pr., 1983), 100.

[8] Arthur R. Moore, *A Careless Word ... A Needless Sinking* (Kings Point, N.Y.: American Merchant Marine Museum at the U.S. Merchant Marine Academy, 1990), 134.

[9] Ian A. Millar, "Sparks," *In Praise of Merchantmen*, 1982. Poetry Collection of Ian A. Millar.

[10] Lillard Waddle, "The Liberty Ship *John Carter Rose*, 1997." Collection of Lillard Waddle.

[11] James J. Fitzpatrick, "Sinking of the S.S. *Julia Ward Howe*, 3 December 1997." Collection of James J. Fitzpatrick.

[12] Millar, "Merchantmen Like Thee," *In Praise of Merchantmen*. Poetry collection of Ian A. Millar.

[13] George Paxton, "Purser - S.S. *Andrea Luckenbach*, 1996," Collection of George Paxton.

[14] Browning, *U.S. Merchant Vessel War Casualties*, 297.

[15] Moore, *A Careless Word*, 17.

[16] Burton Drew, *Diary of Burton Drew*, 15 - 16 March 1943, Collection of Burton Drew.

[17] Moore, *A Careless Word*, 31.

[18] Edward T. Woods, "A Teenager Goes To War, September 1998." Collection of Edward T. Woods.

[19] Henry W. Moeller, "Sinking of the *Atlantic Sun*, 13 July 1999." Collection of Henry W. Moller.

[20] Millar, "The Grey Wolves of the Morn," *In Praise of Merchantmen*. Poetry Collection of Ian A. Millar.

Chapter 6, Northern Russia

[1] John Gorley Bunker, *Liberty Ships: The Ugly Ducklings Of World War II* (Salem, N.H.: Ayer Company Publishers, Inc., 1990), 62.

[2] Samuel Eliot Morison, *History Of United States Naval Operations In World War II. Vol. I. The Battle of the Atlantic* (Boston: Little, Brown, and Company, Inc., 1966), 158.

[3] John Creswell, *Sea Warfare 1939-1945* (Berkeley : University of California Pr., 1967), 197.

[4] Bunker, *Liberty Ships*, 69.

[5] Ibid., 65.

[6] Morison, *History Of United States Naval Operations Vol. 1*, 164.

[7] John F. Brady, "Murmansk Russia Run: Nine Long Months," 14 February 1997, Collection of John F. Brady.

[8] Arthur R. Moore, *A Careless Word ... A Needless Sinking*, (Kings Point, N.Y.: American Merchant Marine Museum at the U.S. Merchant Marine Academy, 1990), 132.

[9] Ibid., 279.

[10] Bunker, *Liberty Ships*, 77.

[11] Robert M. Browning, Jr., *U.S. Merchant Marine War Casualties Of World War II* (Annapolis, MD.: Naval Institute Pr., 1996), 490.

[12] Air Ministry Meteorological Office, "Record of Pressure 17-27 February 1945," Collection of Carl L. Hammond.

[13] Carl L. Hammond, "A Murmansk Convoy, 6 April 1997." Collection Carl L. Hammond.

[14] L.A. Sawyer and W.H. Mitchell, *The Liberty Ships, 2d ed.* (London: Lloyds of London Press Ltd., 1985), 80.

[15] Adolph G. Rutler, "The Difference Between Doc and the Dock, 9 November 1996." Collection Adolph G. Rutler.

[16] Sawyer, *The Liberty Ships*, 80.

[17] John J. York, "Angel of Archangel, 1 November 1996." Collection of John J. York.

[18] Sawyer, *The Liberty Ships*, 54.

[19] John J. York, "Non-Angels of Archangel, 28 November 1996." Collection of John J. York.

[20] Robert E. Gustin, "They Treated Us As Heroes, 22 July 1994." Collection of Robert E. Gustin.

[21] Ian A. Millar, "North Russia," *In Praise of Merchantmen*, 1982. Poetry Collection of Ian A. Millar.

Chapter 7, The Mediterranean

[1] John Gorley Bunker, *Liberty Ships: The Ugly Ducklings Of World War II* (Salem, N.H.: Ayer Company Publishers, Inc., 1990), 113.

[2] Ibid., 125.

[3] Samuel Eliot Morison, *History Of United States Naval Operations In World War II. Vol. IX. Sicily-Salerno-Anzio* (Boston: Little, Brown and Company, 1968), 159.

[4] Jurgen Rohwer, *Axis Submarine Successes 1939- 1945* (Annapolis, MD.: U.S. Naval Institute Pr., 1983), 238.

[5] Peter Cremer, *U-Boat Commander: A Periscope View of the Battle of the Atlantic* (Annapolis, MD.: Naval Institute Pr., 1984), 219.

[6] Ernest Standridge, "A World War II Voyage Remembered, 1996." Collection of Ernest Standridge.

[7] Robert M. Browning, Jr., *U.S. Merchant Vessel Casualties Of World War II* (Annapolis, MD.: Naval Institute Pr., 1996), 258.

[8] Rohwer, *Axis Submarine Successes,* 147.

[9] Arthur R. Moore, *A Careless Word ... A Needless Sinking* (Kings Point, NY.: American Merchant Marine Museum at the U.S. Merchant Marine Academy, 1990), 263.

[10] Burton Drew, *Diary of Burton Drew,* 12 December - 7 February 1943, Collection of Burton Drew.

[11] Peter Dykovitz, "S.S. *Evangeline* - January 1943 to August 1943, 17 February 1996." Collection of Peter Dykovitz.

[12] Glenn B. Infield, *Disaster At Bari* (New York: The Macmillen Company, 1971), XI.

[13] Robert Harris and Jeremy Paxton, *A Higher Form of Killing* (NewYork: Hill and Wang, 1982), 118.

[14] Constance M. Pechura, "The Health effects Of Mustard Gas And Lewsite, " *JAMA* 269 (January 1993): 453.

[15] Karen Freeman, "The VA's Sorry, The Army's Silent," *The Bulletin of the Atomic Scientists* (March 1993): 39-43.

[16] Harris, *A Higher Form of Killing*, 118.

[17] Infield, *Disaster At Bari*, 56.

[18] Ibid., 58.

[19] Ibid., 59.

[20] Ibid., 61.

[21] Ibid., 62.

[22] Leroy C. Heinse, "Hell and Back," 5 September 1997. Collection of Leroy C. Heinse.

[23] E.S. Land, Letter to Cadet-Midshipman Leroy C. Heinse, 22 July 1944, Collection of Leroy C. Heinse.

[24] Moore, *A Careless Word*, 395.

[25] R.H. Farinholt, Letter to Mrs. Ann Flaker, 18 June 1945, Collection of Nancy E. Smith.

[26] Oscar T. Davies, Letter to Mrs. Ann Flaker, 28 June 1945, Collection of Nancy E. Smith.

[27] Wendell Flaker, "Telegram to Mrs. Wendell Flaker," 13 April 1945, Collection of Nancy E. Smith.

[28] Karl Hamberger, "We Learned That the S.S. *Charles Henderson ...,* 11 April 1998." Collection of Karl Hamberger.

Chapter 8, The Indian Ocean

[1] Edward Von der Porten, *The German Navy In World War II* (New York: Thomas Y. Crowell Company, 1969), 109.

[2] Hans-Adolf Jacobsen and Arthur L. Smith, *World War II Policy and Strategy* (Santa Barbara, CA.: Clio Books, 1979), 215.

[3] Ibid., 194.

[4] Arthur R. Moore, *A Careless Woord ... A Needless Sinking* (Kings Point, NY.: American Merchant Marine Museum at the U.S. Merchant Marine Academy, 1990), 256.

[5] Moore, *A Careless Word*, 574.

[6] Stanley Willner, "Veterans Application for Compensation, 1988." Collection of Stanley Willner.

[7] Moore, *A Careless Word,* 256.

[8] Ian A. Millar, "Sawokla," *In Praise of Merchantmen*, 1982.

[9] Millar, "The Death Railway," Ibid.

[10] Jurgen Rohwer, *Axis Submarine Successes 1939-1945* (Annapolis, MD.: U.S. Naval Institute Pr., 1983), 270.

[11] Ibid.

[12] Robert M. Browning, Jr., *U.S. Merchant Vessel War Casualties Of World War II* (Annapolis, MD.: Naval Institute Pr., 1996), 345.

[13] Moore, *A Careless Word,* 237.

[14] Jesse C. Crawford, Letter to Jack Fry Marshall, 1 September 1943, Collection of Jack F. Marshall.

[15] Edward S. O'Connell, "Thirteen Days On A Raft, 23 October 1943." Copy of original report in collection of the U.S. Merchant Marine Academy.

[16] Ibid., Letter to Gerald Reminick, 3 December 1996, Collection of Gerald Reminick.

[17] Peter Cremer, *U-Boat Commander: A Periscope View of the Battle of the Atlantic* (Annapolis, MD.: Naval Institute Pr., 1984), 231.

Chapter 9, The Pacific

[1] Samuel Eliot Morison, *History Of United States Naval Operations In World War II. Vol XII. Leyte* (Boston: Little, Brown and Company, 1966), 412.

[2] James F. Dunnigan and Albert A. Nofi, *Victory At Sea: World War II In The Pacific* (New York: William Morrow and Company, Inc., 1995), 331.

[3] John Gorley Bunker, *Liberty Ships: The Ships of World War II* (Salem, N.H.: Ayer Company Publishers, Inc., 1990), 140.

[4] Robert Carse, *The Long Haul: The United States Merchant Service in World War II* (New York: Norton, 1965), 38.

[5] John Gorley Bunker, *Liberty Ships*, 140.

[6] Ibid., 150.

[7] Emory Scott Land, *The United States Merchant Marine At War: Report of the War Shipping Administration to the President* (Washington, D.C.: 15 January 1946), 32.

[8] Milton H. Houpis, "The Battle of Tarawa, 1996." Collection of Milton Houpis.

[9] John Gorley Bunker, *Liberty Ships*, 146.

[10] Glen Trimble, Letter to Gerald Reminick, 15 September 1996, Collection of Gerald Reminick.

[11] Arthur R. Moore, *A Careless Word ... A Needless Sinking* (Kings Point, NY.: American Merchant Marine Museum at the U.S. Merchant Marine Academy, 1990), 26.

[12] L.A. Sawyer and W.H. Mitchell, *The Liberty Ships, 2nd ed.* (London: Lloyds of London Press, Ltd., 1985), 67.

[13] Arthur R. Moore, *A Careless Word*, 346.

[14] Ibid., 375.

[15] Ibid., 363.

[16] Ibid., 357.

[17] Ibid., 337.

[18] Ibid., 116.

[19] Glen Trimble, "*Witness to the Birth of the Kamikaze, 1988.*" Collection of Glen Trimble.

[20] Paul A. Tumminia, "The Sea Saga of the Juan de Fuca, 1982." Collection of Paul A. Tumminia.

[21] Arthur R. Moore, *A Careless Word*, 312.

[22] Alvin Lee Welch, "My First Visit to the Philippine Islands — Diary — November 12 - December 22, 1944. Collection of Alvin Lee Welch.

[23] Ibid., "The *Henry White*," Poem. 15 January 1945, Collection of Alvin Lee Welch.

[24] Richard Hanly, "Warning Stealing U.S. Gov't Property Is Punishable By 10,000 Fine And 10 Years Imprisonment, 17 June 1989." Collection of Richard Hanly.

Chapter 10, Storms and Heavy Weather

[1] Elmer Vick, "S.S. *Luckenbach*, 4 June 1992." Collection of Elmer Vick.

[2] Arthur R. Moore, *A Careless Word ... A Needless Sinking* (Kings Point, NY.: American Merchant Marine Museum at the U.S. Merchant Marine Academy, 1990), 171.

[3] Jack F. Marshall, Letter to Mother, 9 February 1944, Collection of Jack F. Marshall.

[4] "Crew Goes All Out For "Guy With Guts" Norris Wainwright, Merchant Marine, " *Ossining Citizen Register*, 12 April 1945: 1.

[5] Matthew S. Loughran, "I Heard A Loud Thud and the Ship Lifted Slightly, October 1997." Collection of Matthew S. Loughran.

Chapter 11, Life At Sea and In Port

[1] Emory S. Land, *The United States Merchant Marine At War: Report of the War Shipping Administration to the President* (Washington, D.C.: 15 January 1946), 51.

[2] L. Roy Murray, Interview by Gerald Reminick, 8 December 1997, Collection of Gerald Reminick.

[3] Land, *The United States Merchant Marine*, 66.

[4] Winfield H. Adam, "Good For A laugh In The Arabian Sea, 14 June 1996." Collection of Winfield H. Adam.

[5] L.A. Sawyer and W.H. Mitchell, *The Liberty Ships, 2nd ed.* (London: Lloyds of London Press, Ltd., 1985), 69.

[6] Richard Hanly, "T'was The Day Before Thanksgiving - And All Through The Ship, Everyone Was Hungry!! 1996." Collection of Richard Hanly.

[7] Joe S. Harris, "My Journey Began On September 28, 1943, 1992." Collection of Joe S. Harris.

[8] Fred Allen, "The International Hotel, 10 November 1997." Collection of Fred Allen.

[9] Ibid., "The Registration Book," *Salty Dog Newsletter*, May 1995: 7.

[10] Thomas M. Quinn, "Kid Chicago, 17 March 1997." Collection of Thomas M. Quinn.

[11] Peter Salvo, "Sea Story, [n.d.]." Collection of the S.S. *John W. Brown* Archives.

[12] George H. Marks, Sr., "Unusual Ship — U.S. Army Transport — *State of Maryland*, 1 May 1996." Collection of George Marks, Sr.

Chapter 12, D-Day

[1] Tony Hall ed., *D-Day: Operation Overlord: from landing at Normandy to the liberation of Paris* (New York: Smithmark Publishers, Inc., 1993), 22.

[2] Emory S. Land, *The United States Merchant Marine At War: Report of the War Shipping Administrator to the President* (Washington D.C.: 15 January 1946), 22.

[3] Ibid., 32.

[4] Lester E. Ellison, Letter to Gerald Reminick, 15 February 1996, Collection of Gerald Reminick.

[5] Lester E. Ellison, "Biography, 1 November 1997." Collection of Lester E. Ellison.

[6] Lester E. Ellison, "Speech ofTugs and the Normandy Invasion. Presented at the U.S. Merchant Marine Academy and the Seamen's Church Institute, 30 April 1994.

[7] Richard R. Powers, "D-Day 1944," *Clarksville Leaf-Chronicle*, 6 June 1994.

[8] Peter J. Dilullo, "Tug 247, 1997." Collection of Peter J. Dilullo.

[9] Arthur R. Moore, *A Careless Word ... A Needless Sinking* (Kings Point, NY.: American Merchant Marine Museum at the U.S. Merchant Marine Academy, 1990), 48.

[10] Ibid., 350.

[11] Walter W. Luikart, "S.S. *Nicholas Herkimer*, 1996." Collection of Walter W. Luikart.

[12] L.A. Sawyer and W.H. Mitchell, *The Liberty Ships, 2nd ed.,* (London: Lloyds of London Press, Ltd., 1985), 164.

[13] Edward Macauley, "An Open Letter to the American Seamen," [n.d.].

Chapter 13, The Last Trip

[1] William Erin, "Last Voyage, 1996." Collection of William Erin.

[2] L.A. Sawyer and W.H. Mitchell, *The Liberty Ships, 2nd ed.,* (London: Lloyds of London, Press, Ltd., 1985), 130.

[3] Peter Dykovitz, "Suddenly The War Came To An End, 26 February 1996." Collection of Peter Dykovitz.

[4] Bernard C. Flatow, "10,000 Tons of Ammunition, 1997." Collection of Bernard C. Flatow.

[5] Sawyer, *The Liberty Ships*, 127.

[6] Ian A. Millar, "The Unsung Heroes," *In Praise of Merchantmen*, 1982, Poetry Collection of Ian A. Millar.

Epilogue: I Remember

[1] Glen Trimble, "Recollections Of The Sea, [n.d.]." Collection of Glen Trimble.

[2] Melvern Schroeder, "Of Time And The Sea, 1994." Collection of Melvern Schroeder.

[3] Peter Salvo, "House of Frankenstein, [n.d.]." Collection of the Maritime Museum Archives, Piney Point, MD.

[4] George R. Canaday, Letter to Gerald Reminick, September 1997, Collection of Gerald Reminick.

[5] Ibid., "A Salute To The Merchant Marine of World War II," [n.d], Pamphlet of the United States Merchant Marine Museum, Anderson, Indiana.

[6] Joseph Chomsky, "A Grateful Nation Remembers, 1995." Collection of Joseph Chomsky.

[7] "Welcome Home Our Many Heroes," Author Unknown.

BIBLIOGRAPHY

Adam, Winfield H. "Good For A Laugh In The Arabian Sea, 14 June 1996."

Air Ministry Meteorological Office. "Record of Pressure. 17-27 February 1945," Collection of Carl Hammond.

Allen, Fred. "The International Hotel, 10 November 1997."

—. "The Registration Book." *Salty Dog Newsletter,* May 1995: 7.

Barrus, Merton. Letter to Mr. and Mrs. Vail, 18 October 1942, Collection of Oysterponds Historical Society, Orient, New York.

Bauer, Jack K. *A Maritime History of the United States: The Role of America's Seas and Waterways.* Columbia, S.C.: University of South Carolina Pr., 1988.

Brady, John F. "Convoy To USSR: U.S. Navy Fight Off Attack Off North Cape Of Norway," Oil on canvas, Collection of John F. Brady.

—. "Murmansk Russia Run: Nine Long Months, 14 February 1997."

—. "Refueling Russian Warship," Oil on canvas, Collection of John F. Brady.

—. "Tanker S.S. Beacon Hill," Oil on canvas, Collection of John F. Brady.

—. "Under Attack in White Sea," Oil on canvas, Collection of John F. Brady.

Browning, Robert M. Jr., *U.S. Merchant Vessel War Casualties Of World War II.* Annapolis, Md.: Naval Institute Pr., 1996.

Bunker, John G.. *Heroes in Dungarees: The Story Of The American Merchant Marine In World War II.* Annapolis, Maryland: Naval Institute Pr., 1995.

—. *Liberty Ships: The Ugly Ducklings Of World War II.* Salem, N.H.: Ayer Company Publishers, Inc., 1990.

Burton, Trina. "The Merchant Marine Memories of Dick Burton: Worthy To Serve, Lexington, Kentucky, 1996."

Canaday, George R. *A Salute To The Merchant Marine of World War II.* Pamphlet [n.d.].

Canaday, George R., Letter to Gerald Reminick, September 1997.

Carse, Robert. *The Long Haul: The United States Merchant Service in World War II.* New York: Norton, 1965.

"Chief Lynn R. Fullington." *Anderson Daily Bulletin,* 2 August 1943.

Chomsky, Joseph. "A Grateful Nation Remembers, 1995."

"Committee Reports Seamen Lack Discipline." *Scholastic,* 5 February 1938: 15S.

Crawford, Jesse C., Letter to Jack Fry Marshall, 1 September 1943.

Cremer, Peter. *U-Boat Commander: A Periscope View of the Battle of the Atlantic.* Annapolis, MD: Naval Institute Pr., 1984.

Creswell, John. *Sea Warfare 1939-1945.* Berkeley: University of California Pr., 1967.

"Crew Goes All Out For "Guy With Guts" Norris Wainwright, Merchant Marine." *Ossining Citizen Register,* 12 April 1945.

Davies, Oscar T. (Mrs.), Letter to Mrs. Ann Flaker. 28 June 1945. Collection of Nancy E. Smith.

Dilullo, Peter J. "Tug *247,*1997."

"Disaster At Bari." *Time,* 27 December 1943.

Drew, Burton. *Diary of Burton Drew.* 12 Dec.-7 Feb., 1943.

—. *Diary of Burton Drew.* 15-16 March, 1943.

Dunnigan, James F. and Albert Nofi. *Victory At Sea: World War II In The Pacific.* New York: William Morrow and Company, Inc., 1995.

Dykovitz, Peter. "*S.S. Evangeline* January 1943 to August 1943, 17 Feb. 1996."

—. "Suddenly The War Came To An End, 26 February 1996."

Ellison, Lester E. "Biography, 1 November 1997."

—. Letter to Gerald Reminick, 15 February 1996.

—. "Speech of Tugs and the Normandy Invasion." Presented at the U.S. Merchant Marine Academy and the Seamen's Church Institute, 30 April 1994.

An Encyclopedia of World History. 1968 ed. S.v. "Naval Blockade, 1939-1944."

Erin, William. "Last Voyage, 1996."

Farinholt, R.H., Letter to Mrs. Ann Flaker, 28 June 1945. Collection of Nancy E. Smith.

Fitzpatrick, James J. "Sinking of the S.S. Julia Ward Howe, 3 Dec. 1997."

Flaker, Wendell, Letter to Mrs. Wendell Flaker, Telegram. 13 April 1945. Collection of Nancy E. Smith.

Flatow, Bernard C. "10,000 Tons of Ammunition, 1997"

Freeman, Karen. "The VA's Sorry, The Army's Silent. *The Bulletin of the Atomic Scientists* March 1993: 39-43.

Gustin, Robert E. "They Treated Us As Heroes, 22 July 1994."

Hall, Tony, ed., *D-Day: Operation Overlord: from the landing at Normandy to the liberation of Paris*. New York: Smithmark Publishers, Inc., 1993.

Hammond, Carl L. "A Murmansk Convoy, 6 April 1997."

Hanly, Richard. "T'was The Day Before Thanksgiving— And All Through The Ship, Everyone Was Hungry!!, 1996."

—. "Warning Stealing U.S. Gov't Property Is Punishable By $ 10,000.00 Fine And 10 Years Imprisonment, 17 June 1989."

Harris, Joe S. "My Journey Began On September 28, 1943, 1992."

Harris, Robert and Jeremy Paxton. *A Higher Form of Killing*. New York: Hill and Wang, 1982.

Heinse, Leroy C. "September 1997."

—. "Hell and Back, 5 Sept. 1997."

—. *S.S. John Bascom* - Loss of. Letter. 17 March 1944.

Horodysky, Dan and Toni, eds. *Merchant Marine Casualties of WW II*. 20 July 1999, <http:www.usmm.org/>

Houpis, Milton H. "The Battle of Tarawa, 1996."

Hughes, Terry and John Costello. *The Battle of the Atlantic*. New York: The Dial Press/James Wade, 1977.

Infield, Glenn B. *Disaster At Bari*. New York: The Macmillan Company, 1971.

Jacobsen, Hans-Adolf and Arthur L. Smith, Jr. *World War II Policy and Strategy*. Santa Barbara, California: Clio Books, 1979.

Jaffee, Walter W. *Appointment In Normandy*. Palo Alto, CA: Glencannon Pr., 1995.

Kellett, William, Letter to Gerald Reminick, 23 Aug. 1996.

—. *Diary to Dear Mom.* 15 Feb.- 31 March, 1945.

Kennedy, Joseph P. "New Blood in American Shipping." *Vital Speeches of the Day.* (3) 15 June 1937: 532-535.

Land, Emory Scott, *The United States Merchant Marine At War: Report of the War Shipping Administration to the President.* Washington, D.C.: January 15, 1946.

Loughran, Matthew S. "A True Veteran." *Newsday* 16 March 1996.

—. "I Heard A Loud Thud and the Ship Lifted Slightly, October 1997."

Luikart, Walter W. "How I Got Into The Merchant Marine, December 1996."

—. *"S.S. Nicholas Herkimer, 1996."*

"Lynn R. Fullington." *Anderson Daily Bulletin* 2 Aug. 1943.

Macauley, Edward. An Open Letter to the American Seaman. [n.d.].

MacIntyre, Donald. *The Naval War Against Hitler.* New York: Charles Scribner's Sons, 1971.

Marks, George H. Sr., *"Unusual Ship - U.S. Army Transport - State of Maryland,* 1 May 1996."

Marshall, Jack F., Letter to Mother, 9 February 1944. Collection of Jack F. Marshall.

Millar, Ian A. "The Death Railway." Poem. *In Praise of Merchantmen,* 1982.

—. "Forgotten Men." Poem. Ibid.

—. "The Grey Wolves Of The Morn." Poem. Ibid.

—. *In Praise of Merchantmen.* 1982.

—. "Merchantmen Like Thee." Poem. (For James F. Fitzpatrick).Collection of James F. Fitzpatrick.

—. "Merchantmen All." Poem. *In Praise of Merchantmen,* 1982.

—. "North Russia." Poem. Ibid.

—. "Sawokla." Poem. Ibid.

—. "The Unsung Heroes." Poem. Ibid.

Moeller, Henry W, *"Sinking of the Atlantic Sun,* 13 July 1999."

Moore, Arthur R. *A Careless Word... A Needless Sinking.* Kings Point, NY: American Merchant Marine Museum at the U.S. Merchant Marine Academy, 1990.

—. Interview with Gerald Reminick, 14 November 1997.

Morison, Samuel Eliot. *History Of United States Naval Operations In World War II. Vol. I. The Battle of the Atlantic....* Boston: Little, Brown, and Company, 1966.

—. Ibid. Vol. II *Operations in North African Waters....,* 1965.

—. Ibid. Vol IX. *Sicily-Selerno....,* 1968.

—. Ibid. Vol. XII. *Leyte....,* 1966.

Murray, L. Roy. "Rescue At Sea: The Odyssey of the S.S. *Nishmaha* and the Rescue of the Survivors of the Torpedoed British Cruiser HMS *Dunedin* Before the United States Entry Into World War II, 1995."

—. Interview with Gerald Reminick, 8 December 1997.

New, Al. "Maiden Voyage Of The Jonathan Trumbull, 1987."

O'Connell, Edward S. Letter to Gerald Reminick, 3 December 1996.

—. "Thirteen Days On A Raft, 23 October 1943."

Paxton, George. "Purser - S.S. *Andrea Luckenbach*, 1996."

Pechura, Constance M. "The Health Effects Of Mustard Gas And Lewisite." *JAMA.* (269) 27 January 1993: 453.

Powers, Richard R. "D-Day 1944." *Clarksville Leaf-Chronicle*, 6 June 1944.

Quinn, Thomas M, "Kid Chicago, 17 March 1997."

Reminick, Gerald. "Reunion Speech at U.S.Merchant Marine Academy, 20 April 1996.

Riesenberg, Felix Jr., "Communists at Sea." *Nation* 23 October 1937: 432-434.

—. *Sea War: The Story Of The U.S. Merchant Marine In World War II.* New York: Rinehart & Company, Inc., 1956.

Rohwer, Jurgen. *Axis Submarine Successes 1939-1945.* Annapolis, MD: U.S. Naval Institute Pr., 1983.

Rutler, Adolph G. "The Difference Between Doc and the Dock, 9 November 1996."

Salvo, Peter. "House of Frankenstein. [n.d.]," Collection of the Maritime Museum of Piney Point, MD.

—. "Sea Story." Liberty Ship Archives of the S.S. *John W. Brown.*

Sawyer L.A. and W.H. Mitchell. *The Liberty Ships.* 2nd ed. London: Lloyds of London Press Ltd., 1985.

Schroeder, Melvern. "Of Time And The Sea, 1994."

"Sell Wartime Ships." *Business Week* 17 July 1937: 42.

Standridge, Ernest S. "A World War II Voyage Remembered, 1996."

Stevenson, James. *Fact Sheet: U.S. Merchant Marine in W.W. II — "The Fourth Arm of Defense."* 1995.

Swados, Felice. "Seamen and the Law." *The New Republic* 9 March 1938: 124-126.

Trimble, Glen, Letter to Gerald Reminick, 15 September 1996.

—. "Recollections Of The Sea. [n.d.]."

—. "Witness To The Birth Of The Kamikaze, 1988."

Tumminia, Paul A. "The Sea Saga of the Juan de Fuca, 1982."

U.S. Department of Commerce. Maritime Administration, *The United States Merchant Marine: A Brief History*. 1972.

U.S. Maritime Service. *This is Sheepshead Bay: The Picture Story of the U.S. Maritime Service Training Station.* Sheepshead Bay, N.Y., [n.d.].

Vick, Elmer. "*S.S. Luckenbach*, 4 June 1992."

Von der Porten, Edward. *The German Navy In World War II*. New York: Thomas Y. Crowell Company, 1969.

Waddle, Lillard. "The Liberty Ship John Carter Rose, 1997."

Welch, Alvin Lee. *My First Visit to the Philippine Islands. Diary-Nov. 12- Dec. 22, 1944.*

—. "The Henry White." Poem. 15 January 1945.

"Welcome Home Our Many Heroes." Poem. Author unknown.

Willner, Stanley. "Veterans Application for Compensation, 1988." Collection of Stanley Willner.

Woods, Edward T. "A Teenager Goes To War, September, 1998."

Woodward, Thomas M. "America's Maritime Power." *Forum and Century* May 1939: 282-286.

York, John J. "Angel of Archangel,1 November 1996."

—. "The Non-Angels of Archangel, 28 November 1996."

INDEX